LEISURE CONSUMER PSYCHOLOGY

JOHN LOK

Copyright © John Lok
All Rights Reserved.

Copyright

Contents

Foreword

Introduction

Nowadays, on movie and opera art performance lesiure market, our leisures businesses have many different kinds to let consumer individual choice, for example, movie, opera art management, football performance, swimming , bicycle competition performance etc. indoor leisure activities. How can persuade audiences to buy ticket to see any one of these indoor leisure performance? We need to learn audience psychological factor and indoor environment factor if leisure businessmen hope to increase their audience number easily.

On future space city new tourism development market, space cities will not be science fiction, it will be achieved in possible. Whether what benefits it can bring to our future next generation. In this book, I shall explain what is the development differences between smart city development and space city development, then I shall indicate that what challenges to space city development will encounter , next I shall research view points to argue whether space city development is value or not as well as investigate what the actual aims to this space city development. How to learn space city tourism lesiure to let travelers feel more attractive to compare general earth travelling lesiure.

On airport indoor passenger staying shopping market, nowadays, global travel entertainment/leisure needs increase rapidly. Different countries people like to go to strange countries to travel. Exciting and enjoying travelling feeling is needed to satisfy to travellers. Hence, global airline industry service must be needed to improve to satisfy future global travellers' needs when they catch air planes to go to any countries to travel.

It brings this question: How to improve global airline services in order to satisfy travellers' comfortable and enjoyable catching air planes feeling in order to attract them to catch any airlines' air planes to go to any countries to travel often. I shall indicate some methods to attempt to explain whether what factors can influence airlines service performance or service level to be raised either better or worse.

On computer useful tool leisure market, I shall give reasons to explain how to develop future computer market. I shall indicate what factors will influence computer consumers' laptop purchases behavior as well as explain whether culture factor can influence computer consumer choice behavior. Also, I shall indicatw what service will be future computer related service need market.

In my this book,I shall attempt to explain how to apply audience psychological and indoor environment factors to help indoor leisure activity businessmen how to entertain to achieve persuade many audiences to chooce to buy ticket to see their performance as well as how to design new space city tourism leisure to develop new traveller market. Readers can have more fresh lesiure psychological knowledge to know how to operate leisure service business.

Prologue

Table of content
Chapter 1
Movie and opera art performance leisure
consumer psychology

● Why has theatre become such an important art-form?
● THE PSYCHOLOGY OF PERFORMING ARTS:THEATRE AND HUMAN EXPRESSION
● What is the role of spectacle in performing arts?
● Designing a Good Theater to influence audience seeing movie or opera art performance positive emotion feeling factor
● What is theatre's economic role?
Chapter 2
Publish Market Reader behavior

Analysis of factors influencing online newspaper reading behavior
How electronic versus traditional print
textbook influence of university students'
learning behavior
Factors influence child reading habit
How to change future e-reader study habit to feel better
Factors influence child reading habit
Chapter 3
Persuading traveller space city travel leisure choice
Undiscovered planets adapting

The possible undiscovered similar
Mars planets number

The possible short time methods
exploring undiscovered adapting
human living planets

Is exploring Mars the most important factor

to influence traveller space travel lesiure choice

The comparison benefit
and risk between space
travel and space exploration

Mars exploration failure factors

Space exploration possible
economic benefits

What is space city tourism

Is Developing space city possible

Developing space city tourism aim

Chapter 4
Computer tool useful leisure Consumer Behavior
● Why China's computer manufacturing and product development industry will be global leader to compete US computer dominant market. p.61-83
● Factors influence consumers' laptop purchases behavior.
● Can culture factor influence the computer consumer choice behavior?
Bibliography and further resources
● Computer industry related service market development
● What kinds of technologies innovation products will impact our future lives.
● Autonomous automatic vehicle
● 3 D printer
● Massive open online course education
● Future computer innovative and sustainable food source market
Future computer industry market related business strategy trends
● Government (public) and private partnership property development strategy
● Online Tourism partnership

● Higher education marketing, enrollment,
branding and recruitment strategy

Internet market development trend
    ● What is Internet entertainment function
    ● What is Internet learning function
    ● What is internet for searching information
function
    ● What is internet for online office
Function
    ● What is internet for ecommerce
Function

Computer technology related service consumer
negtive emotion factors

● Technology negative influence reasons
Online technology negative influence
● How technology could contribute to bring poor standard
of living to influence our societies
How to avoid to technology brings negative influence on children
● Technology negative influence to low knowledge learner to feel difficult
to adopt future new technological labor market
● The negative impact of smartphones/ mobiles and desktop /laptop on
human health and life
Avoidance to driving and speaking mobile at the same time
What are the negative effect of electromagnetic waves on human brains
from smartphone influence
The laptop and desktop negative influence
Chapter 5
    Airport indoor travelling staying
shopping market
    Emotional labor factor p.84-100

Airports service environment
factor

Lean maintenance repair

and manual error factor

Influence of airside and off
airport to airport geographical
choice factor
     Influencing air connectivity
to service quality factor
     How to measure and rise airline
service quality

CHAPTER ONE

Movie and opera art performance leisure consumer psychology

What does theatre leisure ? Why we need to enter theatre to see movies or enter opera art performance hall to see opera art performance ? Theatre is a place where one group of people- on stage- tell stories to another group of people who are sitting... usually in an auditorium... usually in the dark... listening to, and watching these stories.Since human beings started to gather in groups and communities, they sensed the necessity to transmit their experiences and knowledge- fundamentally- through storytelling. The transmission of these stories, through the ages moved from shamanism to modern forms of art on and off stage.

Theatre is a tool that has existed for thousands of years. I imagine that from the first moments people wanted to transmit their experiences of the hunt, or their father and grandfather. It is both the wish and necessity of human beings to tell stories.Theatre is an art form that brings people together to celebrate, challenge and provoke through the telling of stories. Theatre is unique, you see transformation right in front of you- created in the moment. In a book; you pick it up, put it down and it remains – similarly with film- but with theatre, what you witness in any given moment is unique and only you and the audience will ever experience that.Theatre is a moment of intersection between people where events collide or reveal conflict through storytelling. It is an art-form that always has, and always will be, important and relevant.Theatre is a sense of escape, it transforms you into a new space. It can however, be many things. Theatre can be a source of intellectual learning, inspiration, and can even reflect your life.Theatre is live, and that's important. So much of our art is consumed through live-streams, through computers and so on – and this misses that extraordinary atmosphere, and sense of grounding and presence that theatre gives.

Why do we need to see opera art performance? Going in front of an audience- be it small or large- is a performance?you have to captivate people with what you say, do or whatever! This is the basic of performance.Not everyone can perform. The people who do it have a virtue that they can exploit to get that attention from people. Performance is about having the capability to captivate an audience with whatever means you can see with words, theatre, dance, music and so on.

What does leisure consumer behavior? How to persuade leisure consumer individual feels to enjoy the kind of leisure activities? I shall attempt to indicate art opera performance or movie lesiure example to explain how to persuade audiences feel leisure enjoyment to see the movie or see the opera art performance. For movie or art performance leisure, instead the movie or opera art performance, the artors individual performance attitude whether they can attract any audiences that they can feel enjoyment or leisure seeing feeling and the movie or art opera performance content whether they can attract their leisure emotion factor, the movie and opera art performance whole length of time factor is also important because if the movie or opera art performance time is too long, e.g. above two hours, then the long time movie or opera art performance can not persuade audiences to feel attractive, otherwise, they will feel boring when they feel that they need to sit more than two hours time to see the movie or see the art opera performance in the cinema or art opera performance hall. Unless, the audiences feel very enjoyment to see the movie or art opera performance.So, it explains why general movie or opera art performance time can not exceed two hours. Because instead of performance cost reason, audience individual boring feeling reason is another important audience leisure psychological factor to influence whether the movie or opera art performance can attract or persuade many audiences to choose to to buy ticket to see the movie or the art opera performance.

CINEMA MOVIE AUDIENCE LEISURE PSYCHOLOGY

Theatre is a collaborative art-form with writers, producers, directors, lighting designers, costume makers and so on. When all those pieces coincide, and when the performances are great, the lighting is great, the music is great, the design is great.... when all those different creative activities fuse into one emotional and intellectual delivery- that's when great theatre occurs.

Different films need to arrange different audience individual leisure taste to adapt their seeing movies or opera art performances raising enjoyment feeling.Each year a small number of new release films, 6-10 titles, become 'events'. These films such as the new James Bond, the latest Disney family feature and other big action titles such as the Marvel films or 'sagas' such as Twilight and The Hunger Games, are the bedrock of commercial cinema. These are mass appeal films created at huge cost and supported by massive marketing effort. They provide a disproportionately large amount of a cinema's annual income and they generally appeal strongly to the youth audience (16-24 year olds). 'Event' films are shown widely at multiplex cinemas but often perform poorly in local independent cinemas when shown a few weeks after the initial high profile release although some people will be prepared to wait if they have seen the film trailered at a favourite cinema.

In contrast a large number of high quality, independent and foreign language films are released annually but invariably they earn much less at the box office. These films appeal more to 30+ year olds and can prove to be very popular with particular audiences in individual cinemas. However,in recent years the 45+ age group has become one of the largest growth markets in UK cinemas with films such as The Best Exotic Marigold Hotel with more mature characters and strong storylines aimed at a multi-generational market. Young people, although still the multiplexes mainstay audience, are increasingly consuming film online through downloading or streaming services.

In fact, films based on literary works or specific aspects of social history or parts of the country are often well received by local audiences who prefer cinemas with comfort, character and the opportunity to have a coffee or a bar drink.Young children enjoy cinema going. Sometimes they attend with a group of friends. Often they are accompanied by parents or relatives. Films for the younger age groups are important for local cinemas and may attract sell-out audiences for morning or matinée performances, especially at weekends and during school holidays. Many cinemas now have a regular slot for this audience and operate it like a 'club' to encourage repeated visits. Local cinemas have to be capable of adapting to whatever is currently in the news and available to them. This requires skill and showmanship on the part of the cinema manager and staff in addition to a well designed building. Why has theatre become such an important art-form?

In my imagination this goes back to the time when we lived in caves. I'm pretty convinced that two people, three people or one person sat on one side of a fire, providing the lighting- while a lot of other people sat on the other side of the cave or dwelling... and from time immemorial stories were told by one or several people, to a larger group of people. These stories may have been history, myths or legend.... they may even have been about religion or about grappling with the seasons.

Stories have always been told by live human beings to other live human beings, that's what makes it such an important and enduring form of art in my view.The unique selling proposition of theatre is the fact that there are live humans in a space, speaking to other live humans. It's not online, not in a cinema, not on some tablet... it's there. As a member of the audience, you are in the same space as the people who are- in the broadest sense of the word- telling stories. The very fact that humanity is at the absolute centre of theatre in tangible flesh and blood terms means that there is intrinsic beauty in that art-form because the human form, human voice and human ability to imagine stories (and their repercussions) is the stuff of art!

The aesthetic and beauty of theatre are very subjective. Performance and theatre can take many forms. It may be a play on the street or- as you saw during the early 19th century- a form of Opera where many forms of art were gathered into a single performance. The aesthetic of the elements of a performance when they are brought together depend on the culture of the people receiving it and where the piece itself is performed.The aesthetic and beauty of a piece of theatre lies almost completely in the eyes of the person watching.Theatre doesn't have to be beautiful. Some of the most fantastic and thought-provoking pieces are ugly. There is an aesthetic in the staging and design- which should enhance the stories or design of the production- but it doesn't have to be beautiful. Also, the notion of beauty in the theatre is- as in life- defined by the perspective of the viewer. For me, beauty may be defined by other simplicities... stripping away all the white-noise of circumstances and just focussing on human action. That's where I find moments of beauty in theatre, where those absolutely pristine quiet pin-drop moments occur... where the audience, story and artist collide in a moment of truth. These moments of beauty dig deep into an essence. Hence, we each have our own personal aesthetic- but for me the simplicity of storytelling and the collision of human events is where beauty and aesthetic occur in theatre.Theatre always has, and always will be, important and relevant.

THE PSYCHOLOGY OF PERFORMING ARTS: THEATRE AND HUMAN EXPRESSION

Theatre is an arena in which we can mentally play, acting out our fears and fantasies in an experimental way. It excites new ideas and perspectives and provides us with rehearsal for life. In the broad sense, theatre can be taken as referring to films and TV as well as live theatre - indeed, any sort of entertainment that includes performers and audience (sometimes intertwined in complex ways) and which requires imagination to make it real.

Central to much of theatre is human conflict - the characters struggle to attain their ends against opposition, mostly from other characters. Role-playing puts us into the head of each character in turn, allowing us to see things from their viewpoint. By observing how they deal with their problems, sometimes adaptively, sometimes self-destructively, we learn lessons in how to choose among our own options. An important function of theatre is stimulation. Theatre adds magic and thrills to our mundane lives - whether it be disturbing (tragedy & horror), ridiculous (comedy) or romantic (esp. musicals). Modern civilisation has become overly safe. From time to time we need to rock the boat and test the alarms - to try out novel, challenging experiences and sample danger, albeit within a safe context. Theatre and films give us a chance to rehearse reactions to rare, dreaded occurrences such as rape, earthquake, fire or death of a loved one, helping us to cope with such events should they occur in real life. So, the audience leisure need difference between opera art performance and movie. Movie lesiure audiences visual enjoyment needs are whether the movie content is attractive or/and the or artistes their performance skills are proficient. Otherwise, the opera art performance artistes need have the actual time performance skills, because they need to perform to let their opera art performance audiences to feel visual leisure enjoyment immediate, if they can not persuade their opera art performance audiences feel happy or visual leisure feeling, otherwise, they feel boring when they are seeing their opera art performance immediately. They must decide to leave the opera art performance hall. So, all opera art performance artistes need know every opera art performance audience individual emotion, whether he/she is enjoying or boring when he/she is seeing their opera art performance on the performance hall.

What is the role of spectacle in performing arts?

Spectacle is largely a question of means, but it also brings an accent to a presentation or to the way of doing a show. At the beginning of Cirque, we were just a group of street-performers- not great acrobats, so the spectacle was little! As we went along, we were able to add artificial spectacle which was connected to the performance and enhanced with better acrobats- improving the whole experience. Now it would be very hard to go back to 1984 where we were just street-acrobats, people expect and accept spectacle from our performances now.

What is the role of the actor in theatre?

The actor is the person who tells someone else's story, he is the messenger of the story; regardless of whether that story was written by a composer, a lyricist or an author. He is the human-conduit to convey the story to the audience. His or her choices are therefore crucial in making that story as vivid as it can be. Also, the performer and his performance are the skeleton of our production. We can put muscles over this in the form of costumes and lights... we will add music, light and invoke the emotion of this skeleton by bringing it to life, but the performance is at the centre of all of this. Moreover, actors are communicators, storytellers, inventors and commentators. They have many roles in their art, depending on the story they are telling and the genre of the play. Actors are there to entertain, but also to deliver the story as the writer (or they, themselves) would want.As an actor, you are an artist. Greatness comes from the quality of the transformation, experience and how they can access and communicate emotion to effect a change in the audience.

Hence, theatre is an art-form that is meant to be heard. It is a collection of words and moments that are defined by the writer, but ultimately given voice by the actor. For me while it's always story first; the actor is the instrument for those stories coming to life. We each have our own notion of truth, but the great actors are the ones who make truth the through-line of their work. They are the ones who make the boundary between actor and character invisible- immersing themselves in the story. They are the ones who allow the audience to do the same. A great performance is not full of noise, but full of context and story. The actor must be generous, and give with abandon. Real theatre and real performance exists when you have a meeting of the performer and the audience as receiver. The audience are an active participant, theatre is a relationship between the production and the audience- audiences are not just consuming. For example, a piece of theatre is not complete until the audience is in the room. The work is changed by the presence of an audience. When you are making work you see rehearsals and so forth, but what the piece becomes when an audience joins the process translates it to another stage. Whether the audience know it or not, they are active in the process. They clarify things, deny things, join with ideas and more. Moreover, the audience are not passive consumers of theatre, it is a circular relationship.It is extremely important that an audience and a story become one. You often hear people describe the experience of 'losing themselves' in the story; I- personally- would call it 'finding yourself'. My guess would be that if you talk to the average audience member or artist, those unique moments that keep us coming back to theatre are relatively rare; yet we keep going. We want that moment where we get so immersed.. where all the people in the audience and the production come together... that is what resonates with us for years to come.

Designing a Good Theater to influence audience seeing movie or opera art performance positive emotion feeling factor

Instead of learning how to produce one good movie or opera art performance content and the artor individence performance skill and length of performance time arrangement factors, the designing a Good theater location factor will be one important factor to influence audience individual emotion. They may include as below:

Since humanity started gathering to tell stories and represent scenes from everyday life in front of an audience, the need for a space to perform such activities began to increase. Theater design developed from the open-air amphitheaters of the Greeks and Romans to the incredible array of forms we see today. Though some forms work better for particular types of performance, there is no ideal shape or size of a theater. The choice of the best form and scale depends on the functional purpose (movies, lectures, stage performances, musical presentations), the size of the staging required and the number of the audience to be accommodated. Let's see which are the basic parts that comprise a theater and the most common types of today's theater design.

1. Design a functioning Auditorium according to the type of performance and the number of the audience

It is the part of the theater accommodating the audience during the performance, sometimes known as the "house". The house can also refer to an area that is not considered playing space or backstage area. This includes the lobby, coat check, ticket counters, and restroom. The amount of space required for each auditorium depends on a number of factors but the following guides, based on modern seating design can give you an idea of the area needed

2. Keep the standard distance for a comfortable audience seating

The aisle is the space for walking with rows of seats on both sides or with rows of seats on one side and a wall on the other. In order to improve safety when the theaters are darkened during the performance, the edges of the aisles are marked with a row of small lights

3. The stage is important: choose wisely

The stage is the designated space where actors and other artists perform and the focal point for the audience. As an architectural feature, the stage may consist of a platform (often raised) or series of platforms. In some cases, these may be temporary or adjustable but in theaters and other buildings devoted to such productions, the stage is often a permanent feature. There are several types of stages that vary as to the usage and the relation of the audience to them:

Thrust theater stage :

A Stage surrounded by audience on three sides. The Fourth side serves as the background. In a typical modern arrangement: the stage is often a square or rectangular playing area, usually raised, surrounded by raked seating. Other shapes are possible; Shakespeare's Globe Theatre was a five-sided thrust stage.

For greater intimacy with the audience, go with the Thrust Stage

A thrust stage is one that extends into the audience on three sides and is connected to the backstage area by its upstage end. A thrust has the benefit of greater intimacy between the audience and performers than a proscenium while retaining the utility of a backstage area. The audience in a thrust stage theater may view the stage from three or more sides.

End Stage:

A Thrust stage extended wall to wall, like a thrust stage with audience on just one side, i.e. the front."Backstage" is behind the background wall. There is no real wingspace to the sides, although there may be entrances located there. An example of a modern end stage is a music hall, where the background walls surround the playing space on three sides. Like a thrust stage, scenery serves primarily as background, rather than surrounding the acting space.

Arena Theatre stage:

A central stage surrounded by audience on all sides. The stage area is often raised to improve sightlines.

The Proscenium Stage or End Stage :
It is the most common type of stage and it is also called a picture frame stage. Its primary feature is a large opening, the proscenium arch through which the audience views the performance. The audience directly faces the stage and views only one side of the scene. Often, a stage may extend in front of the proscenium arch which offers additional playing area to the actors. This area is referred to as the apron. Underneath and in front of the apron is sometimes an orchestra pit which is used by musicians during musicals and operas.

Flexible theater stage:
Sometimes called a "Black Box" theater, these stages are often big empty boxes painted black inside. Stage and seating not fixed. Instead, each can be altered to suit the needs of the play or the whim of the director.

Keep your theater flexible
Flexible stage theaters are those that do not establish a fixed relationship between the stage and the house. They can be put into any of the standard theater forms or any of the variations of those. Usually, there is no physical distinction between the stage and the auditorium and the audience is either standing, intermingling with the performance or sitting on the main floor.

Profile Theatres stage:
Often used in "found space" theaters, i.e. theaters made by converted from other spaces. The Audience is often placed on risers to either side of the playing space, with little or no audience on either end of the "stage". Actors are staged in profile to the audience. It is often the most workable option for long, narrow spaces like "store fronts". Scenically, a profile theater is most like an arena stage; some staging as background is possible at ends, which are essentially sides. A non-theatrical form of the profile stage is a basketball arena, if no-one is seated behind the hoops.

Sports Arenas stage :
Sports arenas often serve as venues for Music Concerts. In form they resemble very large arena stage (more accurately the arena stage resembles a sports arena), but with a retangular floorplan. When used for concert, a temporary stage area often is set up as an end-stage at one end of the floor, and the rest of the floor and the stands become the audience. Arenas have their own terminology

Keep the scenery low for better visibility
In the Theater in the round or the Arena Stage Theater, the stage is located in the center of the audience, with the audience members facing it from all

sides. The audience is placed close to the action, which provides a feeling of intimacy and involvement. However, this type puts major restrictions on the amount and kind of visual spectacle that can be provided for a performance, because scenery more than a few feet tall will block the audience view of the action taking place onstage.

4. Sound quality is as important as visibility

Although theater performances are a visual medium, poor sound quality will ruin even the better plays. The sound is an area often overlooked but, just as you need good sightlines, you also need good sound-lines. Apart from the obvious comfort and size considerations, External sound insulation (how many times have you heard traffic noise, trains or building works over the soundtrack of the film you are watching?) Internal sound insulation – this is particularly important with multiple screens where a loud soundtrack can leak into the adjoining auditorium.Services and equipment noise control – noises such as air conditioning, lifts, toilets and projection equipment need to be controlled. Acoustics – acoustic design in theaters should be considered from feasibility stage – location, auditorium planning etc. through to final commissioning.

What is theatre's economic role?

Every single independent tourist review that is written about reasons why people should come to the UK and London starts with heritage/royalty and then immediately moves on to theatre.... Specifically theatre.... not the arts, not entertainment, not shopping, not restaurants... the theatre. Alongside the fact that theatre employs many people in many diverse and different jobs, it's also a great regenerator of town-centres. If you speak to any government or local-government official that is trying to regenerate cities and towns further, theatres are at the centre. From time to time I get interviewed by an unnamed newspaper about the death of the West End. I always offer to take the journalist around London in a taxi where I can show them boarded up shops, boarded up offices, boarded up factories and boarded up pubs.

However, theatre is growing globally, and people want it globally. How the work of theatre develop will be a fascinating blend of cultures, it's an incredible opportunity. We currently have three proposals from Shanghai asking us to build, operate and convert theatres as a central core-magnet to retail, residential and other developments. This is alongside conversations we are having in Korea, Hong Kong and more. Around the world, more theatres are being built now than at any other time in history. Theatre will lose the London and New York concentration. Hamburg, Vienna, Melbourne and Sydney are already great theatre cities. Hong Kong is growing into a great theatre destination too. There is also a huge opportunity across Canada and other territories. I see theatre essentially following an upward trajectory in terms of number of cities and venues.

People worldwide now acknowledge theatre is good for society economically and socially.

What does the next 50 years hold for theatre or opera art performance leisure need ? I think the essential core of theatre.... the unique selling proposition of being there to see it, having to perform in a space... will remain the same.... However what that core is saying and doing will depend on the message and story of the artists of the future. The activity of theatre has lasted for many thousands of years. As long as human beings have the need to hear stories, and to tell stories, it will remain. We're in very difficult times at the moment in terms of funding. This does however mean that we tend to get better at what we do. The work gets tougher, leaner and better. I would hope however that regional-theatre funding improves in the future, and we're left with a secure theatre network.

In fact, Theatre is ultimately about conflict between people and circumstances... you can wrap it in a different package and bow, but these principles have remained the same for hundreds of years.In the off-Broadway scene of the 1960s, you saw a trend of self-generating theatre in store-fronts and unusual venues. They were still going after the essence of theatre, but taking it everywhere. If you look today at the influence of technology in theatre, we are now able to do some of the things we used to do by hand- but more easily... for example, throwing a light cue by computer rather than moving dimmers by hand. However, technology gives us more tools to get to the core event, but ultimately the fierce passion the artist has to reveal the story is what powers the theatre.

How do artists cope with the mental pressures of perfection?

I would contest that we all have one or two 'issues' with our mental health, perhaps that is just the normal being of being a human. The discipline of ballet gives you the ability to manage your emotions, and an outlet for them. Ballet is a way to go through your emotions with the permission to exploit your frustrations, investigating them, using them and exposing them.Society faces dangers when people have doubts and questions, and cannot investigate them. When people hold-on to their emotions, and don't become malleable to them.. they become fragile, and can break, like glass.

What is the role of digital technology , how it can influence audience emotion from online movie or opera art performance online watching channel in the modern world?

Digital technology is making us insular. We think we have relationships through Facebook, Twitter and Instagram, but they are not real. There is no physical connection. We are human, we need physical connection. Participating in public performance, where you are a part of something with other people is more important than ever. It's more important than ever that we encourage young people into the arts in a meaningful way where they feel they want to go, and can afford to go. Right now, we can't even get young people through the door- and that's hard.

Looking even further to the future, we are entering the world of artificial intelligence and robotics. There is a chance that machines will be performing many of our world's most physical tasks. Wouldn't it be better if we guarantee the future of our children with creativity? That's the one thing machines can't compete with us on. Human beings will live maybe 100 years, and we leave school when we're 16, 17, 18. We need to teach kids to enjoy learning, to be curious, and to always want to learn. Not one iota of what they will become can be taught by us. The most important thing is that children enjoy the process of discovery. The more we encourage creativity, the more digital technology encourage young age audience group to imagine alternate realities when they can see movie or opera art performance from internet channel, the more our futures will all be brighter.

How has art changed your world-view?

Art has changed my world-view completely. I have travelled the world, not for tourism but to work. I have worked with so many different people, from so many different cultures and backgrounds and I have had my mind opened about humanity.I don't feel that I am a particular person from a particular part of the world. I was born somewhere, grew-up somewhere else, and lived in a few more places. I am a person of the world. Art has allowed me to live with myself, and to make sense of the fragility of humanity's desires and traits. I'm just a human being, and art has given me the space to be OK with that.

What inspires you as an artist? How you are as artist , you feel you may perform your movie or opera art performance to attract audience attention? Working with choreographers and producing stuff that really makes people think, and changes their ideas, and takes them to another place... that's powerful for me. for dance performance example, dance in itself is a social skill that everybody should appreciate and enjoy, our bodies are made to move. If you choose to specialise in the field- you're like an athlete. You have to be built for the technique. The role of the body is important and for dancers, it's about the joints, flexibility and muscular strength. The proportions of the body are also important; that's part of the aesthetic, and you can't help that- this is a visual art. How would be your art performance message to the next generation? You really have to devote your life to theatre. It doesn't mean you can't have a family and so forth... but it isn't like some activities in life where you can get a healthy work-life balance, as much as we would like to encourage it. Theatre is your life as well as your work, and if that doesn't fit with you, then theatre isn't right for you. Whatever your talent... music, movement, whatever... if you have the drive to continue and develop and become a great performer then you should. It's a lot of work- my father used to tell me that in life you need a little bit of talent, but lots of hard work. If you have a little talent, prepare yourself for hard work to develop it, and you may attain greatness; but don't forget that the road to greatness is long. You should make the work that tells the stories you feel are important to you and your generation. The role of a theatre maker is to tell the stories of our lives. You should try and grab the whole of the gamut of emotions, it's not just to entertain. The mix and bravery by which you grab those emotions makes theatre exciting. Moreover, you must be fearless and brave. You must be willing to express what you feel, and to do that with thought. People have a fear of expression, and we must encourage them to do the hard, hard work it takes to overcome this and know they are empowered to make work. All great work comes from this principle, new forms are made, new theatre is created.... When someone stops to write... or stops to raise some money? those are the moments where greatness is created. Also, you have to be curious and learn as much as you can from as many people as you can. You can even learn from people who don't know what they're doing; at least you will then know how not to do something. You have to be kind to yourself. You do not have to suffer or punish yourself to be a great artist. The sooner you can accept yourself, the sooner you can progress and discover what you're capable of. Life is so short, and goes so fast, you have to enjoy it. Life will throw you in so many directions, and goals are not the end; they are simply gateways to more questions, and this process of discovering answers and new questions is never complete, that's life. People have a lot of inhibitions, and are hugely preoccupied with what other people are thinking. Dance gives you a space to forget that, and enjoy being you. I always think you should dance with others, but it's amazing how happy you can be dancing on your own. For me however, the entertainment and enjoyment is dancing with friends or even strangers. Dancing breaks-down so many barriers, and makes you more comfortable with people around you. People let their guard-down when they dance, and it opens a lot of doors for communications. I have a fitness and dance programme that we take into state-schools. We let kids try anything they want in dance and let their creativity flow. They can do any genre from around the world- the aim is to find something that they can connect with to give them a feel of what dance can do. When you see the reaction? My God, it's the happiest they've ever been! They're testing their bodies like they've never done before, and finding skills that they didn't think they had. It gives them a space to enjoy being themselves, without peer-pressure, without the stresses that can impact their lives so negatively at this early stage.

However, art is one of the most valuable assets of human society, yet the truth is that while we may attach art to a time and a place; it's true provenance and relevance remain intangible. We can look at the raw materials (the paint, the instrument?, the composition (the brush strokes, the music) or even the act of consumption (viewing, listing? – but the thing that we observe only becomes art within us. The phenomenon of art emerges within the intangible mix of experience and cultural inputs that create our mind. A fact not lost on the ancient Greeks who simultaneously originated the concepts of philosophy (the love of wisdom) and theatre (the place for viewing) c.6th century B.C.

The images of other arts are constituted in quite different ways. This engagement has a metaphysical aspect in that the image between the performer and the audience adds up to more than the sum of its various parts. A materialist criticism that does not recognise these 'metaphysical' qualities of theatre is lacking critical force. For the 'beyond physical', the numinous, the spirit, the aura of art, however it is described is a material response to art not just ideological or 'imagined'. This 'something more' than the thing itself is attested to by too many people without deference to gender, race or class. And to ignore it, as though it will go away, and leave us with the quantified, the material and the manipulable, in the name of dogmatic sectarian objectives, is to impoverish the terms on which theatre might be most valuably and pleasurably thought and practiced. This metaphysics of theatre is what is not seen, beyond the practiced, beyond the mind's eye it remains unwritten. It is the domain which both makes theatre worthwhile and simultaneously jeopardises its effects. For it is in this hinterland of the undocumented and discreet that the fallacies of theatre are nourished. This 'something more' of the image does not disconnect the experience of theatre from its place of performance, nor from the everyday. Theatre remains bound by its context precisely through the unique relationship images create between audience, performer and everyday life." He adds that, "To value theatre, is to value life, not to escape from it. The everyday is at once the most habitual and demanding dimension of life which theatre has most responsibility to. Theatre does not tease people out of their everyday lives like other expressions of wish fulfilment but reminds them who they are and what is worth living and changing in their lives every day." (Theatre and Every Day Life, 1993)

The concept of everyday life here is critical. Human beings are cursed with the knowledge of agency. We know without a shadow of a doubt that our immediate experiences are limited simply to ourselves. In many philosophies this is even manifest as the discussion of how one is trapped in the body- able to only experience the substantive world which we have ingested through our limited senses. With this in mind, we quickly see the real power of theatre. Prof. Erin Hurley describes how, "Theatre allows for and offers vicarious experience: the experience of someone else experiencing something?We know that witnessing another's actions and emotional experiences can create the same neurological imprint as doing or feeling them oneself. Joseph Roach provocatively recasts the history of theatre in terms of the good of what he calls 'synthetic experience', a cognate to vicarious experience. The theatre is a port of entry into another's life and another kind of living." (Theatre and Feeling, 2010)

On conclusion, art is the medium by which we- as human beings- are able to relate to each other. Art allows us to understand things that are more than ourselves, and imagine life through the agency of others. Theatre- as perhaps the most human of all the arts- has the profound ability to engage us immediately in the experience of someone else's agency- at any point in time, at any place. It breaks down the loneliness of being a self, and allows one to realise that not only are there others- but that the self can be them too. Art Business Charity conflict creativity culture. So, any movie or opera art performance businessmen need to educate our next generation needs to considerate art performance movie or opera art performance lesisure industry needs to be continued to develop in order to let they can learn more new art culture and build positive charter role in our society, then crimes number will be influenced to reduce when they can see any health movie or opera art performance after they buy tickets to enter cinemas or opera art performance hall and let they feel that it is valuable economic spending time to see the movie or the opera art leisure performance.

CHAPTER TWO

Publish Market Reader behavior

Nowadays, publish market includes these main book service aspects to let readers enjoy reading interest, such as ebooks online reading channel, traditional book shop books purchase channel, library books lending service. I shall analyze how these books leading or borrowing and send hand or new books purchase choice to influence readers reading behavioral need change.

● Library Services in the Digital Age

The internet has already had a major impact on how people find and access information, and now the rising popularity of e-books is helping transform Americans' reading habits. In this changing landscape, public libraries are trying to adjust their services to these new realities while still serving the needs of patrons who rely on more traditional resources. In a new survey of Americans' attitudes and expectations for public libraries, the Pew Research Center's Internet & American Life Project finds that many library patrons are eager to see libraries' digital services expand, yet also feel that print books remain important in the digital age.

The availability of free computers and internet access now rivals book lending and reference expertise as a vital service of libraries. In a national survey of Americans ages 16 and older:

1. 80% of Americans say borrowing books is a "very important" service libraries provide.

2. 80% say reference librarians are a "very important" service of libraries.

3. 77% say free access to computers and the internet is a "very important" service of libraries.

Moreover, a notable share of Americans say they would embrace even wider uses of technology at libraries such as: Online research services allowing patrons to pose questions and get answers from librarians: 37% of Americans ages 16 and older would "very likely" use an "ask a librarian" type of service, and another 36% say they would be "somewhat likely" to do so.

Apps-based access to library materials and programs: 35% of Americans ages 16 and older would "very likely" use that service and another 28% say they would be "somewhat likely" to do so.

Access to technology "petting zoos" to try out new devices: 35% of Americans ages 16 and older would "very likely" use that service and another 34% say they would be "somewhat likely" to do so.

GPS-navigation apps to help patrons locate material inside library buildings: 34% of Americans ages 16 and older would "very likely" use that service and another 28% say they would be "somewhat likely" to do so.

"Redbox"-style lending machines or kiosks located throughout the community where people can check out books, movies or music without having to go to the library itself: 33% of Americans ages 16 and older would "very likely" use that service and another 30% say they would be "somewhat likely" to do so.

"Amazon"-style customized book/audio/video recommendation schemes that are based on patrons' prior library behavior: 29% of Americans ages 16 and older would "very likely" use that service and another 35% say they would be "somewhat likely" to do so.

When Pew Internet asked the library staff members in an online panel about these services, the three that were most popular were classes on e-borrowing, classes on how to use handheld reading devices, and online "ask a librarian" research services. Many librarians said that their libraries were already offering these resources in various forms, due to demand from their communities.

These are some of the key findings from a new national survey of 2,252 Americans ages 16 and older by the Pew Research Center's Internet & American Life Project and underwritten by a grant from the Bill & Melinda Gates Foundation. The interviews were conducted on October 15-November 10, 2012 and done on cell phone and landlines and in English and Spanish.

● Public priorities for libraries

Asked for readers or students thoughts on which services libraries should offer to the public, majorities of Americans are strongly in favor of: Coordinating more closely with local schools: 85% of Americans ages 16 and older say libraries should "definitely" do this. Offering free literacy programs to help young children: 82% of Americans ages 16 and older say libraries should "definitely do" this. Having more comfortable spaces for reading, working, and relaxing: 59% of Americans ages 16 and older say libraries should "definitely do" this. Offering a broader selection of e-books: 53% of Americans ages 16 and older say libraries should "definitely do" this. These services were also most popular with the library staff members in our online panel, many of whom said that their library had either already implemented them or should "definitely" implement them in the future. At the same time, people have different views about whether libraries should move some printed books and stacks out of public locations to free up space for tech centers, reading rooms, meeting rooms, and cultural events: 20% of Americans ages 16 and older said libraries should "definitely" make those changes; 39% said libraries "maybe" should do that; and 36% said libraries should "definitely not" change by moving books out of public spaces.

Americans say libraries are important to their families and their communities, but often do not know all the services libraries offer. Fully 91% of Americans ages 16 and older say public libraries are important to their communities; and 76% say libraries are important to them and their families. And libraries are touchpoints in their communities for the vast majority of Americans: 84% of Americans ages 16 and older have been to a library or bookmobile at some point in their lives and 77% say they remember someone else in their family using public libraries as they were growing up. Still, just 22% say that they know all or most of the services their libraries offer now. Another 46% say they know some of what their libraries offer and 31% said they know not much or nothing at all of what their libraries offer.

● Changes in library use in recent years

In the past 12 months, 53% of Americans ages 16 and older visited a library or bookmobile; 25% visited a library website; and 13% used a handheld device such as a smartphone or tablet computer to access a library website. All told, 59% of Americans ages 16 and older had at least one of those kinds of interactions with their public library in the past 12 months. Throughout this report we call them "recent library users" and some of our analysis is based on what they do at libraries and library websites. Overall, 52% of recent library users say their use of the library in the past five years has not changed to any great extent. At the same time, 26% of recent library users say their library use has increased and 22% say their use has decreased. The table below highlights their answers about why their library use changed:

● How people use libraries

Of the 53% of Americans who visited a library or bookmobile in person in the past 12 months, here are the activities they say they do at the library:

73% of library patrons in the past 12 months say they visit to browse the shelves for books or media.

73% say they visit to borrow print books.

54% say they visit to research topics that interest them.

50% say they visit to get help from a librarian. Asked how often they get help from library staff in such things as answering research questions, 31% of library patrons in the past 12 months say they frequently get help, 39% say they sometimes get help, 23% say they hardly ever get help, and 7% say they never get help.

49% say they visit to sit, read, and study, or watch or listen to media.

46% say they visit to use a research database.

41% say they visit to attend or bring a younger person to a class, program, or event designed for children or teens.

40% say they visit to borrow a DVD or videotape of a movie or TV show.

31% say they visit to read or check out printed magazines or newspapers.

23% say they visit to attend a meeting of a group to which they belong.

21% say they visit to attend a class, program, or lecture for adults.

17% say they visit to borrow or download an audio book.

16% say they visit to borrow a music CD.

These survey indicated that African-Americans and Hispanics are more likely to say libraries are important to them and their families, to say libraries are important to their communities, to access the internet at the library (and feel internet access is a very important service libraries provide), to use library internet access to hunt/apply for jobs, and to visit libraries just to sit and read or study. For almost all of the library resources we asked about, African-Americans and Hispanics are significantly more likely than whites to consider them "very important" to the community. That includes: reference librarians, free access to computers/internet, quiet study spaces, research resources, jobs and careers resources, free events, and free meeting spaces.

When it comes to future services, African-Americans and Hispanics are more likely than whites to support segregating library spaces for different services, having more comfortable spaces for reading, working and relaxing, offering more learning experiences similar to museum exhibits, helping users digitize material such as family photos or historical documents. Also, minorities are more likely than whites to say they would use these new services specified in the charts below.

Statistical analysis that controls for a variety of demographic factors such as income, educational attainment, and age shows that race and ethnicity are significant independent predictors of people's attitudes about the role of libraries in communities, about current library services, and about their likely use of the future library services we queried. In addition, African-Americans are more likely than whites to say they have "very positive" experiences at libraries, to visit libraries to get help from a librarian, to bring children or grandchildren to library programs.

● Second hand book market

Why is used car market similar to second hand car market consumer behavior ? When one publish decides to sell one used book. It will concern that how much the used book sale price and it won't need to concern the author can receive any royalties and have no economic interest in the text – when you buy the text, not a single penny goes to me. It's designed to be a "disposable," one-use text in order to keep the price down. (The used book market actually drives up the price of texts – to see why, think of what would happen to car prices if used car sales were not permitted.) How does the used car markets drive up the price of the good? With an used market, the buyer is willing to pay more, knowing that he can resell later. However, without an used market, everyone is forced to buy new cars, raising demand, and thus raising the price of new cars. How to think about these countervailing effects? It seems that second had book and car markets , they have similar characteristics to influence consumer behaviors.

Are the used books and used cars market actually analogous like the professor suggests? The professor and his publisher have a monopoly on the new textbook, but no one controls the new car market. Therefore, if people keep reselling text, the publisher will use their monopoly and raise the price of new books to compensate. In contrast, car manufacturers can't do so due to competitive pressure.Imagine that there are two kinds of people, rich and poor, and no market for used books. Rich people are willing to pay more for new textbooks. Poor people cannot afford to buy new textbooks. In the absence of a market for used books, poor people will not buy textbooks.

Imagine now that there is market for used books. Poor people are now able and willing to pay second hand textbooks. And rich people now have someone to sell the books too once they are done using these books. A market for second hand textbooks raises the price of textbooks because some people are not able and willing to buy new textbooks but are willing to buy second hand textbooks. In the absence of such a market, they'll spend their income on other goods that they deem more important.

Think of it otherwise this way. In the absence of a market for used textbooks the full value of a textbook is not exploited because some people who would wish to trade with one another cannot trade with one another. From what I can understand, in the context of the used books market, lets assume that there is set, finite amount of demand for the books. When there is a used books market, the demand first goes to the used books market and finishes up the supply in that market. The remaining demand then goes to the new books market (the professor/publisher). To compensate for the loss in demand, the publisher would therefore have to raise prices of the new books.

Now for the cars market, when there is no used cars market, everyone is indeed forced to buy new cars which raises demand and consequently price. However, you are assuming that cars are a necessity and that the demand transfers 100% from used cars to new cars. Some people maybe only purchasing cars from used cars market because they see the value in the lower price. When there is no longer a used car market, if the price of the new car remains the same, then people would deem that price to be too expensive since they are unable to resell it later on and ultimately choose not to buy at all or opt for alternatives. This actually reduces demand. To capture the market of such consumers, the car companies would ultimately reduce prices to get the market share. This is from the Bertrand competition model point of view.

● Is It Best to Buy or Borrow Books?

In gneral, reader will choose either to visit library to borrow books or visit book shop to buy book. In any readers' reading behavioral choice process, they will compare whether the book shop has same book to sell or library has same book to borrow, if the book can be sold or borrowed in shop or library. Then, the reader will compare the price between the library's the book list price and the shop's the book sale price. Hence, if the library's the book list price is more expensive to compare the shop's same book's sale price. Then, the reader will choose to visit the book shop to buy the same book in possible. So, his earlier borrowing the book desire will be changed to visit the book shop to buy the same book because the book shop's same book's sale price is cheaper than the library's same book.

Unless, the reader does not visit the book shop , so he believes that the library's the book can not be sold from any book shops.

One major positive of buying books is more money in the pockets of authors, who — unless they're someone like Harry Potter creator J.K. Rowling — tend to need all the sales they can get. Plus you're giving business to bookstores. Then there's the pleasure of adding another title to your home shelves — where the book is always available for reading, for impressing guests with your superior taste in literature.

But taking out titles from your local library has advantages, too. It's free — an especially nice price in these grim economic times. It's eco-friendly, because many people eventually peruse the same copy. And it can lead to more reading, because there's a deadline for when the books need to be returned. Sure, you can renew a book. But I try to avoid that. If I borrowed four library books the month before, I'll stay up late a few nights before the due date to finish that last one. I read approximately 10 more novels a year that way. Last but not least, library users are supporting an important government institution at a time when many right-wingers want to close or privatize almost everything that's not making a profit for greedy corporations. America needs democratic places that welcome everyone, not just people with lots of money.

I first came across this comparison on a popular sales psychology website [link below], and it got me thinking... how do these kind of (genius) persuasion techniques apply to your career as an author? You see, whatever people might say, books – especially ebooks – are cheap. Most self-publishers who sell books on Kindle (or wherever) set the bar at $2.99 – $5.99 per title. And I just know you break out in nervous sweats at the thought of charging more than that. I know I do. But price isn't the only thing readers care about. In many cases, it isn't even their top priority. Raise your hand – ever dropped your book prices down to 99c in the hopes of picking up some much-needed sales? I know I have. But the main problem isn't to do with price. $2.99 or $3.99 or $5.99 isn't a lot of money. It just isn't. The problem is all about POSITIONING.

Car market is similar to book market. In car market, that is, making your prices seem like a good deal. And that's where your sales message comes in. In the case of the car advertisements above – the sales messages focus on what's important to the prospective buyer and frame it as a benefit. The Rolls-Royce drivers want opulence and calm. The Land Rover crowd want power and ruggedness (which they associate with a noisy engine).

In education and car markets, Think about it like this – millions of people spend $50,000 – $100,000 on a college education. Or $30,000 on a new car. Or $500 on marketing and advertising for their business. Or $200 on a new cover design for their book (you can substitute your own numbers – but you get the idea). And this doesn't feel like a bad deal. Because you're getting what you expect at the price you expect to pay for it. You trust the person or business selling to you. It feels like a good deal, and you're more than happy to pay.

Which brings me to my main point. There are three types of reader in this world:

– First, those who will buy ANYTHING you publish without even thinking twice.

– Second, those who will NEVER buy from you.

– Third, those who aren't ready to buy... yet.

Hence, any paper book shops or publishers need to consider that they must have ebook publishers and libraries to be their competitors. Any readers can choose to go to libraries to borrow to read or pay visa to buy the epublisher's ebooks to read from internet. So, technology had influences any readers' reading habits to change from traditional paper book reading method to ebook reading method. Technology factor will influence readers or book buyers their reading behavioral change. So, any authors' paper books prices can not be raised rapidly , even their prices can not charge more than ebook prices. Otherwise, readers or paper book buyers can choose to read any ebooks to replace paper books from internet channel. Because ebook publishers have more effort to replace any paper book publishers, when paper book readers are influenced to accept to apply internet channel to read any ebooks in popular. So, traditional paper book publishing will change to ebook publishing market in the future.

● Online vs offline book shop different development trend

Nowadays, online book publishing is one kind of popular sale method to global publishing. For example, Amazon publish is as a business model with many potential advantages, relative to a physical operation. It held out the potential of lower book inventing and distribution costs and reduced overhead. Consumers could find the books, they were looking for more easily and a variety book topic choices could be offered for sale. It can accept and fulfill orders from almost any domestic location with equal ease. And most purchasers made on its site would be exempt from sales tax. One Amazon strategy hand, it would have to make its returns and redress processes transparent and reliable, and offer other ways for clients to learn, as much about the book possible before buying. Future online book market development trend, such as Amazon, Barnes & Noble etc. online book shops. How closely would their clietns find book ordering, as a substitute for visiting book stores?

In fact, Amazon is global the largest ingle online booksellers and sells many other products. Otherwise, Barnes & Noble, have been market share diminsh obviously. In the future, Noble & Barnes both will have their market share diminish continue obviously. There are also many fewer specialty re lowest. Hence, it seems online and offline both publishing methods will be competitive. It brings this questions: What is the trend between online book sale channel, its size relative to offline book sales channel, growth rate and the charcteristcs of reders who by online in the future? How book market's online channels are economically different , due to e-commerce's effects on online book market and supply fundamentals? How an online book sales channel might be expected to change equilibrium market outcomes?

I believe online book channel based sale activity varies considerably on these aspects: Sales in manufacturing printing cost, online sale services and online demand print book sale book topic choices. Such as author online advertising, change more or less sale price, online paper book shippng cost, visa card discount or online book shop member card discount book purchase, what welfares to online book buyers are.

Why readers chooce to buy books from internet habitally? In tradition, online book buyers habitally hope to use the internet to buy. Generally, they have these characteristics: They hope to use the internet to buy electronic books at home, they enjoy to read electronic book from computer, it is in any regular capacity , not ncecessarily to visit book shops to find books to buy and they can search any electronic from internet, electronic book is convenient to read from computer or laptop when they catch transportation or going to anywhere. Usually, internet users are higher income, more educated and younger. It seems that education is a sizeable determinant of who is online, even controlling for income. However, gender does not seems to be a factor in explaining internet use. Moreover, many of book qualitative patterns are seen for online book purchases in general are observed for electronic book products on on demand printing book products in particular.

Predition in future, many of the traditional online products , such as electronic or print on demand books, computer hardware , electronic airline tickets, saw more modest , but still substantial growth. In the future, online sellers trend to be newer online book stores and have less brand or reputation capital to signal or famous brand quality. These factors can create in online book sellers, which also often involve delay. However, there are many reasons for online book purchasing. The most obvious is that readers don't have opportunity where unobservably inferior point of electronic or demand on print book purchases.

● Pricing strategy in online and offline
book retailing

The book price represents consumer behavior on price. On one hand, the model contains two probability fuctions which render consumers' reservation prices for each individual channel. On the other hand, it is based on numerous book distribution which represent probabilities from and to each online or offline book store separate channel. Price strategy of book sale concerns how readers select a particualr book? Both offine and online book information seeking price strategies point out the challenges for information systems development. Hence, book price decision based on readers' age, e.g. children book price will be chealer than adult book price, due to children book content is usually simple and papers page is less. Otherwise, adult book content is more complicated or difficult to understand and page number is more than children book page number. However, online book store disadvantages are that : information system still often fail in supporting the users in causal leisure situations. In order to improve online book search system. Online book stores need to be better understood user strategies and performance and translate them into purposeful features.

A common analysis approach is to compare price and user strategies and interactions in the digital environment with those that occue in similar physical environment. If online bookstores hope to decide more reasonable electronic books or on demand printing books sale prices to compete with offline bookstores. Since, the physical environment (in this particular case bookstores) usually preceds the development of digital environments, processes and strategies from interaction in the physical environment have already stabilized and experiences can be translated into patterns for digital information system development. Thus, some only digital electronic bookstores , such as Amazon publish' disadvantages are : It lacks physical bookstore environment sale experiences. Otherwise, some owning themselves physical book and online book sale environment bookstores, bookstores that can compare only either paper books or electronic books bookstores to predict what the reasonable sale book sale price more easily. Are these differencs between online/digital book discovery environments and offline (neighborhood bookstore) services? Are researching recommendation strategies differences between observable in online and offline book search sessions? In general, interactive users studies based on user interactions in a ISBS developed web-based book discovery information system are aggregated cross multiple researcher groups. In order to provide a realistic book discovery environment, book collection should be large and comparable to other book discovery systems ,such as online book sale. For example, Amazon library book collection is used consisting of approximately 1.5 million books. Each book contains general metadata (title, authors, publisher, publication , year, etc.) subject metadata (classification, code), subject headings , user generated content (Amazon publish user reviewer, library thing user tags).

How does India book market trend?

Thus, I believe that online or offline bookstore different book research method will also influence readers' preferable book choices, then their choices behavior will influence how many times to find the book easily. If the online or offline readers can find the book topic or author name or contents etc. information easily. Then, the sale chance of the book will increase. Thus, price can increase more. For high population country, e.g. India, China . Does it have more sale chance, due to many people are living in these countries? What us online book store trend in India? Online book can let readers to buy new books and old books from internet, rent or borrow books from internet or access it in the form of e book, e.g. Amazon publish is the big player of online book business in India today. India where dynamic technologies like mobiles are prevalent, e-book readers may soon make into average household. Some of publishing houses which predicted that it would be long journey for e –books to become part of life needs to India readers. Thus, India will be one potential e book market. India is the third biggest market for English books. However, there are challenges of online bookstore in India. IN fact, online book market has changed the way reading consumer use internet for knowledge. Nowadays, people prefer e books are accessible anywhere, any time for creating flexible and secure online bookstore for online bookstores that need to concern to sell their e books to India markets because India readers shall concern visa card payment method where it is safe to pay to read any e books from internet.

Besides, online information searching has touched every field of human life. In the future, it is possible that purchased via mobile are clothing/footwear and e book or on demand print books. Also , due to e book is one kind of popular reading product to be enter India market. Currently, the online book market in India is offering exciting and renewed services to the internet users. India readers can accept to buy old books to read from online sale channel. Thus, India will be one new second hand online book store market to follow developed countries, such as US, UK etc.

Trend and development in the global book market

Under the influence of internet, new media , social networks. The way in which search to satisfy our needs. Internet is the high technological search method to change at the level of products and services, such as e book (electronic book or demand on print electronic paper book) and online e book rent service , online library e book borrowing services. Thus, in the future, global book market will be popular on concentrating selling e books or online print on demand paper books more than general walk in offline book shop paper books sale only method. Due to, internet changes traditional readers' reading habits to enjoy to read e books from mobiles, laptops, desktops more than paper book reading. Thus, the global book market will be predicted online electronic book sale format more than visiting walk in book ship sale format. The digitalization of information enables us to bring into discussion today contents separated from the physical, materials, paper shapes of the book. Today, books could be found online, read online for free or downloaded as an e book in English or any other language. Practically, the book has changed from paper to electronic book. In until , the internet and the e book , the changes were extremely slow. Today, digitalization produces rapid changes to the entire system of printing, distribution and reading books. Hence, the global book market trend will be the major implication on publishes, distribution, authors and book consumers. The online competition brings major changes to traditional distributors, the bookstores, the author of independent distributors noticeable decreased. The number of big distributors' stores will decrease. For example, Amazon publish is the best known global selling books online. Although, it can sell e books and printing on demand paper books both from internet channel conveniently.

In conclusion, e book market will dominate global online electronic book sale market and the e book publisher number will increase. As the same time, the visiting walk in offline book shop number will decrease, due to readers have accept to use laptops, mobiles to read electronic books from internet channel more than reading paper books. It implies paper book publishers need to change sale method, e.g. adopting internet to sell print on demand paper books, or reducing paper book sale price to attract e book readers to choose to buy paper books to read.

Web vs School campus book store development trend

Why do students choose to buy textbooks online? What factors motivate students choose online textbooks purchase? Nowadays, many online book retailers, such as Varsity books.com and Bigword.com ,. Amazon publish.com are now capturing more of the textbook online store market. What is motivating this behavior changes to student market , instead of children story market, entertainment or travel or sport book market etc. topic market. What causes students to choose purchase textbooks online ? Can likelihood to make purchases online by predicted by various social and personal characteristics of consumers? The online textbook purchase growth is allowing online retailers to capture a substantial portion of sales in some sectors. What motivates consumers to shop on the web? But, what if these factors are nor significant , such as better product availability, lower cost, as is that case when comparing on offline textbook purchasing. There is no significant price advantage to buy textbook online, it is there an availability issue, given that textbook can be purchased in the campus store (Foucault et al., 2000).

I shall assume that precious positive online purchase is positively correlated with the likelihood of an individual purchasing textbooks online. Hence, it influences why readers choose to buy textbooks online again. Following , other factor web consumers are likely shop online to save time and/or money, but what of those consumers who shop online when an equally time and cost efficient alternative is present. With regard to textbook purchasing, the time invested in researching for the appropriate books is likely to be similar, regardless of whether the student bookstore or through an online textbook. With regard to textbook purchasing, the time invested in researching from the time invested in searching appropriate books is likely to be similar: regardless of whether the student chooses to shop in the campus bookstore or through an online textbook retailer. If time from purchase until use counts, online textbook shopping could be considered less time efficient than its offline counterpart. Due to the readers need to turn on computer to link to internet to read electronic books or wait the print on demand to buy paper books from the electronic book store web site to wait the paper books to post to the online book buyer's home. Otherwise, offline bookstores can reduce time spending to wait the books to be posted to the buyer's home, after who pay money to take the paper book from the bookstore immediately. So, the non-waiting post book issue is still the text bookstore's strength to attract students to buy.

Prediction of direction of electronic books future trend

What is future trend of electronic book publishing development? To answer this question, we need to know what benefits of (electronic books) can attribute to human's needs. Nowadays, electronic books (e-books) are one way to enhance the digital library with global 24 hours a day and 7 days a week access to authoritative information, and there enable users to quickly retrieve and access specific research materials easily, quickly and effectively. Evenm some ebooks publishers choose to let readers who can borrow ebooks to online readers to read from online libraries to earn profit. For example, Amazon publisher lets every Amazon readers only pay about US$5 per month. Then, who can borrow unlimited ebooks to read from Amazon publisher private online member library website convenently.

Thus, it is one ebooks online borrowing strategy to compette with offline book stores and public library and school library in publishing industry. Due to offline book stores lack borrowing books services to any walk in readers. However, some countries' publich libraries also have similar ebooks borrowing to read services. An an ebook providers' electonic online libraries, online computer library center has been involved in the selection, catalogue and distribution of ebooks. Library users can able to remotely search, locate and checkout ebooks from the library's online public access catalogues. Thus, ebook publisher will have another public library competitor which can provide similar ebook borrowing service to online ebook readers from public library websites.

It means ebook publishers need to adopt any attractive ebook library sale borrowing service strategy to attract public library readers. However, as with any new opportunity, new challenge utilizes the internet opportunity to deliver new book content is no exception, Integrating ebooks into the digital library has created challenges and opportunities for librarians, publishers and ebooks providers for librarians in this ebook library borrowing service market to earn extra ebook lending service income. Because, online borrowing service library can have ebooks borrowing service, then why online ebook readers need to choose independent ebook publisher individual borrowing book service website to replace traditional public library paper book borrowing service. The reasons possible include that the readers can borrow ebooks to study from ebook publisher individual library borrowing website at home conveniently, but it is possible that they can not find any paper books to borrow from public libraries which are the same ebooks to be borrowed from any one ebook store to read, also ebook publishers can let whose ebook borrowers to borrow unlimited ebooks to read and there are longer extend borrowing ebook return days more than public libraries borrowing book return days and ebook readers have no penalty when they return ebooks too late and they can choose to pay little borrowing ebook charge in the month, if who do not expect to borrow any ebooks in the month, who can choose to stop to pay borrowing ebook charge in the month. Hence, they can choose to continue to borrow unlimited ebook numbers from ebook publishers and they are permitted to return ebooks longer time to compare traditional public libraries. For example, when the ebook reader pay only US$5 ebook library service fee to the ebook publisher in the month , then who can borrow the number of ebook up to 50 maximum number in the month as well as who can return the all ebooks to the ebook library within 60 days, it is longer return days to compare traditional public libraries. If the ebook reader can not return all these ebooks after the return day of 60 day. They can permit to extend more 60 return days. After this another 60 return days, they only need to pay US$5 penalty to the ebook store. Thus, it is one attrative ebook library borrowing service strategy in this competitive book publishing industry.

There is no doubt that the same trends that adopts ebooks and e-readers to US ebook publishing market are having a similar effect in other countries as well, such as Mobile ebook or laptop ebook technical development of reading devices that provide an reading experience similar to that of reading an actual book, the increasing penetration of the internet in all areas of life, which is significantly changing reading patterns and reading behavior. The increasing extent to which ebook or demand on printing book consumers are open to new technological reading trends, for which in particular that availability of attractive mobile devices, such as smartphones, portable games consoles, and MPS players are responsible to ebook reader tools.

Future trend will be that publishers and authors need to build close digital cooperation relationship. Publishers, bookstores and device manufacturers should take the opportunity to provide the market now with innovative ebook publishing products. And authors should explore opportunities for digital distributions and support publishers in their efforts to publish content. Publishers should also design a giving strategy and attractive ebook sale website that attracts customers without undermining the value of content. A well-thought out pricing strategy may also help publishers and content gain new customers, those who would not have purchased a traditional book , but may be inclined to buy an ebook that costs less, offers additional features , and works on a digital device . They already own there, usually the ebook price compares to traditional paper book price which have similar content, ebook price will be cheaper them the similar content of traditional paper book sale price.

In the future, ebook publishers will need to position themselves as content providers, and not just the suppliers of physical books. They will have to make content available on multiples media, in multiple formats, on multiple platforms. This content may not be limited to the text of a book itself, it may also include videos and games. This additional content may lead to incremental revenue.

In fact, the only lesisure activities more popular than reading books were watching television, listening to music such the radio and reading newspapers and magazines. Thus, every one should need to choose to enjoy to do what kinds of leisure activities every day. For example, if one person chooses to spend much time to either watch television or listen the music and radio or read newspapers and magazines in the whole day. I believe that he will spend less time to read book in the day. Then, it implies that ebook or paper book readers , the paper book or ebook buyer number will be decrease, due to they spend less time to read or without any reading behavior in the day. Thus, how to persuade every one to feel that reading book habit is attractive or important which can be one factor to influence the paper or electronic book readers, even electronic or paper book buyer number. Thus issue will be an attractive topic to concern for every ebook or paper book publisher on book publishing industry. If these both kind of publishers can persuade any person to feel reading book habit can bring benefits to themselves. They will spend less time to leisure activities. Then, ebook or paper book sale number or ebook borrowing service income will raise in the future. Thus, these both kinds of publishers need to concern how to persuade people to choose to spend some time to read books habitually every day. Consequently, psychological factor will be one important direction to raise book buyer number in publishing industry.

What are the factors to influence sales and marketing strategies for publishers?

I feel that how to predict book buyers which is driven by book buying experience and the publisher's credibility (loyalty) factors which will influence the any book buyer whose make final decision to buy the book from the publisher. As a publisher, a major goal is to extend whose readership and extend whose readers' influences, but where to start? How do publishers understand and serve diverse readers and decision makers in different countries? Whether can readers find the kind topic of book from publishers only, when find the kind topic of book from the university libraries or public libraries? Hence, due to offline and online publishing industry competition is high, global publishers will need to develop a sales plan to satisfy readers' reading taste. For publishers need to conduct book exhibition activities, visit different author's decision makers to research what who like to write negotiate terms to publish books with individual authors, secure sales and manage orders etc. different regulations of publishing to every author.

I recommend online or offline publisher ought concern how to publish every book before they decide to sel their every electronic book or paper book to any countries' readers. The marketing strategy includes to develop plan every book sale projection, SWOT (strengths, weaknesses, opportunities, or threats) to every book to be published to the country's readers to implement the plan. Book sales program, email communication marketing, lead generation to analyze the results, eg. every book purchasing trends, customer profiles, marketing sementation for every book to follow up and bedrief: Measuring ROI, setting priorities and develops tastics, finally customer needs analysis foe every book sale, it includes GAP analysis, ebook online library visits numbers to experience the ebook and focus groups. The, it is cycle to the develop plan again. Thus, if the publisher can have a better understanding of pricing strategy plan which can create price plan to be strengthed changes or cancelled for every paper book or electronic book sale marketing price strategies. Bringing potentially and disastrous reading experience to readers , this factor can be one good method to increase reader number and book sale price and sale number method. Then, the ebook or paper book publishers can make more accurate ebook or paper book sale price to every sale market, e.g. US or UK which is better book sale market, which kind of book can be the popular to these either market, whether UK readers like to read ebooks more or US readers like to read ebooks more or US readers like to read paper books more or UK readers like to read paper books more. Thus, the ebook or paper book stores can gather these data to analyze whether what every book topic sale price is more accurate to achieve the highest sale number and income.

Consequently, more appealing offerings can be developed to broader every publisher's audience and enhanced whose every publisher's image, segments of reader research, e.g. reader age, book reading taste. This is a measure level of penetration of journals and identity opportunity for growth GAP analysis marketing strategies will be popular methods to future book publishing. Based on first hand, expensive visiting and surveying librarians around the world, examing factors unique to each country and culture and make to recommendations integrate in every publisher's communication plan. For example, ebook trends pecentage of ebok spending in online ebook borrowing libraries is a publishing extra income from ebook borrowing readers. It is such one part of the overall electronic book market share income in the electronic book publishing market. In conclusion, internet technological innovation can bring new publishing business chance to ebook development , but it also brings competition to traditional paper book stores. So, paper book stores need have good marketing strategies to win their new ebook competitors.

Analysis of factors influencing online newspaper reading behavior

Nowadays, online newspapers will be popular to let readers to read any newspapers' news from internet. It showed that for online newspapers reader's intention is influenced by performance expectancy, habit and the habit of reading a print newspapers. So, newspapers consumer personal reading behavior was influenced by intention and habit. Some reading behavioral researchers showed some reasons to explain why traditional paper newspaper readers will like to change habits to study online newspapers.

Hence, changing reading habit will be one factor to influence traditional paper newspaper reader individual reading behavior changes to online newspapers reading habit. In fact, high technological communication media will influence mobile phone and internet both new communication media causes. These new communication medias will bring new print electronic media causes, such as print newspapers, online book products. Some of traditional paper newspaper readers will choose to read any news from online newspapers. The reasons include free charge, reading at home in convenient, not need go out newspapers, online newspapers do not need the reader's hands to touch the black word paper newspaper to be dirty, and waste less time to buy every day to achieve economic benefit.

Every online newspaper reader will have this factor to influence whom to change traditional paper newspaper reading habit. The factor shows that attitude has a direct effect on intentions, and is influenced by performance expectancy and effort expectancy or related personal online reading acceptance conceptions. Because of whose acceptance of online newspaper reading attitude is as an important in technology user online newspaper reading attitude was included.

Additional, every online newspaper reader self-efficacy and anxiety are expected to be minor issue to influence the online newspaper reader to change whose attitude to choose not to internet tool to read of an online newspaper. However, different age reader either he/she is young or old age factor will have influence whom to choose online newspaper to read, e.g. old age readers will feel difficult to apply internet technology to read newspaper, otherwise, young age readers will feel easy to apply internet technology to read newspaper. So, the old or young age traditional paper newspaper readers, when the acceptance new technological online newspaper to them, they will adopt online newspaper reading attitude to replace traditional paper newspaper reading habit more easy. So, their acceptance new technological of online newspaper reading attitude will have a direct effect on online newspaper reading intention and are influenced by both paper and online newspapers reading enjoyment performance expectation and online newspapers reading effort expectation, when their expectations were needed to be satisfied more these past traditional paper newspaper reading experience. Moreover, past paper newspapers reading behavior and habit should be noted. Then, these two expectation factors will encourage or persuade the traditional paper newspaper readers change whose reading attitude, reading habit and reading behavior to read online newspapers. Hence, the online newspaper readers' psychological factor will influence whose traditional paper newspapers readers whose reading behavioral changes. Also, it means that expectation factor will influence the traditional newspaper readers to change whose counter intentional paper newspaper reading habit.

However, online newspaper will bring much knowledge to compare traditional paper newspapers , e.g. real newspapers news data, more meaningfulness news, providing the nature of visiting a news website, which can let online news readers can feel different read model primary on frequency with relatively little spread in the amounts of time spent at the site.

What are the main factors to influence online newspaper reading behaviors? Same testing indicates for moderation by the online newspaper age, gender and online newspaper reading experience will bring the online reading newspapers habit influence. The testing also indicates male gender and young age group , this group likes to apply internet to find or seek or search any news matters. Hence, this internet user group will bring to have interest to read newspapers from internet channel. The reason is possible because this young male internet users like to contact new technology, e.g. internet. They think the online newspaper is useful and it is more useful to read the online newspaper to compare to paper newspaper.

The two reasons : liking to contact new technology and feeling the online newspaper is more useful which can support why young male online internet users feel to expect reading online newspaper expectancy were more concrete.

Additional online newspapers usefulness are more considered on unclear concept to explain why this reader group feels more like to study online newspapers. What exactly is the usefulness of reading an online newspaper?

The testing also indicated that some online newspaper readers responded to use the online newspaper to feel natural, it showed to be related to attitude as well as to habit , which seems to hold face validity as a natural feel can be considered on attitude on the online newspaper. So, online reading attitude and online reading habit can reflect why man young male like to read online newspapers more than paper newspaper reason.

Another reason indicated that when the young male readers want to read the news, the online newspaper is an obvious choice for him/her. So, many online newspaper young male readers had felt online newspaper is one another newspaper reading choice to replace traditional paper newspapers.

In conclusion , free charge online newspaper is not the main factor to influence both traditional paper newspaper readers to change their reading habit to choose online newspapers to read suddenly. There are other factors to cause them to choose online newspapers to read, such as more usefulness feeling, contacting new technology, online reading habit, positive online reading attitude etc. different psychological factors which will have more influences to cause their paper newspaper reading habits to be changed. Hence, the free price economic gain actor must not only one main factor to persuade readers to choose online newspapers to read.

How electronic versus traditional print
textbook influence of university students'
learning behavior

When one university student was accepted by electronic text book learning channel to replace traditional paper text book learning channel (methods). Electronic text book will bring what positive or/and negative influence to impact whose learning behavior changes. For example, electronic text book learning method will bring positive impact to raise the student's examination grades and perceived learning scores or it will bring negative impact to fall down the student's examination grades and perceived learning scores. The mean scores indicated that students who choose to text books for their learning aim. It will have significantly higher perceived affective learning performance and examination results. Thus, the purpose of student learning and teacher teaching method, every university needs to examine whether it is efficient to raise student learning effort to replace paper text book learning method in any learning environment, e.g. many students and one teacher classroom learning environment or the independent student learns himself/herself at home learning environment or library learning environment.

Can text book reading tool bring absolute advantages to university students or bring some disadvantages to them? When a student needs to apply e-text book to learn, who needs access e-text book in a static location, such as a computer or on a mobile device. So, the e-text book in a static location factor, it will have influence to each student reading or learning behavior to bring negative and/or positive both impacts.

The e-text book was distributed on a CD and installed on a located computer. This limited the user to accessing the e-textbook in a single location and eliminated the potential access to the e-text book on due to the lack of mobility. So, it seems that the location of limited to e-text book will bring negative impact to let the student can only learn in a fixed location because he/she will feel difficult to move heavy computer to other places to learn more than on paper text book. So, e-text book location can not allow the student to leave the classroom to learn more easier if he/she had chose to use to computer to install the CD to learn in the classroom. Supposing the student 's teacher needs the student often to leave the classroom to discuss any matter suddenly, it is not very convenient to the student to use e-text book to learn because he/she can not move the computer to leave the classroom with him/her easily. Then, it will be possible to influence the student can bot be attention to read the e-text book, when the teacher needs the student to leave the classroom (none book bringing) to discuss any time any time immediately. Otherwise, if the student used one paper book to read/learn in the classroom, if the teacher needs whom to leave the classroom often to discuss immediately. He/she will feel convenient to learn because he/she can bring the light paper book to leave the classroom to discuss with the teacher in any location easily.

Hence, it seems e-text book learning will bring not convenient fixed location learning environment to every e-texting learning student in classroom, when, he/she needs often to leave the classroom to discuss with the teacher any time.

Other disadvantage of e-text learning will bring students feel difficult in possible. In the past, some learning researcher experiments indicated results demonstrated that student participants in both groups had similar recall and ability to reinterpret information suggesting that retrieval of information is not effected by kindle e-book reader e-text book, a tabled computer e-text book or a print version.

Hence, it seems that e-text book can not help or assist recall the student's learning memory to remember the e-text book content more easier. Due to it is one e-text book machine, the student will fell to difficult to find any unclear or important information in any page(s) to write for learning/reading record more easier than one paper text book.

Another disadvantage of e-text book is the inefficacy or inefficient reading challenge to the e-text book reader. The efficacy of e-text books in a higher education environment will be one interesting discussing question. Passage length is one difference that impact the results. Studies involving shorter reading sessions indicated no substantial variance with respect to reading comprehension and understanding.

Conversely, studies involving longer reading passages indicated prior comprehension, when reading longer e-text , eye fatigue and mental workload are also concerns. Hence, e-text book reading will be possible to let students feel eye fatigue and mental workload in their reading process.

Due to machine e-text book words are more small size and unclear more than paper text book words to print to let students to read every words or sentences in computer. Consequently, studies indicated that e-text book readers need to spend much nervous and time to read longer and poor comprehension in whole e-text book reading process. When, university students need to spend time to read longer e-texts from computers. For example, they need to choose to reads hundreds of papers of e-text books on a screen, whether on a computer or handheld electronic device compared to print versions may contribute to eye fatigue. The consequence, eyestrain and mental fatigue could be poorer comprehension and have a poor eye, nervous health influence and every student's e-text learning behavior can bring negative reading habit to whom, when every one need to apply desktop or laptop or mobile electronic tools to read any words from e-textbooks. Hence, it seems e-text book reading method has possible to bring poor health challenge to every student.

So, above all these e-learning reading factors to bring this question: Does e-learning influence the student's negative reading behavior to cause poor final examination grades results? In fact, every student needs to change whose traditional learning method from paper text book reading habit or reading behavior to e-text books. He/she needs to change whose reading habit. He/she must need to spend long time to accept how to adopt this kind of new technological reading method as well as effect may change through a new technological learning experience itself and impacts the acquisition of knowledge leading to reading behavioral change.

As I indicated the e-learning will bring poor health and poor nervous negative influences when the student often needs to apply electronic product to read long time. So, it will be possible to influence the student health to be poor to bring examination low grades results in possible be cause he/she has poor health to exam.

It is possible that it has relationship to influence the student to exam low grade between e-learning habit and poor health causes. The reason is based on that efficacy of textbook format is defined grades. I assume that all these negative e-text book reading factors can influence every e-text book reader's health to be poor when he/she needs often read e-text book s to cause long time reading habit. So, I mean that e-text book reader individual health changes to poor, it is only depend on how long time e-text book reading habit factor. So, if he/she only spend less time to read e-text books and he/she also has habit to read paper books sometimes. Then, he/she won't be influenced to be poor from e-learning method easily.

It means that it has none direct relationship between less time e-text book reading habit and low examination grades result. Hence, low examination grades result to the student, it only depends on long time e-text book reading habit and the student's long time e-text book reading habit needs to confirm that whose long time e-text book reading habit causes poor health to the student effect. Why do I believe that efficacy of textbook format can influence the student's examination grade? Based on above analysis, the e-text book reading format and paper book reading format is very different. For example, the efficacy of textbook is very different between paper text book reading format and electronic text book reading format. Such as one sickness student needs to spend more nervous to read one e-text book more than one paper text book . This reason is because machine reading method is difficult to compare paper reading method. When the student has sickness, who must need to spend more time and nervous to read one e-text book more than one paper text book. If my assumption is right, then the e-text book sickness reader's reading efficacy to each paper must be poor to compare the paper text book sickness reader , due to the sickness e-text book reader needs to spend long time and much nervous to read each paper more than he/she chooses to read one paper book. When he/she is sickness to finish whose reading . Due to his/her memory will be poor and tries, when he/she feels sick, so whose reading effort must be poor when he/she needs to apply computer tools or mobiles to read.

How to change future e-reader study habit to feel better

Nowadays, publishers, internet bookstores manufacturer e-readers have high expectations for digital future of book industry. If they expected e-book publishing industry success, they need to considerate how to assist to future e-readers to let them to feel whose reading habit to be better in order to persuade or attract them to choose to read e-books more easily, due to doctors indicated that long time e-books reading will cause eye poor health and tired and poor nervous reason in possible and paper book price competition and more topic choice reason. It is one value consideration question that e-book publishers need to considerate.

For example, in the US Amazon publish has improved the reading market by producing e Reader that is easy to use and making it easy for clients to purchase a wide variety of books at competitive prices. It will bring digital reader technology as an opportunity to open new target markets and create new e-readers. The question is how Amazon publish , such as e-book publishers change future e-reader reading habit to feel to choose e-books reading method is better than paper books reading method. The successful factors may include as below:

E-book reading market is similar to e-music listening market. They need every e-book reader and/or digital music listen listener to discover why to apply this kind of new digital technology reading or listening method which is better to enjoy to read every e-book content and/or listen every digital music song in order to adopt new listening and/or reading digital technological learning habits or experiences. So, this new digital technological reading or/and digital music listening process, every e-book reader or digital music listener needs to learn how to adopt this kind new digital reading or/and listening products to change from his/her traditional paper book reading or/and CD/DVD music song listening method to this new technological digital reading or listening methods from computer tool channel.

In this changing habit process, every e-book reader or/and e-music listener needs to spend some time to learn how to apply internet technological tool to help whose to read digital book or listen digital music from computer channel. So, he/she must attempt to change whose habit from traditional paper book reading habit and/or CD/DVD listening music habit to e-book reading habit and/or e-music listening habit.

Furthermore, e-book publishers also need to know whether which kind of book topics are be favorable popular to be chose to read for either student reader target to read or mature age reader target to read or old age reader target to read. Who will purchase the topic to read to be e-Reader? Will they be designed to appeal to be a group of e-reader customers or only to those who have a high degree of comfort with technology to enjoy e-reading method? Will people who read once in a time be purchased by the small group of e-reading clients who buy and read a high volume of e-books? What reasons, readers will choose to read the topics of e-books more than paper books? Will publishers be able to use e-books and e-readers to extend the many different age e-reading clients, e.g. young, mature, retirement, old, student age e-readers? Will publishers ever more to all readers are only choose digital e-reading model habit or who are a half digital e-reader and a half paper book reading habit clients to them?

Hence, one successful digital publisher needs to consider how to persuade every traditional paper book habit readers to change their reading habit to read digital e-books from computer. Because changing habit is one challenge to influence the e-book publisher 's e-book reader number. How to persuade the paper book reading habit readers to change whose attitude to choose to read e-books , it is one considerate question to every digital publisher? Some readers may feel difficult that who needs to learn new knowledge how to read e-books from computer tool, e.g. old age reader group. This reason will influence they still choose paper books to read in habit. So, any e-book publisher has responsibility to teach new digital technological knowledge learning method to let the e-book desire readers can feel easy to apply internet to read e-books from computer tool.

Another factor is e-book price, normally every e-book price will need to be sold cheaper to compare the similar paper book topic in order to persuade paper book readers choose to buy the similar topic of e-books to read more easily. Because if the reader discover the e-book topic is similar to the paper book topic contents, but the e-book price is charged high than the similar paper book topic content, then he/she will possible to choose to buy the similar paper book topic to read.

Another factor concerns how to raise e-books attraction. E-publishers will need to position themselves as content providers, and not just to be similar to the suppliers of physical books. They will have to make content available on multiple media, in multiple formats, on multiple platforms. This content may not be limited to the text of a digital book itself, it may also include audio, video, image and sound speaking digital books to attract e-readers' attention.

Another factor is that I recommend e-book publishers need to let all e-book readers to feel reading e-books are leisure time habit to let them to enjoy life every day in popular. Intention is such as good tool for anyone to apply to entertainment, for example people linked using internet to read books, watch movies, play video games from computer tool. They are some main points. They have same main points. They tend to spend leisure time with electronic media, such as apply internet to watch television which is such as to apply internet one more choice to assist readers to read e-books from computer media tool conveniently at home.

However, this is one example e-book attraction point to e-reader. Every e-book needs have e-pub files to allow readers to control the size of the text or their computer screens. If the e-reader feels the text is small size and computer screen is small size in difficult to read. Then, he/she can use mouse tool to change the e-book text number to be high number, e.g. from 18 to 20 or more number and he/she can apply mouse tool to move the computer screen to be wider more easily. Hence, it is e-book attraction point to e-book readers to feel when he/she feel the text is small size to read in difficult. Otherwise, every paper book print text(word) size is fixed, all word size can not be changed to read and every paper book wide size is also fixed. All it is every paper's unattraction point to every paper book reader.

Consequently, every e-book publisher needs have its attraction point to let its every e-book reader feels it is different to the other paper book publishers. It needs to solve these challenges to let its every reader to accept to choose its e-book reading channel. The challenges may include how to let the e-reader feels its e-book reading media can provide a more comfortable e-reading experience to compare other e-book publishers' reading media, how to let its e-readers feels its all e-books can provide one precise and stable e-book reading characteristics, how to let its ebook readers to feel its every ebook displays does not require any background lighting and one easy to read, even in direct sunlight environment, and it e-reading tool can spend less energy from laptop battery or desktop electricity to compare other e-book publisher reading tool, it means that the e-book publisher's ebook reading tool can provide a recharged power desire which can be used for several thousand pages or seveal weeks e-reading function. Hence, it the e-book publisher's e-book reading tool can provide more clear words and text image as well as less electricity consumption function to let every e-reader to read to compare other ebook publishers from laptop, destop or mobile media. Then , the ebook publisher's competitive effort will raise to win its other ebook publishing competitors. However, any ebook publisher needs have attraction points to persuade its ebook readers to read its any ebooks feel comfortable and providing fun ebooks choices and easy to read its every ebook text more clear if it expects to win its competitors in ebook publishing industry.

Factors influence child reading habit

Reading failure is a serious educational problem to influence every publisher success because if the child chooses to buy its books to read, but its child readers can not feel its books can help them to assist their learning success or failure examination or low grades result. Then, it will influence its child reader number to be reduced. However, the factors cause reading failure, it is not only considered to the publisher's poor book content quality factor, it can include the other factors such as: It is simply be attributed by poverty, immigration or the learning of English as a second language. What factors will influence child read in wrong habit to bring reading failure, even learning failure in effect? It is one question to every publisher needs to know in order to avoid they feel failure examination emotion after read their e-text books. Hence, how to design every text book content is one important issue to ever publisher.

A study by Yankelovich found most children are reading, but they are not reading enough. It indicated only about 3 in 10 children can be classified as high frequency readers who read books for fun ever day. Age 8 children are less to see benefits t oreading for fun, girls are more likely boys to have positive attitude about reading and feel fun. The benefits of reading are evidenced by the attitude of high frequency readers to achieve future learng success. More than 40% of children ages 5 to 8 say they are high frequency readers, by ages 9 to 11 that proportation drops to 29%. Almost half of the 15 to 17 year old (46%) are low frequency readers compared with 14% of 5 to 8 year old age. So, this study investigation reflected that building good learning habit has relationship between frequency reading and feeling fun to read to every child. It seems that one fun content book can attract the child to read the whole book all content really. So, publisher needs to consider how to design and write attractive content books to let every child to read.

What factors cause every child feel barriers to read? Some investigations indicate that young children tend to maintain high expectations for success, even in the face of regarded failure, when old students don't, also to older students feel failure following high effort appears to carry more negative inplications. Moreover, all students individual attitude about their capabilities and their interpretation of success and failure is further factor to affect their willingness to feel fun to read in themselves learning proceses.

So, it concludes this fun book content design method can persuade young people feel fun to read really. Moviated readers hold positive benefits about themselves attitude or reading habit which will bring positive and attractive reading emotion to influence them.

What are the book publishers and teachers' responsibilities to improve student individual negative habit to have positive reading habit or positive learning attitude? The ultimate goal in teaching and reading book is to raise students comprehend te ideas in a piece of text as they need. So, any publisher has responsibility to publish one fun and meaning book in prior, because every teacher will teach whose students by the text book content. If the text book content is fun and attractive and meaning, then the teacher can teach to let every students to learn more easily.

Training every student owns good reading habit which can help whom expand their thinking skills, learn to concentrate and enlarge their vocabulary and effectively better their learning environment. The good reading habit ought be trained from the child stage in beginning. So, when the child has is growing up, when he/she is needed to go to primary, secondary, even university to study, he/she had been built good reading habit from the publishers' fun and meaning book content influence in order to let they further learn any new knowledge to feel more easily. So, publishers have responsibilities to sell fun and meaning content books to let every child to read to raise whom reading interest to further young and mature learning stages.

However, the problems, children experience learning to read are often not related to their ability to learn, but to their awareness. Their ability to hear the English language and their expose to the English words. So, repeating to spell the English words will assist the child to raise memory to remember to write the English words more easily. So, book publishers have responsibilities to express every book content to attact child readers to feel interest or fun to learn to remember to spell every word as well as teachers have responsibilities to train students how to hear the words, he/she assist every child to learn to spell the English word more easily. So, teachers ought often speak every word or speak every sentence loudly from every book content to let students to listen easily in order to let they can raise every word memory more easily.

Consequently, instead of child's parents and child himself/herslf has responsibility to help the child self to build good reading habit, teachers and book publishers have also responsibilities to help them to build good reading habit because fun and meaningful books which bring more attraction to influence every child to read, when the book is fun and meaningful , then the teacher can follow its content to teach whose students to attract them to learn more easily. However, the good reading habit includes elements of reading comprehension to every book content , such as: identifying and summarizing the main idea, comparing and contrasting, identifying supporting facts and details, making influences and drawing conclusions, predicting outcomes, recognizing fact and opinion, identigy cause and effect recognizing sequence of events, identifying story / case elemetnts, such as main characters, settings, conflict, and resolution, identifying the another's purpiose and point of view, interpreting literary devices, such as imagery , symbolisms.

Hence, publishers ought to follow above these elements to design their every book content in order to let child readers to feel fun and meaningful and easy to read. Because reading comprehension elements will be one important factor to train every child or mature student reader to build good reading habit or attitude more easily and effectively in order to raise their future good reading effort in their every learning stage in success.

CHAPTER THREE

Persuading traveller space city travel leisure choice

Undiscovered planets adapting human living chance

There are still thousands of undiscovered planets, systems, suns, etc. all within the Sol region alone! Don't forget, there are 400 Billion(!!!) star systems and most of them contain planets and often even several stars. I doubt we will ever find everything in this huge galaxy. With that being said, I found undiscovered stars, planets and even completely undiscovered systems not even 300 LY away from the next star system which had a station in it. I also found undiscovered stars only about 50 LY away from the inhabited systems. It literally takes you only minutes to get there. But you really have to pay attention and keep searching. You will find discovered stars and planets even thousands of LY away from inhabited space, but every now and then you stumble across undiscovered stuff in between. There are just too many stars and planets to be discovered. Now if you venture REALLY far out, you will eventually come across completely undiscovered systems everywhere but it will take you quiet a long time to fly there. The map is so freaking huge there is probably more than thousands of stuff that are unexplored. So, we have possible to attempt to find one another earth to be adapted to human to live if scientists can spend long time to search another planet to live in space.

I shall indicate the reasons to explain that why space ought have some planets which can be similar to earth to allow human to live as below:

● There are many undiscovered planets exist in space

Space scientists had been experimenting a long range exploration to find whether inhabited space has any planets which can adapt to allow human to live in possibility. The VAST majority of data that they indicated that the hard numbers that frontier developments has, but if they had to guess and peg a percentage to the amount of galaxy explored, maybe somewhere around 9%. To put that in perspective, that may actually be a bit high, that would be upwards of 36,000,000,000 (That's 36 billion!) explored systems! Even in the very off chance they had explored that much, there are still 364,000,000,000 to go! There's still a lot of exploring to do 9% is extremely high. Breaking it down further, if they could assume an active player base of 10,000 (again, that's hardly an official number, it's just something I pulled out of my head) that means every single player would have had to have explored and scanned 3,600,000 systems, just to get to 9%. considering the number of active full-time explorers doesn't number anywhere near 10 thousand, and over 3 million systems fully scanned would be an absolutely impressive achievement very few people would have accomplished, (even among full-timers) means we are very probably at significantly LESS than 9% explored. So, it mean that space scientists still need to spend long time to attempt to find any planets' locations to carry on implementing further scientific experimentation in order to ensure whether the planet can provide good natural environment, e.g. fresh air, clean water, warm weather to provide human to adapt to live in possible. Because the undiscovered planets number is too many, so any one undiscovered adapted living planet still have high chance to exist in space.

● There are many planets can provide good weather natural environment to provide human to live in possible

What undiscovered parts can provide good weather is similar to earth natural environment? Space scientists had ensure that there are many planets' weather is similar to our earth's weather. It mean that any one of the good weather natural environment planets may provide fresh air, clean water and land natural resource to satisfy human's basic life needs. Today the most inaccessible parts of the planet such as the deep Congo or the New Guinea highlands have had at least some contact with the outer world, and it's doubtful a population of Neandertals could sustain themselves in such a limited area. Back in the 1970s there was a sensation when a tribe called the Tasaday in the Phillipines were thought to be survivors of an ancient population dating back to paleolithic times. It turned out however that they probably had only been in their present area for a few hundred years.

Not likely. The climate has changed too much and they either adapted or became extinct. With the progress and technological improvement in Gene splicing, It will be possible to assemble genetic material to clone one.

It would take three generations. The problem is to develop a climate and environment in which they can survive. If they do not die out too quickly, some people are carrying more Neanderthal genetics than others. Climate, environment, and improvements in nutrition and medicine are aiding in eliminating the best carriers.

The Earth Provides Four Resources for Every Human Being

- Air to breathe
- Water to drink
- Food to eat
- Space in which to live

Each of these resources is compromised because of the large numbers of people now living on the earth whose consuming lifestyles have a negative impact on our natural resources. We must make changes now in how we live so that the earth can continue to sustain our needs and be a healthy and safe place for everyone.

Air: Every day you bring chemicals into your home that are meant to do good. You bring them in to clean your home, manage pests, care for your clothing, or enhance your appearance. Find out how to make sure these chemicals are the safest and most effective in accomplishing your intentions. First, read the labels. If the ingredients are labeled "dangerous" choose another product to bring into your home.

Topics to Explore: integrated pest management, safer cleaning supplies

Food: Consider Michael Pollan's quote: "Eat food, not too much, mostly plants" from Food Rules: An Eater's Manual.

Topics to Explore: healthy eating, local food, organic food, diet for a small planet

Water: The water we drink and use comes from our local surface water or sometimes from water sources underground. Using local water rather than bottled water transported from elsewhere is one example of positive environmental sustainability. Use the water from your faucet rather than drinking from bottled water or other bottled drinks. Take steps to learn about water and how to protect it. Every step we take to improve the quality of our surface water or ground water will improve someone's drinking water, perhaps our own.

Topics to Explore: storm water retention, watershed, ground water, water use cycle

Space: You use space both in your home and in your community. Help the earth provide quality space for your use.. Improve the quality of the space around you by walking rather than driving, cleaning up a park, or promoting civic pride. Connect to your local community by participating in local events.

Topics to Explore: supporting local businesses, protecting the watersheds, "transition town", alternative energy, energy conservation

● Reducing energy use and

● Protecting water in Pennsylvania (Marcellus Shale gas drilling)

Is it possible for a planet's atmosphere to be so thick that things could float in it like an ocean? What might that atmosphere be composed of?

Space scientists had confirmed that indeed it is, at least in principle. It has been suggested that Venus could be colonized by buoyant cities floating in the atmosphere at rather more comfortable temperatures than are to be found at ground level. Space scientists indicate that Venus planet has below these characteristics :

Venus' Atmosphere: Venus' Atmosphere: composition, Climate and Weather

Venus has the distinction of being the hottest planet in the solar system, and the fault lies solely with its atmosphere. What is it about the air on Venus that keeps the planet cooking?

Atmospheric makeup

The atmosphere of Venus is made up almost completely of carbon dioxide. It also includes small doses of nitrogen and clouds of sulfuric acid. The air of Venus is so dense that by mass, the small traces of nitrogen are four times the amount found on Earth, although nitrogen makes up more than three-fourths of the terrestrial atmosphere. This composition causes a runaway greenhouse effect that heats the planet even hotter than the surface of Mercury, although Venus lies farther from the sun. When the rocky core of Venus formed, it captured much of the gas gravitationally.

In addition to warming the planet, the heavy clouds shield it, preventing visible observations of the surface and protecting it from bombardment by all but the largest meteorites.

Although Venus and Earth are similar in size, someone standing on the ground on Venus would experience air about 90 times heavier than Earth's atmosphere; pressures are similar to diving 3,000 feet beneath the ocean. The most Earth-like atmosphere in the solar system occurs 30 to 40 miles (50 to 60 kilometers) above the surface of Venus. Both oxygen and hydrogen rise above the heavier gas layer covering the ground, and the pressures are similar to our planet.

Chemical composition:
- Carbon dioxide: 96 percent
- Nitrogen: 3.5 percent
- Carbon monoxide, argon, sulfur dioxide, and water vapor: less than 1 percent

Climate and weather

Winds of about 224 mph (360 kph) keep the clouds of Venus in constant motion. Though the planet spins slowly, only once every 243 Earth days, the clouds zip around the top of the planet's atmosphere every four days. But wind speeds drop closer to the surface, where they only move a few miles per hour.

On Earth, seasons change based on the planet's tilt: When a hemisphere is closer to the sun, it experiences warmer temperatures. But on Venus, most of the sun's heat fails to make it through the thick atmosphere. As such, the planet not only doesn't experience significant temperature changes over the course of the year, it also keeps things constant from night to day. The clouds of Venus appear bright white or yellow. Unlike Jupiter or Saturn, there are no discernable bands or storms visible to the naked eye.

Hence, due to Venus planet has above these characteristics ,hence space scientists believe that Venus's weather and climate is similar to our Earth's weather and climate. It implies that Venus has possible to provide good natural environment to allow human to adapt to live in possible. However, Venus is not one planet in space. There are too many undiscovered planets are existing in space. Also, it can imply that it has possible that there is another planet , it can provide better natural environment to compare Venus this planet to allow us to live in possible.

The possible undiscovered similar Mars planets number

How many can our undiscovered planets which be similar to Mars to exist in space to supply natural resource, such as air, water, food, land, good weather or climate to allow human to live in possible? Nowadays, scientists discover possible existence of new planet the size of Mars in our solar system. Astronomers believe they have discovered a new planet in the solar system the size of Mars.

Recent research paper claims there is a massive object lurking on the edge of our solar system that is likely to be a
previously undiscovered world.It follows suggestions last year that another planet – nicknamed Planet 9 – appeared to be orbiting the sun from the

outer regions of the solar system. Scientists discovered Planet 9 after noticing that something was exerting a gravitational force on objects in the Kuiper Belt

– an area of comets, the dwarf planet Pluto and huge ice objects beyond Neptune that encircles the whole solar system. The unusual

orbits of the objects could be explained by a planet with a mass 10 times that of Earth exerting a gravitational pull on them, researchers said Now a similar analysis has revealed the possibility of a second new planet, dubbed Planet 10.

On a study to be published in the Astronomical Journal, Kat Volk and Renu Malhotra from the University of Arizona discovered that a number of Kuiper Belt objects (KBOs) are not orbiting in the way they would normally be expected to, suggesting something in the region is exerting a strong gravitational force on them. Imagine you have lots and lots of fast-spinning tops, and you give each one a slight nudge," Professor Malhotra said. "If you then take a snapshot of them, you will find that their spin axes will be at different orientations, but on average, they will be pointing to the local gravitational field of Earth." Scientists said the most probable explanation for the discrepancy was the existence of a planet, similar in size to Mars, to the edge of the solar system. The most likely explanation for our results is that there is some unseen mass," Dr Volk said. "According to our calculations, something as massive as Mars would be needed to cause the warp that we measured."

Scientists hope the launch of the Large Synoptic Survey Telescope will help them spot the two new planets, should they exist.

Scientific models suggest most planets that enter our solar system would be ejected without causing a significant impact.

Hence, it seems that our space has at least one planet, it is possible existence of new planet the size of Mars in our solar system. Although, scientists can not confirm that it does not represent it has good weather, climate, clean water, enough land, fresh air etc. natural resource to provide us to live, although it's size is similar to Mars. But, we can make more accurate prediction that it is possible that there are other planets are possible existence of new planet

the size of Mars in our solar system. If scientists can confirm that this new planet's size is same or similar the size of Mars.

Then, it implies that there is possible that many new planets the size of Mars are also existence in our solar system. Even, if this new planet the size of Mars, it can not provide good weather , climate , provide good weather , climate , fresh air, clean water, ocean, enough land, food etc. natural resource environment to supply to human to live. There is possible that we can also discover another possible existence of new planet the size of Mars in our solar system any location later. Then, it will has another possible to provide good weather , climate , fresh air, clean water, ocean, enough land, food etc. natural resource to supply to human to live. Because if one planet's size is similar to Mars, although it can not provide good weather, climate, fresh air, clean water, ocean, enough land, food etc. natural resource environment to supply to human to live the planet.

It can not represent that another planet's size is similar to Mars and it must not supply good natural resource environment to allow us to live in the planet. So, I believe that it is possible that space scientists ought have much chance to find the another planet , its size is similar to Mars, even it can provide the good weather, climate, natural resource environment to let us to live in possible, due to our solar system is very large and it is continue expanding. It means that the planets number will possible be increasing when our solar system is also expanding to increase its space or area to let many large planets to locate in our solar system in possible.

In conclusion, I believe that the possible undiscovered similar Mars planets number in our solar system won't be zero, even it is more than one. Even, space scientists can find another Earth to let us to live in possible. My conclusion is based on these reasons: our solar system is expanding to allow enough space or area to let increasing planets number existence in our solar system and the causing similar Earth planet chance is more,
scientists had found one planet, its size is similar to Mars, it implies that our solar system ought existence another planet, its size is similar to Mars size or our Earth size in possible, as well as I suppose that when space scientists can discover one planet, its size is similar to our Earth or Mars, then it will have more opportunity to own our Earth's same natural resource environment to allow us to live.

So, the another Earth planet is possible existence in our solar system. The question is : Do we need how long time to discover our another Earth in solar system? So,
space scientists ought need to find the best method , which can spend the shortest time to find any planets' existence locations in our solar system. Because if they need long time to find any planets' existence location in our solar system. Then, we need to wait long time to discover the another Earth

existence in our solar system really.

● The possible short time methods exploring undiscovered adapting human living planets

What methods can space scientists can use to search any possible adapting human to live planets existing in space in the shortest time? Nowadays, space scientists had discovered that this solar system of seven Earth-sized planets may be the best place to look for alien life. Around 40 light-years away, seven Earth-sized planets have been spotted orbiting closely around a small,

ultra-cool star. It's one of the largest solar systems that's ever been discovered outside of our own, and it's a particularly enticing find in the ongoing search for extraterrestrial life. Six of the planets in the system may have the right temperatures for liquid water to exist on their surfaces, and astronomers are confident they'll be able to get a more in-depth look at these seven worlds with future space telescopes.

Particularly enticing find in the ongoing search for extraterrestrial life the solar system, detailed today in a study in Nature, isn't a completely new find. In fact, the discovery of this system was announced last year by the same researchers. But at the time, they thought they had only found three planets around the star, named TRAPPIST-1. When the researchers took a closer look at the system with more precise telescopes, including NASA's Spitzer Space Telescope, they found more planets nearby. The space scientists got plenty of new data, and we went from three to four to five planets," Michael Gillon, research associate for the Belgian Funds for Scientific Research and lead author of the Nature study, tells The Verge. "Then we got this Spitzer data that showed there were, in fact, seven planets."

Since these planets are roughly the same size as Earth, the researchers think they may be rocky like our own world. And three orbit within the star's habitable zone, where temperatures are just right that there could be whole oceans on the planets' surfaces.
Given that liquid water is such an essential ingredient for life here on our planet, astronomers are eager to find it on other worlds outside our Solar System.

The presence of liquid water on an exoplanet could mean that life has thrived there as well, so that makes these seven planets now top candidates in the search for alien life.

The astronomers say there's a good chance they'll get some answers, since they'll be able to study these exoplanets and their atmospheres in greater detail. In the grand scheme of the Universe, 40 light-years is a relatively short distance, which makes observing this system a bit easier with our telescopes. Plus, peering into the planets' atmospheres is less challenging since these planets orbit around a star that's much smaller and fainter than our yellow Sun. If they orbited a star the size of ours, the intense starlight would make the worlds and their atmospheres difficult to see. "Of course it's super exciting, but what makes the system so special is that all these seven planets are suited for detailed atmospheric characterization," says Gillon space scientist.

This is why small, super-cool stars — known as red dwarfs — have become popular targets for exoplanet hunters; it's easier to study the planets around them. Over the past couple of years, Gillon and his team have been focused on looking for worlds around red dwarfs using the TRAPPIST telescope at the La Silla Observatory In Chile. Less than a couple years ago, their search led them to TRAPPIST-1, a star just a little bigger than Jupiter.

The space scientists found three worlds orbiting TRAPPIST-1 by watching the planets as they passed in front of the star — a process known as transiting. Whenever a planet transits in front of its host star, it slightly dims the star's light. That dimming is incredibly small, but with the right instruments,
astronomers can sometimes pick up these minute light changes from Earth. Through this process, astronomers can use the dimming to calculate the size, mass, and orbit of a passing planet.

The astronomers decided to keep observing the system and have spent more than 1,000 hours spying on the star and its planets with other telescopes.
The new data has helped bring the rest of the planets into view, with NASA's Spitzer Telescope revealing two planets that could not have been seen from telescopes on the ground. (The telescope's location in space allows it to bypass Earth's noisy atmosphere and gather more precise data.) The follow-up observations also revealed that some of the scientists' original findings had been misinterpreted. One of the original three planets the team had identified turned out to be multiple planets.

The planets all orbit closer to TRAPPIST-1 than Mercury orbits the Sun the planets, which have been named alphabetically from b to h, all orbit closer to TRAPPIST-1 than

Mercury orbits the Sun. The closest planet takes just 1.5 Earth days to complete one orbit, while the farthest planet takes around 20 days to circle the star. Because of this, they're all a super tight bunch. When TRAPPIST-1f and TRAPPIST-1g are at their closest to one another, they're just at three times the distance between the Earth and the Moon. So if you were to stand on TRAPPIST-1f, sometimes TRAPPIST-1g would look twice as big as the Moon in the sky. "It's remarkable that you could see another world right there," Amaury Triaud, an exoplanet fellow at the Kavli Institute at the University of Cambridge and a study author, tells The Verge.

If there is an abundant amount of H20 in an exoplanet's atmosphere, then chances are there is liquid water on the surface below. "If we see water vapor in the atmosphere, we're going to be very excited," Sara Seager, an exoplanet expert at MIT, tells The Verge. "We couldn't prove 100 percent, but we'd be pretty sure that there's liquid water on the planet." So far, liquid water has never been found on an exoplanet. The next step after that is to look for other gases

that don't belong in the atmosphere — especially ones that could be coming from biological life. "Our favorite one is oxygen," says Seager. "Without life on Earth,

we wouldn't have oxygen at all. So we'll go down our list of things we're looking for, kind of like a triage."

If we see water vapor in the atmosphere, we're going to be very excited. We couldn't prove 100 percent, but we'd be pretty sure that there's liquid water on the planet."

To get these tantalizing answers, the astronomers hope to use NASA's upcoming James Webb Space Telescope (JWST). When it launches, JWST will sit at more than 1 million miles from Earth and will observe the Universe in the infrared. It's a type of light that can't be seen but can be felt as heat. Observing star systems in the infrared makes it much easier to pinpoint when light is coming from a star and when it's being reflected off of a planet. Plus, JWST will be the most powerful space telescope ever built, seeing cosmic objects with more precision than ever before. However, JWST doesn't launch until 2018. In the meantime, Gillon and his team will be using NASA's Hubble Space Telescope to keep looking at their seven-planet system. "Maybe it will tell us something about the frequency of life and habitable conditions in the Universe," says space scientist Gillon. "This system is really a cornerstone in exoplanetology."

Hence, as above space scientists indiated that they had ensured our solar system had possible existence at least six planets , they have our Earth similar climate and weather,
due to this basic essential requirement, they have possible to cause liquid water to create any life. It's one of the largest solar systems that's ever been discovered outside of our own, and it's a particularly enticing find in the ongoing search for extraterrestrial life. Six of the planets in the system may have the right temperatures for liquid water to exist on their surfaces, and astronomers are confident they'll be able to get a more in-depth look at these seven worlds with future space telescopes.Particularly enticing find in the ongoing search for extraterrestrial life the solar system. So, our space scientists are very clever.

In conclusion, I estimate they shall concentrate on nervous and time and human resource to carry on researching whether these six planets have similar weather and climate to our Earth in order to further life existence researching as well as human living research mission. So, the first step, these space scientists ought follow these steps to attempt to find whether any one of these six planets have our Earth similar climate and weather. Next step, if they confirm that any one of these six planets have our Earth similar climate and weather, then they ought attempt to research whether any one of these six planets has/have any life existence. The final step, if they confirm that there are any life existence in any one of these six planets, they may concentrate on researching whether any one of these six planets has /have any natural resource environment to allow us to live in possible. In conclusions, I believe that this is the shortest time to research the undiscovered adapted human living planet method to our space scientists nowadays, because I believe that instead of our Earth, these other six planets ought have enough natural resource environment to let us to live if any one of them are confirmed to own Earth similar climate and weather in true.

Is exploring Mars the most important factor to influence traveller space travel lesiure choice

Space scientists plan to explore Mars to research whether Mars can provide enough natural resource or right climate or temperature to let us to prepare to live. However, whether our space has only Mars can replace our Earth to live, or it has possible other planets which can also provide any natural resource and provide right climate or temperature to let human adapt more than Mars to live. Because scientists indicate that they discovered at least seven planets which is similar our Earth's climiate or temperature , even any of one can own similar our Earch natural resources. So, it implies that it is possible that it is not only Mars is similar to our Earth. Ought space scientists only concentrate on researching Mars exploration? Are none any other planets replaced to our Earth to live? I shall attempt to explain these two questions as below:

Can we live on Mars? How much possibility do we live on Mars? How much possibility do we discover other planets to replace to live? Why live on Earth when you can live on Mars? Well, strictly speaking, you can't. Mars is a completely hostile environment to human life, combining extreme cold with an unbreathable atmosphere and intense radiation. And while it is understood that the planet once had an atmosphere and lots of water, that was billions of years ago! If we want to expand into the Solar System, we'll need to learn how to live on other planets. And Mars is prime real-estate, compared to a lot of other bodies. So despite it being a challenge, given the right methods and technology, it is possible we could one day live on Mars. Here's how we'll do it.

Space scientists feel Mars is possible the only one planet to us to live, the reasons may include: We also need to go there if we want to create a backup location for humanity, in the event that life on Earth becomes untenable due to things like Climate Change. We could also go there to search for additional resources like water, precious metals, or additional croplands in case we can no longer feed ourselves. In that respect, Mars is the next, natural destination. There's also a little local support, as Mars does provide us some raw materials. The regolith, the material which covers the surface, could be used to make concrete, and there are cave systems which could be converted into underground habitats to protect citizens from the radiation.

The space scientist Elon Musk has stated that the goal of SpaceX is to help humans get to Mars, and they're designing rockets, landers and equipment to support that. Musk would like to build a Mars colony with about 1 million people. Which is a good choice, as its probably the second most habitable place in our Solar System. Real estate should be pretty cheap, but the commute is a bit much. And then there's the great vistas to think about. Mars is beautiful, after a fashion. It looks like a nice desert planet with winds, clouds, and ancient river beds. But maybe, just maybe, the best reason to go there is because it's hard! There's something to be said about setting a goal and achieving it, especially when it requires so much hard work and sacrifice.

However, Mars is possible one poor place , it can not allow us to live. The reasons may include: Mars is pretty great... if you're not made of meat and don't need to breathe oxygen. Otherwise, it's incredibly hostile. It's not much more habitable than the cold vacuum of space. First, there's no air on Mars. So if you were dropped on the surface, the view would be spectacular. Then you'd quickly pass out, and expire a couple minutes later from a lack of oxygen. There's also virtually no air pressure, and temperatures are incredibly cold. And of course, there's the constant radiation streaming from space. You also might want to note that the soil is toxic, so using it for planting would first require that it be put through a decontamination process.

Assuming we can deal with those issues, there's also the major problem of having limited access to spare parts and medical supplies. You can't just go down to the store when you're on Mars if your kidney gives out or if your sonic screwdriver breaks. There will need to be a constant stream of supplies coming from Earth until the Martian economy is built up enough to support itself. And shipping from Earth will be very expensive, which will mean long period between supply drops. One more big unknown is what the low gravity will do to the human body over months and years. At 40% of Earth normal, the long-term effects are not something we currently have any information on. Will it shorten our lifespan or lengthen it? We just don't know.

So, it bases on above reasons, it seems that we will feel difficult to emigrate to live Mars successfully because Mars has poor climate and temperature to human feel adapt to live as well as it may be difficult to grow any vegetable, food , even building any houses on lands, or dirty water and difficult to produce oxygen to let we breathe in this planet.

There's a long list of these types of problems. If we intend to live on Mars, and stay there permanently, we'll be leaning pretty hard on our technology to keep us alive, never mind making us comfortable. Scientists will need have these solutions, if they expect to explore Mars to let us to live successfully.

Hence, if space scientists expect to explore Mars to let us to live successfully. They ought attempt to solve these major problems in Mars, they may include as below:

In order to survive the lack of air pressure and the cold, humans will need pressurized and heated habitats. Martians, the terrestrial kind, will also need a spacesuit whenever they go outside. Every hour they spend outside will add to their radiation exposure, not to mention all the complications that exposure to radiation brings.

For the long term, we'll need to figure out how to extract water from underground supplies, and use that to generate breathable air and rocket fuel. And once we've reduced the risk of suffocation or dying of dehydration, we'll need to consider food sources, as we'll be outside the delivery area of everyone except Planet Express. Care packages could be shipped up from Earth, but that's going to come with a hefty price tag.

We'll need to produce our own food too, since we can't possible hope to ship it all in on a regular basis. Interestingly, although toxic, Martian soil can be used to grow plants once you supplement it and remove some of the harsher chemicals. NASA's extensive experience in hydroponics will help.

To thrive on Mars, the brave adventurers may want to change themselves, or possibly their offspring. This could lead to genetic engineering to help future generations adapt to the low gravity, higher radiation and lower air pressure. And why stop at humans? Human colonists could also adapt their plants and animals to live there as well.

Finally, to take things to the next level, humanity could make a few planetary renovations. Basically, we could change Mars itself through the process of terraforming. To do this, we'll need to release megatons of greenhouse gasses to warm the planet, unleashing the frozen water reserves. Perhaps we'll crash a few hundred comets into the planet to deliver water and other chemicals too.

This might take thousands, or even millions of years. And the price tag will be, for lack of a better word, astronomical! Still, the technology required to do all this is within our current means, and the process could restore Mars to a place where we could live on it even without a spacesuit. And even though we may not have all the particulars worked out just yet, there is something to be said about a challenge. As history has shown, there is little better than a seemingly insurmountable challenge to bring out the best in all of us, and to make what seems like an impossible dream a reality.

To quote the late, great John F. Kennedy, who addressed the people of the United States back when they was embarking on a similarly difficult mission: We choose to go to the Moon! ... We choose to go to the Moon in this decade and do the other things, not because they are easy, but because they are hard; because that goal will serve to organize and measure the best of our energies and skills, because that challenge is one that we are willing to accept, one we are unwilling to postpone, and one we intend to win.

So, if space scientists can not solve above problems to explore Mars, than I believe that the possibility of exploring Mars chance , it will be low. Also, it brings this question: Whether does concentrate on exploring Mars worth? Does attempt to explore other planets worth if any one of them have absolute possibility natural resource environment requirement better than Mars? I shall indicate some reasons to explain whether attempting explore other planets (another earth) to live mission is better than concentrating on only exploring Mars as below:

Do the benefits of exploring Mars outweigh the risks? I shall indicate that the risks of space travel do not outweigh the risks example. In space anything can happen conserving the astronauts health or the rocket he or she is flying in. To conclude, not only will the astronauts have to commit leaving there Earth life for their job but many things in your body work differently in space. Their are risks of an exploding appendix but common cold, weak bones, and fluids floating upwards in your body rather than down due to the zero gravity in space. So, such as that the benefits of exploring mars outweighs the risk of space travel because our world is getting more in bad shape because of pollution and other things. If our world dies we would have another place to stay and live. I also believe its more important to spend the money on space travel to save the human race if the world ended. So, I ensure exploring Mars must more important than exploring space travel because if we find resources that can help us on other planets it can save earth.

However, whether space scientists need to concentrate on time and nervous exploring Mars only or concentrate on time and nervous exploring other planets. If something did happen to the earth by this time we would already have a solution to prevent or stop this outbreak. They're is also not enough resources to make that many rockets in short time period of a world massacre. Because we don't have the reliable technology and if we did it would be very expensive and we most likely wont have enough money because the parts are expensive, so space scientists only either choose to concentrate on time and nervous to explore Mars continue or concentrate on time and nervous to explore the other seven undiscovered similar Earth planets.

However, because resources are so little and expensive, and there are quite a lot of people on the planet Earth, not everyone will be able to get out safely. The sad truth is some people will have to die. So, yes for more reasons than one, some space scientists that they should choose to travel to Mars more than other seven undiscovered similar Earth planets. But, if space scientists only consider that limited time and limited money and resource and technological reasons, so they make the limited exploring Mars decision. If the final consequence, they confirm that Mars is not one suitable planet to let us to live. Then, we will lose to explore other seven undiscovered similar Earth planets which any one has really chance to let us to live in possible. Then, human will be failure because if something happens to Earth then we can live on another planet, instead of rushing to find somewhere else to live only Mars in supposing.

I believe that the benefits of exploring Mars outweigh the risks of going into space due to the fact that our world is already in bad shape from our actions. If we explore Mars now, we could have another chance to live on Mars if we really have no other choice in the future. We could help the generations ahead of us. But, in fact, space scientist indicate than there are seven similar Earth planets existence in space. So, it means that we still have other choice to replace only exploring Mars mission.

In economic view, when space have total eight similar Earth existence, such as Mars and other seven undiscovered planets existence. It is not worth only concentrating on spending more time, money, resource, technology, and human scientists to Mars. Economists agree divide investment on these eight planets at the same time. So, when they discover one planet is more similar to our Earth more Mars. Then, they can stop to continue to explore Mars mission, they can change another the more similar our Earth planet exploring mission immediately. I also say that the benefits of exploring Mars outweigh the risks. One day our world will end, and if we haven't found a new world by then the human race will cease to exist. Some people might say that failed missions will cost billions of dollars, but would you rather be rich and dead or alive and on Mars? There are many health problems with traveling through space, like chronic boredom and weaker bones and muscles, but I believe there are ways to fix that, using artificial gravity and centrifugal force.

Of course there will be lots of risks but we need to focus on how we can make sure we save the human race. Then when we have the technology and are able to move anything from people animals or plants we will be ready to move to mars and live a happy healthy life on a different planet instead of focusing on the risk and just staying on earth, and when it ends so will the human race. Also if we do make it onto mars then we can deal with the risks, because you never know what is going to happen until you get there.

Success with this mission will save more people than if we didn't do this. It may cost millions of dollars but it is worth it on how many lives it saves. Some of the problems can be fixed through research and future technology. But, in fact, because we don't have the reliable technology to support that and everything could go wrong from everyone dying to going insane. Also, people may not find the resources to be able to live on mars such as food and easily accessible water. So, exploring on Mars will bring more risk more than exploring other seven undiscovered similar Earth planets after space scientists have found where their locate on space. It means that space scientists do not need to spend long time to find these other seven similar Earth planets. They only need to send space men to invite any one of these planets to find whether any one of their weather environment and natural resource is suitable to provide to us to live more than Mars.

However, some space scientists believe that because we are still developing new technology to travel to mars and have found ways to get water and oxygen. Going to mars will be the first step in traveling to deep space and finding new life. If we never move to mars, we will die here because we can't stop the sun exploding we either go to mars or let the human race go extinct. we can't leave finding a new planet to live on up to a different generation, money and the risk of a few lives doesn't even matter if you put it up to saving the next several generations. This mission will take a lot of money, time, and effort, But if we never spent anything or took any risk on getting something or achieving something, You and many of the people you know probably wouldn't even be alive. There is no way to stop risks and they are dangerous, but how can we possibly be expected to succeed without taking those risks and learning from mistakes. Failure only harmed those who took it as negativity and a stopping point.

Although, I think the risks outweigh the benefits because say the rocket ship blows up going into space that's a lot of people's money getting wasted, but it is worth it so we could one day have a living community on mars. Also people can get boredom and make them have anxiety of leaving earth for the rest of there life. Last people would have to give up most of there life to commit to making mars a living place for humans to go before the world ends. Also the life on earth will never be forever due to resources and lack of O2. But, it is risky and a lot of money will be wasted if this mission does not work out but Earth is not going to lack O2. We get O2 from plants. As long as we have water, plants, and the sun O2 is not going anywhere. Your breathing it in right now as you

However, I think that going to Mars for exploration and colonizing outweighs the risks. Of course, there is always the possibility that you are not right in the first try, but people have overlooked that and become human sacrifices. We can prevent ourselves from the fate of our predecessor, the dinosaurs, as Earth won't last forever and we have to save our future generations. We can find new alien life forms and lots more and many of the risks can be overcome by choosing the right person and creating the right technology. I agree that we read today for some tomorrow zero gravity can cause many harmful injuries like heart failed and liquid poring to the top of your head or eyes. Also on the other hand we need to have options when the sun gets to large them eats its self. We need a home to raise family's and build a new earth. So, Earth will have possible be one dangerous place and we can not live forever. So, exploring another one Earth mission is essential,, but we need to evaluate whether only exploring Mars mission, how much degree we shall be failure. However, I think that going to Mars is a very risky thing to do but we need to move human life somewhere else because Earth is not going to live forever. We will use up all the resources and the earth will then explode. If we do this trip to Mars it could advance our technology and tame our wonders of beyond. We could find out if there is water, human life, bacteria, diseases, and viruses. Soon enough humans might not even need to take almost a year to go to Mars. We could make that like our second earth. Additionally, we are ruining Earth. To clarify, you need to know this first. The planet Venus is the hottest in our Solar System. Why? This is because it's atmosphere is made of entirely carbon dioxide. This gas has the ability to hold in heat from the sun. Thus, the planet is so hot. When coal or oil is burnt through cars or power plants, this releases CO_2 into our atmosphere. This creates holes in our radiation-protective ozone layer and they get filled with CO_2,which brings stores heat. We are also cutting down plants for houses and farming, which eliminates our single method to save Earth's atmosphere. Alongside, nobody is taking the initiative to stop this global warming mess and rather, encouraging it. Also, the population of humans and animals breathing out CO_2 without enough plants to continue the cycle worsens the matter. We pretty much have put ourselves on a path to doom and we are going to turn Earth into Venus, with an atmosphere of all CO_2 all over again, like the origin of the Earth. With all these errors by humans, and no one standing up to fix these mistakes as well as the encouraging global warming, the only way to save our species, the future generations is by getting to Mars.

In conclusion, I believe that the benefits of exploring mars outweigh the risks because we need to explore mars so that we know what to expect when we need to go there. Also we need to start a civilization so that when Earth dies our we will have started a civilization on mars. And we need to experiment to see if there are any living species on mars. Also, it is not safe to send humans to mars and it is not worth the risk. Because the chance of failure, the lives of 100 men and women could be wasted along with billions of tax payer money. To further express my opinion, each passenger on the ships has a large chance of getting sick or chronic boredom. In conclusion, the benefits do not out weigh the risks only, when human ensure exploring mars in success chance is more than exploring other seven similar earth planets.

The comparison benefit
and risk between space
travel and space exploration

When our money, time, technological resource, human resource is shortage, whether we ought concentrate on investing space travel entertainment and space exploration or choice of either one investment only. We need to evaluate whether future how much benefit we can earn more between either space travel and space exploration as well as whether what we will encounter more failure risk between space travel and space exploration. Hence, I feel that space scientists need to compare their benefit and risk both in order to concentrate on choosing only one implementation.

In prior , I shall indicate what the space exploration benefits and risks are. Latter I shall indicate what the space travel benefits and risks are. What does space exploration mean? Space exploration is the use of astronomy and space technology to explore outer space. physial exploration of space is conducted both by human spaceflights and by robotic spacecraft. There are different types of exploration? They may include:

•Arctic exploration •Cave exploration •Desert exploration •Mineral exploration •Ocean exploration •Space exploration •Urban exploration •Mountain exploration these different kinds of exploration. I feel space exploration will bring these possible benefits and risks as below:

On job creation aspect

The possible of space exploration may include as these: the popularly cited benefit of space exploration is "job creation", or the fact that a space agency and its network of contractors, universities and other entities help people stay employed. From time to time, NASA puts out figures concerning how many associated jobs a particular project generates, or the economic impact. Employment can also be full-time, part-time or occasional. So while "job creation" is cited as a benefit, more details about those jobs are needed to make an informed decision about how much good it does.

On education aspect

Teaching has a high priority for NASA, so much so that it has flown astronaut educators in space. (The first one, Christa McAuliffe, died aboard the space shuttle Challenger during launch in 1986. Her backup, Barbara Morgan, was selected as an educator/mission specialist in 1998 and flew aboard STS-118 in 2007.) And to this day, astronauts regularly do in-flight conferences with students from space, ostensibly to inspire them to pursue careers in the field. NASA's education office has three goals: making the workforce stronger, encouraging students to pursue STEM careers (science, technology, engineering and mathematics), and "engaging Americans in NASA's mission." Other space agencies also have education components to assist with requirements in their own countries. It's also fair to say the public affairs office for NASA and other agencies play roles in education, although they also talk about topics such as missions in progress.

On intangible benefits aspect

Added to this host of business-like benefits, of course, are the intangibles. What sort of value can you place on better understanding the universe? Think of finding methane on Mars, or discovering an exoplanet, or constructing the International Space Station to do long-term exploration studies. Each has a cost associated with it, but with each also comes a smidgeon of knowledge we can add to the encyclopedia of the human race. Space can also inspire art, which is something seen heavily in 2014 following the arrival of the European Space Agency Rosetta mission at Comet 67P/Churyumov–Gerasimenko. It inspired songs, short videos and many other works of art.

Instead of tangible and intangible aspects, space exploration may also include these advantages as below:

1. Space exploration allows us to prepare for potential hazards.

The universe is a vast place where hidden dangers could be lurking almost anywhere. Even if you consider only our solar system, there are asteroid and comet threats which could devastate our planet if an impact were to occur. Exploring space gives us an opportunity to locate these hazards in advance to prepare an encounter that could help to preserve our race. Then there are the interstellar items to consider. Oumuamua, or 11/2018 U1, was discovered by the Pan-STARRS1 telescope in 2017 by the University of Hawaii through funding from the Near-Earth Object Observations Program. It was originally thought to be an asteroid, then a comet since it was accelerating, and up to 10 times as long as it was wide. These items could create interstellar impacts as well.

2. It gives us more information about our solar system, galaxy, and universe.

When we take on the effort to start exploring space, then we can discover new truths about our planet and culture simultaneously. The information we obtain from these studies can then be applied to our STEM resources here at home. NASA technologies that were originally developed for space programs include infrared ear thermometers, LED lighting, ventricular-assist devices, anti-icing systems, and even temper foam. Because it requires us to innovate to reach to the stars, our efforts to solve critical problems create opportunities to make life better here on our planet at the same time.

3. Exploring space is one of the few human endeavors that crosses borders.

There are currently 72 countries who claim to have a space program, but there are only three which have an operating government space agency: China, Russia, and the United States. Despite the political conflicts that occur between these nations, their capability of producing human spaceflight provides the gold standard for future exploration efforts. Only 14 of the 72 nations who operate in this space even have a basic launch capacity and six (adding Europe, India, and Japan) have the capability to launch or recover multiple satellites. Because of the expenses and resources necessary to achieve space flight, the remaining nations work together with those who have the capability of a full launch to manage this aspect of human existence. This endeavor is one of the few ways that humans from all nations cooperate without conflict.

4. We can see humanity in a different way with space exploration.

Carl Sagan suggested that Voyager 1 take a picture of Earth while it was 4 billion miles away at more than 30 degrees above the ecliptic plane. In that image, our planet appears as a 0.12 pixel crescent. All of our conflicts, political battles, successes, failures, love, loss, and life occur on this one-tenth of a pixel. In the scope of a universal lens, we are but one small point of light amount countless others.

"Look again at that dot," wrote Sagan. "That's here. That's home. That's us. On it everyone you love, everyone you know, everyone you ever heard of, every human being who ever was, lived out their lives. The aggregate of our joy and suffering, thousands of confident religions, ideologies, and economic doctrines, every hunter and forager, every hero and coward, every creator and destroyer, every king and peasant... every saint and sinner in the history of our species lived there – on a mote of dust suspended in a sunbeam."

5. Space exploration provides us access to new raw materials or undiscovered natural resources.

When we began to launch satellites into space, it allowed us to find new raw material deposits on our planet that we could access to make life easier here. If we apply this technology as an extension to the rest of our solar system, then it gives us the same benefit to find minerals, precious metals, and even new materials that we can use. Although the expense of exploring space is admittedly high, this advantage gives us a way to offset those costs somewhat. There is even the potential that it could become profitable one day if we can provide these efforts with enough capital.

6. Investments into space exploration create real economic benefits at home.

The governments which provide the majority of our space exploration infrastructure employ over 20,000 people per agency who make direct positive economic impacts on their community. There are private companies who look at the potential benefits of this industry and contribute to this advantage as well, such as SpaceX and their thousands of staff. People from all walks of life contribute to space exploration every day, ranging from astronomers to actual rocket scientists. Even though many of these programs receive taxpayer funding, the wages, manufacturing, and indirect investments contribute over 70% more in overall value at the local level compared to each dollar spent in the United States. These opportunities allows us to explore many different fields of study in addition to what is waiting in the universe as well.

7. Anyone can become a space explorer to achieve their dream.

Space exploration doesn't need to involve starships, space stations, or intergalactic travel. If you own a telescope and can look up at the sky, then you can embrace this element of human existence. Our scientists have taken this advantage to the next level with the Hubble Space Telescope, which has made over 1 million observations in almost 30 years of service. We have made some incredible discoveries with this technology already.

•We have a better idea about the age of the universe (around 13.7 billion years).

•Images of the deep universe show that there are thousands of galaxies out there.

•It helped us to discover four of the five moons that orbit Pluto.

•We have a better understanding of planetary seasons in our universe.

•It works to peer into the atmospheres of alien planets so that we know what is waiting for us in our future exploration efforts.

8. Space exploration encourages us to share instead of being selfish.

Being human-first from a space exploration standpoint isn't about dominating other cultures that we might find waiting for us in the universe. It is a way for us to find common ground outside of our physical appearance, cultural differences, or religious preferences. For far too long, we have allowed ourselves to be consumed by our petty problems instead of looking at the big picture. If someone is hungry, then we should feed them. If they are cold, then we should clothe them. If they need a job, then we should help to train them. Space exploration unites us in ways that other global efforts do not because we see ourselves as humans first. This advantage won't solve our problems, but it can shift our attitude toward something that is healthier than our current state.

9. We know more about our planet thanks to our efforts to explore space.

Because space exploration gives us a different perspective, it allows us to look at our planet in a different way. The view from outside of our atmosphere allows us to see the big picture instead of trying to extrapolate information from micro-scale research. This advantage allowed us to discover the problem of ozone depletion in the upper atmosphere, begin the conversations on global warming, and examine the current and future impact of weather pattern changes that may happen because of a changing climate. Space exploration helps us to look inward as well as outward, helping us all to find the changes that are necessary to keep our planet healthy for our children, grandchildren, and beyond. But, space exploration also have these disadvantages, they may include as below:

1. Our current technology makes it dangerous to get into space in the first place.

Several agencies are developing "space tourism" packages that can take people in a comfortable aircraft to the very outer layers of our atmosphere, but that is not an exploration effort. We currently strap astronauts into a vehicle that gets attached to a very large rocket so that there is enough speed available to break the grasp of gravity.

Starting with Theodore Freeman, who was killed in the crash of a T-38 in October 1964, there have been over 20 individuals who lost their lives in the line of duty while advancing U.S. space program interests. There have been two individuals (Gus Grissom and Peter Siebold) who were able to survive a problem that resulted in the loss of a space vehicle.

2. There are cost considerations to look at with space exploration.

The cost of exploring space is one of the biggest criticisms of the efforts to launch a program that takes us beyond our planet. When the space shuttle program was active in the United States, the total cost of the launch was about $500 million. That figure does not include the expenses of postponement that often occurred because the conditions were not right to send a rocket into space.

Manned missions in our solar system could cost 10 times that amount, and that might get us to Mars or one of Jupiter's moons. Technology advancements in recent years could make this issue cheaper for the next generation, but we should ask ourselves if spending billions on space exploration is the right thing to do if we have people dying of hunger on our planet.

3. Astronauts receive exposure to natural dangers while in space.

If the launching process doesn't kill you during a manned space exploration effort, then the natural dangers that are present outside of our planet's atmosphere could become problematic in a variety of ways. The radiation that comes from the sun is a constant danger to astronauts when they are in space, and the weightless environment can change their physical conditioning. Experiments with identical twins, with one staying on our planet and the other spending a lengthy assignment in space, show that there are changes at the cellular and genetic level that occur with space travel as well.

4. Current space exploration efforts could be a one-way trip.

When we sent astronauts to the moon, our technology provided them with a chance to land on the surface and return to their spacecraft. It is possible that we could perform a similar action for asteroids, moons around other planets, and other celestial bodies that do not have an atmosphere. If we are going to start exploring Mars, then that journey could be a one-way trip for the astronauts. Even if this journey does not become a one-way trip, the amount of time necessary to reach a destination beyond the moon makes it virtually impossible to mount a rescue mission if something goes wrong. Our current vision of space exploration requires perfection to create a successful result.

5. There may not be a reason to start exploring at this time.

Human cultures have always had a fascination with exploring space because it satisfies our need to learn more about the universe. Taking long-distance pictures with the Hubble telescope is not the same as visiting the location in-person. What we must ask ourselves right now is if there is a valid reason to begin this effort, and the truth is that there are few pragmatic applications to consider. We could start mining asteroids for their raw materials and mineral content in the future. Planetary colonization could be necessary in future generations. Since we are still dealing with issues like crime and poverty here at home, addressing our immediate concerns might be better than looking at future needs which might never be necessary.

6. Unmanned probes are even a waste of resources.

One of the ways that we attempt to limit expenses with our space travel needs is to send unmanned probes into the dark vastness that lies beyond. There have been some successes with these efforts, most notably the Voyager 1 and Voyager 2 missions that allow us to peer outside of our solar system. This option allows us to almost eliminate the risk to human life entirely as well. There are also disadvantages to consider with this approach, starting with the fact that there is little adaptability to changing circumstances. The Mars Climate Orbiter is an excellent example of this problem. When it received incorrect coordinates for landing, it burned up while entering the atmosphere before sending any data at a cost of more than $120 million.

7. Our current information is well out-of-date.

On February 22, 2017, NASA announced that it had found seven planets the size of Earth in a single solar system. Three of the planets were in the so-called Goldilocks Zone, which means they are at a distance from their star that is not too hot and not too cold. It is called the Trappist-1 group, and this set of planets lies in the Aquarius system. That's about 235 trillion miles away, which is at least a measurable distance.

The problem is that this planetary system is 40 light-years away from us. That means the information that we can observe right now took forty years to get to our scientists. Think about all of the changes that have happened in your life in just the past 5 years, and then apply that concept to a planetary scale. When we start exploring space, we must take into account that this delay is present so that we don't fly into an unexpectedly dangerous situation.

8. It may lead us into future conflict with beings who have superior technology.

Space exploration makes us think in noble terms about what lies in wait for us in the universe. When we sent the Voyager spacecraft into our solar system and beyond, there were two records placed on the devices to communicate with whoever might find them to let that intelligent life know that we exist. Most theorists who seriously consider the pros and cons of meeting alien life say that there are only two possible outcomes that can occur with first contact. That alien species will either be so advanced that their technological presence as led to a peaceful society where an exchange of information may one day be possible, or it will be aggressive and want to access our planetary resources.

9. Space exploration creates a lot of trash or rubbish around our planet.

There are over half-a-million items of trash from over 50 years of space travel and satellite placement which orbit our planet right now. Unless these items fall into the atmosphere and burn up, they will stay in place forever. The ring of debris that we have created makes space exploration more dangerous because an impact with a ship's hull could have deadly results. We will need to clean up this mess in the future to provide better safety to our future explorers, and we have no idea what the expense might be.

Verdict (comparison) on the Advantages and Disadvantages of Space Exploration

Space exploration is beneficial even if we only look at it through the lens of hope. It is an idea that unites us as one race instead of over 190 different countries. We can proceed into the universe as one people, taking the first steps toward new experiences just like we did when we placed astronauts on the moon for the first time. Explorers always face danger, and space is no exception to that rule. The vacuum of the universe was not meant for humans, which means we must constantly adapt and protect ourselves when we are outside of our atmosphere. Then there is the risk of an encounter with alien life to consider too.

The advantages and disadvantages of space exploration must come from a common sense perspective. Other races could harm us, but there is also the possibility that we could be dangerous to other life as well. We should continue with these efforts, but with the understanding that this work is not a race. It is a cooperative effort that will eventually define our humanity.

Similarity, space exploration's benefit and risk may include as these: The benefits of space exploration is it helps man think outside the box as far as the dwindling resources are concerned. The risk is that it can lead to death. The only drawbacks are cost and safety. If you can afford the cost and are willing to take the risk, there are unlimited benefits. To further our knowledge on the ever expanding universes. However, there are so many problems that are associated with space exploration. Some of the problems include the high costs, the risk level is also very high and there are chances of getting negative results. But, space exploration also have these intangible benefits , such as the benefits are that it has more space and more fuel than the Apolo and it gives astronauts a chance to bring whole satilities. Space stations can help in the exploration of space because in space stations they do experiments on things they find in space.

How does space exploration impact us?
Beyond furthering the scientific understanding of how the universe formed, the mechanics involved in galatic, solar, and planetary formations, as well as mapping the universe for potential physical exploration at a later date, the space exploration programs impart a bevy of technologies which are applied to everyday use as well as research benefits that come from zero gravity research (such as medicines or materials development. The commercial impact seen from the space program can be possible brought to our next

generation in the future. What are the reasons for space exploration? In conclusion, I feel that space exploration may bring these intangible benefits. they may include: Space exploration is an important part of our life today. The main reasons for exploring space are: The urge to know what is out there as well as by space exploration, we get to know if there is any harm from the heavens coming our way. Thus, space exploration will bring future intangible and tangible benefits more than present risk. Space scientists ought concentrate more nervous, time , human and technological resources to research how to achieve this space exploration mission more than space travel. Due to space travel present and future risk is more than future benefit as below reasons.

What are the benefits and risks of space travelling? I shall indicate as below:

What is space travel benefit ? Nowadays, human begins feel space travel is one kind of exciting entertainment activity, instead of earth travel. But, due to space travel cost is high, so this kind of travel activity is focus on rich people because they have more extra money to spend this kind of travel entertainment. It is its weakness. Space is fascinating. Humans have been sending objects into space for decades, trying to learn about Earth and what's beyond. But while space travel can be beneficial, there are also risks that come along with exploring the rest of the universe. There have been many more trips to space and the moon, as well as orbits around Earth. Our fascination with the universe beyond our own planet is as limitless as the universe itself. Technology and science have even allowed us to land on and explore Mars - a feat barely imaginable when space travel first began decades ago.

However, space travel also have these kinds of different risks when space travelers are flying rockets to space. The different risks may include as below:

(1) Health risk

The Health Risks of Space Travel

,research into the health risks of space travel may someday make long-duration spaceflights safer for astronauts. But despite such achievements, space travel still involves a myriad of health risks for people. From DNA damage caused by radiation exposure to the bone loss, muscle loss, and blood pressure changes that occur when living in microgravity, to name a few.

(2) Radiation risk

Also, space travel can bring radiation risks. The latest review examines eight NASA evidence reports, with half of the topics focused on the health risks of radiation exposure in space. "The radiation problem is the toughest one to solve and the most concerning," Valerie Neal, Ph.D., a historian at the National Air and Space Museum, told Health line. Neal spent 10 years working at NASA, but she was not involved in the current research. On Earth, Neal explained, we are shielded by the planet's magnetic field and the protective gases in the atmosphere.

However, there's no effective way to shield astronauts from some types of radiation present in space, especially on a long journey such as a trip to Mars.

In particular, there is no technology to protect against galactic cosmic rays, a type of ionizing radiation likely produced by supernovae, or exploding stars. That type of radiation can pass right through the hull of a spacecraft and the skin of people on board.

Astronauts also face radiation risks from solar particle events, which are difficult to predict.

In its current review, the National Academies' committee looked at NASA's evidence reports on radiation exposure and increased risk of cardiovascular disease, cancer, central nervous system disorders, and acute radiation syndrome. For the conditions covered in each report, the committee noted that NASA has well-documented evidence of the risks, although some studies rely heavily on animal models. One area of growing interest is the link between radiation and cardiovascular disease. The committee found that there's now enough evidence, "to support the conclusion that the risk of degenerative diseases from long-term exposure to space radiation may be of much greater concern than previously believed."

(3) Cancer risk

Space travel also brings cancer risk.

Another major area of concern is cancer.

Radiation exposure can cause genetic damage that may increase an astronaut's risk of developing cancer years after their mission.

Currently, NASA sets the radiation limit for astronauts at a 3 percent cancer fatality probability. For a mission on the ISS, where proximity to Earth provides some protection from radiation, women can stay about 18 months and men can stay about 24 months before exceeding the limit. But on a mission to Mars, astronauts would be way over the limit, according to Francis Cucinotta, Ph.D., a professor of health physics at University of

Nevada, Las Vegas, who authored the research on exposure limits.
Cucinotta worked for NASA for more than a decade, and developed a database that tracks astronauts' exposure to radiation and cancer risk estimates. He told Health line it would be a question of ethics whether to raise the risk limit to allow astronauts to travel to Mars.

(4) Mental illness risk

But the hazards of space aren't the only risks astronauts face on a long voyage.

They also have to put up with each other, while maintaining their own sanity in a small, cramped space. The National Academies also examined NASA's evidence reports on mental health issues related to space travel and "behavioral health decrements" when team members aren't working well together.

Another report focused on the health risks associated with sleep loss, circadian rhythm issues, and work overload. Lastly, the committee reviewed evidence on risks related to "vestibular/sensorimotor alterations," which include issues like space motion sickness. Overall, the committee noted that all of NASA's reports were quite thorough, but recommended that NASA pay more attention to the interactions between different types of risks. For example, lack of sleep and being overworked could have a big impact on how well a team of astronauts works together. Teamwork issues are especially important to consider on long-duration missions, according to Neal.

"On a one- to two-week mission you are so busy, you don't have time for interpersonal issues to form," Neal told Health line. But on longer missions, more psychological factors come into play. She noted that being able to call family and friends back home and talk in real time has made a world of difference for astronauts' mental health and well-being.

But those immediate connections wouldn't be possible on a long mission to Mars — which could be a real source of stress for astronauts.

In conclusion, although, space travel is one kind of exciting and new travel entertainment activity, however, it can only let some rich people can enjoy the short time space travel journey. So, poor people won't enjoy this kind of travel entertainment. But, it also bring different risks when space travellers are catching the rocket to fly to the space anywhere to travel. Moreover, any space travellers have life danger when they are catching the rocket to fly to space anywhere to travel, even the cost is expensive, e.g. space travel facility, space travel destination entertainment arrangement.

They need spend too much money to build on the planet when the space travellers arrive the planet to travel. If the space travelling investor can not gain any reward to compensate their expenditure, then they will encounter much loss. Is it still worth to invest more than space exploration? Otherwise, if any space exploration is successful, then it may bring another earth existence in possible and human may attempt to live another planet in possible. So, it seems that space exploration can bring long term benefit more than space travel because space travel is one kind short time individual entertainment enjoyable benefit. Otherwise, space exploration is one kind long time human overall living benefit. It explains that why exploring space is more important than exploring space travel.

Mars exploration failure factors

What are Mars exploration possible failure factors? I shall indicate Mars exploration mission possible failure reasons as below:

On space exploration improvement aspect: US plans for the human exploration of Mars are best seen as a serious human spaceflight effort. It is possible that improvements in technologies will make flights to Mars feasible and survivable, but these technologies are still in development. Robotic exploration provides the scientific benefits to be gained from exploring Mars at lower cost and much lower risk. When these is a manned flights to Mars, serious political interest is lacking. A manned mission to Mars is not likely to occur for at least 10 years, if not longer.

The problem may include: How to provide fast speed space station transportation service between earth and Mars, less dangerous risk or high safety, providing more innovative space manned flight activities lead to space tourism or some other commercial activity involving human spaceflight. Acquiring earth observation satellites for security purposes, providing imagery, electronic intelligence and communications services, spacecraft, robotic and more advanced space shuttles, ability to maneuver in orbit, remain in space for long periods. So, space technology must need to be improved if space scientists hope to explore Mars to achieve to let human to live in possible in future one day.

On space science continue researching and development aspect: Why do space scientists need to continue space science research, if they hope to explore Mars more easily? Because we live in a society which depends on science and technology, those are very essentials seem undervalued perhaps because they are not understood. There are great concern in some quarter about the inadequacies and shortcomings in science funding, science education and the way space science in communicated to the public. For these questions example: Why do we need to choose Mars to live? How do we need explore Mars to live in success? What benefits and risks do we encounter in this Mars exploration process? So, space scientists have responsibilities to let pubic to know because they need people vote to support their Mars exploration mission. If people do not understand engine science , space science, medical science or whatever, then they are not equipped to get knowledgeably on science issues.

In space science, there are two main but not necessarily separate for spending, sometimes referred to collectively as research and development. Research is the acquisition of new knowledge. Development is the application of existing knowledge to new or improved user, such as exploration continue research of any new space exploration knowledge to Mars as well as they also need to learn how to apply existing Mars exploration knowledge to new or improved uses. However, there is no way of knowing where or when any kinds of new Mars exploration knowledge will find a practical application. But they need still continue to research and develop any possible new kinds of Mars exploration new technology.

However, researching and development is impossible without approval and funding. It is safe to say. Then, that some of the most vital work done, such as Mars exploration by space scientists is in preparing their funding applications. Also, space science is a around field, with a vary limited number of resources for cutting edge research. An idea for research and there is a fair chance that someone has already thought or it is already working on other similar earth seven planets , or other undiscovered researching planets which choice has higher successful chance to implement human living another earth mission. So, choice of which one space exploration mission is the best, it needs space scientists compare their benefits and risks in order to make final space exploration decisions.

On space exploration expenditure spending aspect: NASA needs to make budget for everything from launching missions to conducting educational programs, such as human space flight, which includes the shuttle and space station, gets around bit billion of that. Space missions are cheaper today than in earlier times, because the technology is in general cheaper and methods have been improved.

Billion dollar figures naturally keep a lot of people in work, and have an economic influence, but are there tangible returns that the ordinary citizen can consider over the entire range of space based activity, such as whether exploration of Mars mission is the most reasonable choice among other planet exploration choices? How will serious economic effect be influenced by this wrong failure space mission decision ?

One of the first and most obvious results of the space age was the rapid progress in satellite and communications technology, evident today is so many aspects of life that our interface with them is virtually seamless. What is the value of satellites? From weather reports, sports broad casts, and communication networks to geographic information systems, geophysical research and the global positioning system, we can earn the benefits of the space age every day of our lives. If nothing else had some of the space race, we would still have different reasons. In fact, that satellite technology has become a commercial enterprise means that it can pay its own way.

What do we get for our investment in space? The space environment offers conditions of microgravity, vacuum, and temperature extremes, which hold promise for experiments and possess not possible on earth. The vacuum of space , for example is better than the best vacuum attainable on earth. So , space scientists need to find methods how to flight this natural and dangerous space environment, it includes radiation, simulate, progress in developing more versatile , and efficient materials and engineering methods. However, these developments can bring indirect benefits to our space exploration development, such as computers, medical equipment and electronics science in general have all benefited from the space exploration development age.

However, space scientists need to make an analysis of the likely risks and benefits of any one space exploration research. There must be interested to know, for instance, how his/her idea would almost certainly to choose the planet living exploration, any planet living explorations must be at same stage , the come a point where the benefits outweigh the risks and the financial budget can be justified.

Deciding whether a risk is acceptable is necessarily subjective, such as the Mars exploration mission. Rocket testing is done in isolated areas, and launch paths or usually over wide stretches of ocean or sparsely populated land, when the rocket arrives the Mars land. It must need ensure safe and none crash or fire occurrence accident when the rocket arrives on the Mars land. Costly through a failure is the risks in unmanned missions are relatively strategic involving fire or pollution from rocket fuel , and falling space junk. Onboard radioactive substances can certainly give valid cause for concern, but once a craft has left earth orbit, the space men are out of danger, when their rocket arrives on the Mar's land.

By comparison with radio active,if you feel rocket fuel and space plane quickly, the risks do seem minimal probably, they are. We should put those possibilities into perspective, through, e.g. tens of thousands od people live in close proximity to airports, and face the prospect of having a burning airbus coming down coming down on top of them. It is something we live with, such as our solution concerns how to the Mars, when it only has one limit number of space station to let the rocket to land on Mars, and it can not cause any fire occurrence to bring life absolutely dangerous to our life, if we were living on the Mar's land one day. For instance, that microscopic organisms can survive and mutate in the microgravity and higher radiation levels of space stations.

What would happen if Mars people came back to Earth as passengers on an astronaut's clothing? Moreover, we must rightly consider the possibility of dangerous Martian microbes arriving on Earth in samples returned by robot explorer. Will quarantine conditions devised around known standard be sufficient? Suppose some of our own bacteria travel to Mars on our spacecraft survive on the surface, but mutate in the intense UV radiation. What kinds of diseases could they cause when human explorers arrive ?

In conclusion, mutant Earth bacteria will have to be dealt with of and when they are encountered. The possibility of native microbes from Mars arriving, though is already taken seriously enough by some people that an organization dedicated to seeing that samples are not returned is already in existence. Another problem is how adaptable living on Mars problem, how can human adapt to live in Mars in the silence of space environment , but it would be too much for modern city, light weight feeling when human does not need to walk on Mars' land. All of these issues will be human need to face problems, if space scientists can confirm Mars can be one adaptable planet to let us to live to compare other planets in the future possible one day.

● Space exploration possible
economic benefits

What are economic benefits of space exploration? Space exploration may bring these economic benefits as below: The critical drive of technological changes linked to the space industry. Firms may make technological leap that took billions in public funds to finance to carry on continue space exploration research continue in long term into the different kinds of space markets development, e.g. space resource exploration, space living environment exploration, space energy exploration , space tourism expenditure exploration etc.

For new entrants to all one space market, they may be assisted to invest to build their own rocket factories or space stations , how to design and rebuild reusable rockets easily when they anticipate to any kinds of space exploration activities. It can increase cooperation to develop future space exploration missions successful chance as well as expertise is increasingly consolidated within single firms, instead of across a multiplicity of vendors and contractors. Because any one space exploration activity, if there are many different countries' space exploration companies anticipate , it will bring more success in the process of designing, testing and improving products in all those space exploration companies in new and innovative ways.

Then, any one space exploration mission success, it also brings another or other new technological business chance. It helps to create monopolies or at least oligopoly and this provide sufficient incentive to innovate or drive down costs to US space industry sells its any space exploration products into international market as well as creating more space exploration manufacturing workers, space products salespeople, space science teacher etc. positions job opportunity to reduce unemployment ratio and encouraging more students choose space science subject to learn. It can change to the space exploration industry with long-term commercial, scientific and even military security, technical innovation economic benefits to global entrepreneurs, even when any one space exploration technological development reaches mature stage, then it will bring long term profits, as reducing cost and less risky businesses in possible.

In conclusion, it seems that space exploration industry may bring long term economic benefits more than long term economic loss. It depends on this factor whether how many space exploration technological firms can be encouraged to cooperate together. When any one space exploration activity/mission has many space exploration firms anticipation, then the space exploration activity/mission will have high successful chance. Otherwise, there are less number space exploration firms cooperate to carry on researching the space exploration activity/ mission, then it will have high failure chance. Some firms anticipative number will be one important influential factor to any one of space exploration activity/mission.

Image

What is space city tourism

It has different between smart city and space city. A Smart city is an urban area that uses different types of electronic Internet of things (IOT) sensors to collect data and then use these data to manage assets and resources efficiently.

This includes data collected from citizens, devices, and assets that is processed and analyzed to monitor and manage traffic and transportation systems, power plants, water supply networks, waste management, crime detection, information systems, schools, libraries, hospitals, and other community services.

The Smart city concept integrates information and communication technology (ICT), and various physical devices connected to the IOT network to optimize the efficiency of city operations and services and connect to citizens. Smart city technology allows city officials to interact directly with both community and city infrastructure and to monitor what is happening in the city and how the city is evolving. ICT is used to enhance quality, performance and interactivity of urban services, to reduce costs and resource consumption and to increase contact between citizens and government.

Smart city applications are developed to manage urban flows and allow for real-time responses. A Smart city may therefore be more prepared to respond to challenges than one with a simple "transactional" relationship with its citizens. Yet, the term itself remains unclear to its specifics and therefore, open to many interpretations.

Why do our cities need to improved to be smart cities ? It offers a reminder that more than half of the world's population lives in urban areas. With the number of people flooding to cities expected to rise over the coming decades, satellites and space technologies are an increasing vital source of information to help manage the issue of urbanization. For our daily activities why we need smart cities example, during your commute to school or work, try to count how much of what you see has been impacted by space technologies. You would probably have a hard time finishing before you reached your destination.

● Why do we need space cities development?

Space technology is everywhere – whether it is making sure traffic flows smoothly, or improves your favorite commuting method, ESA's contributions have transformed the way we interact with our cities. On World Cities Day we have a look at how space technology can provide the change needed to make urban centers more sustainable. Supporting the United Nation's 11th Sustainable Development Goal (SDG) on Sustainable Cities and
Communities is vital not only because of the role cities play in our lives, but also because of its deep links with the other goals.

Access to accurate and up-to-date information is vital for formulating and implementing good policies. Our Earth observation (EO) missions and satellites, such as the recently launched Sentinel-5P, are a formidable tool. Thanks to optical imaging, radar sensors and filters, satellites help monitor air quality and chart urbanization. This allows us to pinpoint the source of pollution problems, for example a dense traffic zone, and enables long-term and cost-efficient monitoring to observe trends, useful for tackling slum growth or terrain
and building displacements (e.g. in San Francisco). Satellites can also be used to improve connectivity in isolated communities (ECO; Ubisat), for e-governance, and can provide digital solutions for air monitoring, traffic management and coordinated recycling.
ESA will also contribute to the implementation of future innovations, such as 5G, which will revolutionize digital interactivity, such as smart meters, in homes and on the street.

● **Paris Metro Line One and Austria space cities mission development**
Other space applications are already seamlessly fitted into our cities. Innovations brought to life using ESA's technology transfer programs are adapted from space technology to make our urban centers more live able. In Paris, some trains use space cooling technology to cut emissions and increase passenger space.

In Austria, space innovations are being implemented in fuel cells for inner-city delivery vehicles, allowing for more cargo space and eliminating both noise and pollution. Air conditioning, a big contributor to carbon dioxide emissions, is getting the "space treatment", where main-grid electricity is replaced with sunshine as their power source. External partners like Eurisy, the World Bank and the Asian Development Bank use their experience in dealing with policy-makers to bridge the technical gap needed to bring the Agency's projects to local communities. Beyond its business applications programs, ESA's workshops and seminars, such as 'Space for Municipalities', contribute to educating stakeholders about the tools available to them.

Space city means that human builds houses to let we to live in planet, e.g. Mars or human builds offices to let we to work in planet

human builds any entertainment facilities, e.g. swimming pools, cinemas, hotels ,gardens, growing any plants, vegetable, potato, tomato,

e.g. foods to provide us to eat or building water drainage to let us to drink clean water or building playing facilities in any one space planet, e.g. Mars, Moon or other planets in possible. So,

one space city is outside our earth and the planet can provide the essential resources e.g. fresh air oxygen, clean air, clean farm,

save land to let us to live in the planet.

● How to build city in space

Science fiction has delivered on many of its promises. Star Trek videophones have become Skype, the Jetsons' food-on-demand is materializing through 3-D printing, and we have done Jules Verne one better

and explored mid-ocean trenches at crushing depths. But the central promise of golden age sci-fi has not yet been kept. Humans have not colonized space.

For a brief moment in the 1970s, the grandeur of the night sky felt interactive. It seemed only decades away that

more humans would live off the Earth than on it; in fact, the Space Shuttle was so named because it was intended to make 50 round trips per year. There were active plans for expanding civilization into space, and any number of serious designs for building entire cities on the moon, Mars and beyond.

The space age proved to be a false dawn, of course. After a sobering interlude, children who had sat rapt at the sight of the moon landings grew up, and accepted the terraforming space – once briefly assumed to be easy – was actually really, really hard. Intense cold war motivation flagged, and the Challenger and Columbia disasters taught us humility.

Nasa budgets sagged from 5% of the US federal budget to less than 0.5%. People even began to doubt that we'd ever set foot on the moon: in a 2006 poll, more than one in four Americans between 18 and 25 said they suspected the moon landing was a hoax. But now a countercurrent has surfaced. The children of Apollo, educated and entrepreneurial, are making real headway on some of the biggest difficulties. Large-scale settlement, as opposed to drab old scientific exploration, is back on the menu.

Space cities come in three basic models. The classic one is to terraform a nearby Earth-like object, by using massive geo-engineering projects or bio-domes to create a lunar or Martian metropolis. The second is the low-Earth orbit model: this expands upon the currently inhabited region of space. Think of the International Space Station as a government fort, around which commercial trading posts, homesteads and finally urban areas develop. Then there is the free space model, basically floating cylinders with artificial gravity, surviving by digesting the natural resources of outer space. As the saying goes in the space community: once you're out of Earth's gravity well, you're halfway to anywhere.

US Space cities development organization indicated that what O'Neill's vision is. In the 1970s, Princeton physicist Gerald K O'Neill envisioned 100,000-person colonies, stationed at what is known as the fifth Lagrangian liberation point (L5) in the moon's orbit – like a gravitational eddy where things stay put by themselves. Encouraged by fellow physicists Freeman Dyson and Richard Feynman, he posited a "planar cluster" housing four billion people across 30,000km of space. "It is orthodox to believe that Earth is the only practical habitat for Man," he wrote in Physics
Today in 1974, but we can "build new habitats far more comfortable, productive and attractive than is most of Earth." O'Neill called the classic model of colonizing planets proper a "mental hang-up", and suggested it lacked imagination
for the possibilities of open space.

In O'Neill's vision, cable cars would connect communities spaced at 200km intervals. Single-family spacecraft –the minivans of the sky – would act as recreational vehicles. On the inner surface of what would be rotating habitats, strips of land would alternate with windows to let in sunlight. That same sun would provide all of our energy needs (a much bolder statement in the 70s than it is now), while the moon would be mined for aluminum and titanium to use in habitat construction. Asteroids, containing water and other material, could be towed along behind the city in the vacuum. His idea to build such cities in the moon's L5 orbital point inspired the influential L5 Society, which aimed to realise his vision by 1995. Their motto: L5 in '95!O'Neill's dream did not come to pass – not because it was inherently flawed, but because it was an idea before its time. Spaceflight infrastructure was in its infancy, and costs were prohibitive. We simply didn't know enough of the basics to jump straight into urban design.

The central challenge to building a city in space is to create a closed system that can sustain itself for the long haul. Urban areas on Earth survive only by relying on a much larger footprint than their metropolitan boundaries. The more isolated a space city is – the farther from external resupply resources – the more closed its oxygen, food and water loops must be. The ISS, for example, has about 40% efficiency in its oxygen recycling, and even so its ambient CO_2 levels are perpetually high. (Nasa is working on how to convert that CO_2 directly into oxygen.) As for food, any space-based urban plan would require rolling out high-yield agriculture on an unprecedented scale – though 3D printers could, given some fresh ingredients, print a pizza.

● Developing a space city challenge

The other big problem for a space city is how humans would function physiologically. The neighborhood gym would be a popular
destination: though the human species is ill-suited for some aspects of deep space, 14 years of continuous presence on the ISS have advanced our understanding of how to adapt physically for a lifetime among the stars. Early astronauts paid for this knowledge the hard way, as it were, with their bone density. Today's ISS crew train for 2.5 hours a day on a jury-rigged zero-gravity exercise contraption in order to keep their bone density at normal levels. Still, with longer stays in zero gravity, new problems seem to crop up. For example, your cerebrospinal fluid – the clear liquid found in the brain and spine – drifts upward, where it engorges your retina and flattens your eyeball. "I lost two diopters in my eyes," recalls former
astronaut Michael Lopez-Alegria, who spent 215 consecutive days on the ISS. "It's also pretty easy to get something in your eye up there. You just walk into something."

Other problem is space living environment radiation hurt challenge. City walls would be required to shield space citizens from the brutal radiation bombardment of deep space. "Aluminum shielding can actually be part of the problem," says Vince Michaud, Nasa's deputy chief health and medical officer.

"Radiation that makes it through takes some of the aluminum with it." Nasa spends $28m every year in radiation research alone,
including pharmaceutical and nutriceutical countermeasures and magnetic shielding. Bill Paloski, director of Nasa's Space

Life and Physical Sciences division, believes that by 2024 his team will be able to mitigate the health risks of space.

As for actually getting people to the space cities in the first place, it won't be using rockets – basic physics doesn't cooperate. Rather, space elevators, or "beanstalks", promise to close that gap. Vehicles would climb out of the gravity well along a cable anchored to the equator and held under tension by centrifugal force on a counterweight tens of thousands of kilometers high. Until now, materials science hadn't produced the kind of tensile strength required for a space elevator cable – even carbon nanotubes are too weak by themselves – but in 2010 the Nobel prize in physics was awarded for experiments on graphene. A one-atom sheet of pure carbon that is 100 times stronger than steel, graphene is a promising candidate for space elevator cable material.

"We can colonize the moon, Mars ... wherever people want, really," SpaceX chief executive Elon Musk (of Tesla Motors fame) told documentary-makers on the film Orphans of Apollo. "I think Mars is the logical place to go." Musk's company, specialists in space transport, are one of the most serious around; none of this conversation would be happening without SpaceX, and Musk is not alone in thinking of colonizing Mars first. But though it may be easier to generate excitement around the Red Planet, insofar as the moon feels like an achievement already under our belts, several characteristics make Mars harder to colonize.

Martian gravity is three-eighths that of Earth, making landings more hazardous than in the moon's one-sixth gravity. On the Apollo missions, lunar dust got everywhere – the crews inhaled it and got it in their eyes, and it wreaked mechanical havoc – and on Mars the dust is even more problematic, because it is highly oxidised, chemically reactive, electrically charged and windblown. Mars's chlorinated soils would be toxic, for example, to the human thyroid gland.

There was some early speculation that a space city could be buried under the Martian surface to protect its inhabitants from radiation. Pamela Conrad, an astrobiologist with Mars Science Laboratory, contends that we would be digging from a rock into a hard place. "Trying to drill down to shield from radiation might be okay for bacteria, but materials in the core are radiating, too," she warns.

A lunar city, on the other hand, has the advantage of being up to a thousand times closer – practically next door – and as such could participate in Earth's economy to some extent. Possible anchor industries could include space tourism and titanium mining, as well as pharmaceutical factories that require microgravity. The moon is also rich in helium 3, which is rare on Earth and thought to be a potential fuel source for future fusion reactors.

And industry is very much at the top of the agenda. Today the biggest space operation in the world is neither Nasa's nor
that of the US defense department, but DirecTV, valued at more than $48bn. Low-Earth orbit is quickly becoming the realm of the private sector – including the loose agglomeration of companies known collectively as New Space, which have shaken human spaceflight progress out of a sluggish period. Using the window created by the withdrawal of public funds from space programs, New Space has fostered trust with government and increasingly enjoys the blessing of the US State Department, which controls export permits for objects being launched into orbit. Public sector clients like Nasa and the Air Force Space Command purchase equipment and supplies, and depend on the ingenuity and dexterity of the market. Indeed, Nasa has an $800m program to develop the commercial space market. Costs have come down dramatically as a result.

One figure in New Space taking advantage of this new flexibility is hotel tycoon Robert Bigelow. In 2015, the owner of Budget Suites of America will use a SpaceX rocket to send one of his inflatable space habitat modules up for testing at the ISS. These ingenious blow-up houses are capable of operating independently as space stations, and Bigelow wants to lease them as hotel suites (no surprise there), laboratories or for whatever else you might want. Nasa, having no current plans of their own for a moon mission, have given their blessing to Bigelow to use similar inflatable modules to build a lunar base. Inflatable space habitats made by Bigelow Aerospace, whose founder owns the Budget Suites of America hotel chain.

● Russia and China space city mission

If he doesn't get there soon, the Chinese may beat him to it. Whereas Russia has been integrated into the global space community fairly effectively since the end of the cold war, China does not partner with the other big players. Instead, it plays its own game: in December of last year, as part of the country's
12th Five-Year Plan, China's lunar rover Change 3 made the first soft landing the moon has seen since 1976. China is somewhat secretive about its space progress, but among its stated goals is to establish a crewed lunar base.

Rick Tumlinson is head of the asteroid mining company Deep Space Industries, which aims to be the gas station, building-supply center and the air-and-water provider for space settlements. In the 1970s, a young Tumlinson
worked at the Princeton Space Studies Institute, where he came under the influence of Gerard O'Neill and science fiction author Arthur C Clark (known to them as "Uncle Arthur"). He even led the New York chapter of the L5 Society. Deep Space is playing the long game out of a commitment he says he made in 1986 with several New Space entrepreneurs. According to Tumlinson, they pledged their lives and fortunes to "making the human breakout into space happen in our lifetimes".

Tumlinson was one of a group that leased the Mir Space Station commercially from the Russian government for a few months in 1999. Calling it MirCorp, they gave their venture a countercultural, tongue-in-cheek
personality, and sent up a Jolly Roger flag with the first commercial cosmonauts. Nasa and the State Department were not amused. They placed heavy pressure on the Russians to de-orbit Mir in order to focus on the ISS, then under construction. The current crop of space entrepreneurs, like Musk and Amazon's Jeff
Bezos, watched Mir's fire re-entry and breakup in 2001. They have learned from this and dedicate a lot of effort toward diplomacy and government cooperation.

● US Mars space city mission
Speaking at the Humans to Mars conference in Washington last month, Nasa chief Charles Bolden laid out a vision for bringing the US space program out of its first stage, exploration, and into pioneering,
even homesteading. "We are, right now, an Earth-reliant species," he said. "But only multi-planet species survive for a long period of time." Nasa plans to start with an asteroid capture and redirect by 2025, then pick up skills in the proving ground near Earth before venturing to a destination a thousand times farther than the moon. When humans get to Mars in the 2030s (the much-mocked Mars One group aims for the rather optimistic goal of a proper human settlement by 2024, or 10 years from now), the implication is that we will be there to stay.

If large-scale space settlement still sounds a little crazy, consider that from the passing of the Space Settlement Act 1988 until its quiet demise in the Paperwork Reduction Act of 1995, establishing extraterrestrial civilization was the official goal of the US in space. The Space Settlement and Development Act of 2015, currently under draft, would promote economic development in space and work to reverse current strictures against property ownership in space. Which brings us to what might be the biggest obstacle close to being hurdled: who would move to a city on Mars? Well, lots of people claim to be interested, signing up to Mars One's non-binding longlist of candidates to emigrate to the Red Planet. But Lopez-Alegria, the former ISS resident, says that while he could imagine our space presence being scalable, he wouldn't volunteer to live permanently in a space city. "The experience of being in space is magnificent," he says, "but only in the context of being an Earthling and knowing that you're coming back to Earth."

Is Developing space city possible

There are many factors may influence to develop space city in success. I shall indicate the factors as below:

Basically, we need to develop our smart cities in our earth any countries. The reason is simply because if we can not develop smart city in our earth in success, it is more easier and more simply to compare develop and build any cities in any one planet in space , due to they are apart away to our earth and we need to space too much time and nervous and money and resource to invest any one space city development mission.

First , I shall explain how we can develop smart city in success. Then I shall explain how we can develop cities in any one planet in space in success. So, you can know whether why and how space cities development is more difficult to compare smart cities development.

The developing Smart City in any countries, the challenges may include as below:

The first challenge is how to deliver high technological delivering intelligent transportation systems in the country's cities. Draws on the country's experience designing smart cities and delivering intelligent transportation systems internationally. It aims to shed light on the key elements required for cities to develop and implement a successful strategy. "Smart Cities " are already a reality. Government and private sector initiatives worldwide are exploring innovative ways to make cities in the 21st century more efficient, more livable, and more competitive. "We believe that achieving these goals is not just about being technologically advanced –

it's also about urban renewal and citizen engagement."

The another challenge initiative may include whether the country has enough money to invest high technological smart cities building. The discussion will explore best practices for developing smart city strategies and cover topics including transforming neighbor hoods,

infrastructure, public service, and the economy. For UK, London smart cities developing example, it may encounter these challenges, they include: London and Edinburgh are the leading smart cities in the UK, according to a new study.

Analysis by Juniper Research identified the top 10 smart cities in the UK with London coming top of its "smart city UK" leaderboard.

The rankings were calculated over a range of city indices, including transport, healthcare, public safety, energy and productivity. Scores were calculated according to diverse metrics, including present state-of-play variables

(such as congestion and crime levels) alongside smart city rollouts, vision and long-term strategy.

The ranking is as follows:

1 London

2 Edinburgh

3 Glasgow

4 Bristol

5 Manchester

6 Brighton & Hove

7 Liverpool

8 Oxford

9 Birmingham

10 Milton Keynes

With Glasgow ranked in third place, Scotland's major cities were regarded as strong performers across the board. Edinburgh's 16-year smart city journey, for example, has allowed the city to learn from mistakes (such as disparate maintenance of systems and control of systems by separate council units) and apply its "one council" principle in order to better deliver citizen services. "The traffic system is integrated with emergency services, helping save lives. Meanwhile a £ 24m grant was used to plan smart CCTV rollout, using artificial intelligence to detect suspicious objects and terrorist activity."

But Juniper warned that "significant hurdles" lie ahead for the UK smart city market. The report noted that the European Investment Bank (EIB) and Horizon 2020 have contributed over £ 23bn to the UK market over the past three years;

after 2019, alternative funding will have to be found to replace them, the analyst said.

UK government found that funding challenges bring with them issues in scaling projects,

particularly for small-to-medium enterprises. Juniper urged the creation of more 'test bed'

environments in cities, enabling experimentation prior to full roll-out. This would allow more risk-averse players, such as utilities, to enable disruptive service providers to work in partnership with them to develop smart city solutions and new business models.

● Expediting Factors in Developing a Successful Space Colony

One of the most significant challenges facing our society today is the incredible feat of colonizing space. Whether it is for scientific research or in hopes of bettering life on earth, extending humanity's habitable domain has always been at the top of human curiosity and intrigue. Apocalyptic science fiction stories

combined with current technological levels make humans wonder how possible it would be to permanently inhabit space. The vast knowledge and technology needed to accomplish this combined with the profound impact it will have on humans would make a sustainable space colony one of earth's crowning achievements.

Without a doubt, humanity's future will be highly dependent on successes in space and how humans can use the outcomes for the good of society. Conquering the extreme environments of space will not only expand human knowledge of the universe, but will also tell us a great deal about humanity and why humans evolved in such a unique way. This project focuses on the inherent obstacles and possible solutions for sustaining human life outside the boundaries of mother earth. While we do not expect to come up with a viable plan to colonize space, we seek to determine the factors that will contribute to the first space habitat and how creating a second world for humans will shape and come to define humanity.

Space is a promising enterprise for scientific discovery, commercialization, and

expanding the human race in the future. As the United States searches for a dominate
position in space, they mark their territory with caution to any seeking to disrupt their progress.

This will allow for the space sector to be commercialized much quicker and more effectively. Because the goals of the US are to use space any way possible to benefit economic growth, this clause is vital to the purpose of the policy. "If space activity is going to pay off economically, someone other than a government has to provide a return on the government's investment in space infrastructure" . Eventually the profits and benefits of a more privatized space sector will pay off for the government. The billions of dollars and decades spent developing the basic space infrastructure will be offset by a thriving economy and improved quality of life on earth. Hence, it seems that it is only US government has possible to help us to live to space colony to live. However, US government space city colony development mission may encounter these challenges as below:

● THE PROBLEMS Of FEASIBILITY ISSUES

Currently, it is still not technologically feasible to colonize space. Although many countries and a few private corporations have the capability to travel to space,
the high levels of technology needed to sustain human life in space still do not exist.

A more efficient method of propulsion is needed to make space missions more economically feasible. The high cost of launching objects into space, which would be undoubtedly necessary to start a colony, is still a deterrent for large missions. Until more frequent and cheaper ways of sending people and goods into LEO exists,
the planning stages of creating the first space colony will not even be possible. Also,protecting the human body from the harsh conditions of space becomes a much greater problem when the time spend in space is years instead of months. Bioengineering is a key factor that can combat the negative effects on humans.
This can be done either by adapting humans to be more resistant to these effects, or by creating better protective suits and ways to ensure the prolonged health of humans. Even if the propulsion technology and infrastructure were available in space to start a colony, without better ways to guarantee the safety

of humans the first colonies still would not be able to sustain human life.

● THE PROBLEMS OF MONEY AND TECHNOLOGICAL INVESTMENT AND ECONOMIC DEVELOPMENT AND RESOURCE ISSUES

Because of this, the required capital must come from profits acquired in space.

This is why it is so important for initial space activities to be profit oriented. A successful commercial system must also be established before a colony can exist in space.

Without a method of generating profits, sending humans to space will eventually need to stop because the resources and interest will be depleted.

Creating the first colony in space is not something that will happen on its own.

The initiatives must be started to make it feasible, because otherwise the required

technology and investments will never come about on their own. A breakthrough in

propulsion would serve as the catalyst to this entire process. Better means of propulsion

will not only lower the costs of space transportation enough to make commercial efforts feasible but also spark enough interest to improve outdated technology. This would allow for increase human activity and presence in space and would mark the first step in sending humans to live permanently somewhere other than earth.

I shall indicate how US space city development organization shows cost and profit estimates for various commercial ventures in space and act as a starting point for analysis on what is required to make a colony in space feasible as an initial investment and as a long term business opportunity as below:

For space hotel case development example, revenue is cost of stay multiplied by the number of guests per year. When the launch costs to hotel orbit decrease, the cost to stay in the space hotel will drop significantly. This in turn will create much more demand for rooms in the hotel. If we assume a module or room weighs 2000kg and the cost of hotel stay per person equals the launch cost times 250, then only 8 guests would be needed to pay off an additional module launch. This means that regular additions to hotel capacity when launch costs drop would be extremely profitable and would lower costs and increase demand. So space hotel businessmen develop to evaluate the hotel building facilities and the additional model launch flying to the planet expenditure to judge whether they need how long time can earn profit, e.g. how many travelers hope to live hotels when they arrive the planet to live , how long time to every guest who expects to stay in the space hotel, how much charge to the young, child and old age space hotel guest.

As above space hotel business cost and profit evaluation assumption. The trend shows that current launch costs have to be cut by a factor of 2.5 in order for a space hotel to generate any revenue at all (10 years away by current estimates). This is due to the high cost of a stay and corresponding low demand. The real profitable region starts when launch costs are less than a tenth of what they are today. Once this barrier is reached then demand will not be limited to income brackets and the limiting factor will be the hotels capacity. As above space hotel business profit estimation, it indicates that the cost to expand with lowered launch costs is extremely low compared to the expected yearly return so hotels would most likely expand faster than they could be filled. If this business proves profitable over time, then space hotels would grow in size and number until everyone interested in visiting space could have the chance. I believe that this will happen within the next 100 years and will resemble the
first orbiting civilization.

● THE PROBLEM OF SPACE LABS AND SPACE STATIONS EXPENDITURE

By these estimates and assumptions, research labs and space stations would need at least 25 modules to be profitable at any point in their operational lifetime. The ISS has less than this but was not designed to be profitable and is not entirely used for research. As launch costs decrease over time, smaller space stations will be economically feasible and more likely to attract investors. Until this ,
however, large space stations will likely be the only ones considered and such a large capital investment most likely rules out private ventures. Lab revenues, which were fixed for this analysis, are actually more likely to vary than launch cost and could greatly distort these trends.

● THE PROBLEM OF ENOUGH NATURAL RESOURCE SUPPLY ON THE SUSTAINABILITY OF SPACE COLONY

Although the focus now is on how a space colony can be made feasible, the underlying challenge is to make such a colony sustainable. Since the purpose of a colony is to be a long term habitat for humans, then the primary task is to work up to the point when this is possible. A large part of making a colony sustainable is having enough energy and resources to maintain human life and support the activities that the colony was created for.

The main purpose of a colony highly affects these requirements.

A research colony would most likely consist of a medium number of living inhabitants and a significant amount of laboratory and observation equipment. For this settlement, a moderate amount of food would be needed along with a substantial energy source. A mining colony, on the other hand, would consist of heavy machinery, robots and far fewer humans to act as supervisors. Despite needing less food to

sustain this type of colony, a much greater amount of energy would be needed. Finally, if we consider a space ecosystem that's main purpose was to facilitate human inhabitants, the food and nutritional requirements would be a major

concern while energy levels could be low to moderate compared with the other colony applications.

Using the same three colony examples, it is necessary to also compare the required interactions with earth. For this comparison it must be assumed that colonies cannot provide their own food and that these resources

must be sent from earth. Also, communication and any sharing of ideas or information are also considered interactions with earth. If these were not true and a colony could provide for itself then it would most likely already be feasible and sustainable.

Research colonies would need frequent interactions with earth to share new ideas and test out concepts on earth. Since only a medium amount of food is essential to sustaining this colony, the frequency of communication visits would be more than sufficient to transport all needed food and resources. For the mining settlement, there would only need to be somewhat frequent trips from space to earth and vice versa to send the mined resources

to earth and the required food to space. Communication for anything other than emergencies would be minimal because

the people in control of the operation would most likely be in space supervising the operations.

A purely human colony would call for the most interaction with earth because of the high amount of food and resources required on a daily basis.

This type of colony is the hardest to make sustainable. This is due to the fact that there are more humans who need to be kept alive and there is no source of profit to guarantee the feasibility of sustained efforts. From a humanitarian standpoint
ultimate to sustain prolonged human life outside of the earth's ecosystem. It is also the most advanced and expensive colony and it's the farthest off from becoming possible in the future.

Because of this, the very first colony is almost certainly going to be similar to a mining
operation on earth. This would be the most profitable out of the three types, and also the most simple technologically. Such a establishment in space could be used to test out bioengineering advances so that
eventually humans will have the capability to stay in space for longer and longer periods of time, working up to the when a non-profitable human settlement is possible long term.

Propulsion is by far the most significant contributor to making a colony initially feasible,
but it contributes little to making that same colony sustainable. Bioengineering becomes the more important aspect of technological advancement because the protection of human life is the most challenging problem regarding long term stays in space. Commercialization also plays an important role because the sustained funding for these expensive colonies cannot realistically come from government budgets or private investments. If a colony does not have a commercial motive, then it is that much harder to not only sustain but to start in the first place. This is the main reason why a colony for only humans is so difficult to establish.

● THE PROBLEM OF WHETHER HUMAN CAN ADAPT OR ADOPT TO LIVE IN NATURAL SPACE PLANET ENVIRONMENT IN LONG TERM

In order to fully understand the detrimental effects that space has on humans,
testing would need to focus on the aspects of the earth's environment that differ most with those in space. First, humans are very susceptible to radiation so they would either need to be highly protected, or treated that radiation does not have as much of a negative effect on the body. Humans would also have to withstand great temperature variations in space if a suitable environment could not be designed.

Our chemical makeup would have to change severely if unprotected humans

would be able to withstand the harsh temperatures of our solar system. Certain pressures would also have to be maintained in order for our bodies to function normally as they do on earth. The levels of gravity take a toll on human bones and muscles as well, and would have to be increased in space for us to exist for long periods
of time.

Finally, light is a very important but often overlooked factor that contributes to the function of the brain. In order to maintain sanity and normal biological processes, humans in space would need to get the right amount of sunlight. Many of these variables could be tested in the extreme environments on earth to see how
different levels affect the human body, but eventually the research would have to be continued in space to see how versatile our body truly is.

● THE PROBLEM OF SPACE TECHNOLOGICAL IMPROVEMENT

With improved technology in the future, less fuel can be used to achieve the same velocity so it will be possible to use single stage propulsion for comparable missions. Selection of the optimal chemical fuel has provided many challenges in the past because of the vast
tradeoffs between available possibilities. Hydrogen is preferred because it is very prevalent on earth and can be easily burned with oxygen. It is also has a great combustion efficiency, cooling abilities, and low condensed mass compared to other fuels. Although it has the highest thrust to mass ratio of any rocket fuel, it requires very large and heavy fuel tanks which make the structural design of the vehicle much more difficult. This also is a huge setback to decreasing the structure to overall mass ration that is required to make SSTO possible. Therefore future single stage rockets using chemical propellants will not use hydrogen unless a better way to store it is discovered. The space technological challenges may include as below:

For a spacecraft with this weight delivering human to space technological transportation tool example, difference in theoretical maximum payloads is 5000 kilograms. This may not seem like a big difference, but it is remarkable. This extra space could be worth as much as $100 million, which is also the same amount of revenue that was assumed to be needed to attract investors. This would be possible if the payload was used to transport goods made in space to be sold and used on earth. All of the estimates and assumptions used to obtain these values are the same as in the Launch Cost Economics analysis.

Propulsion and transportation have always been one of humanity's greatest challenges and triumphs. Many of the great innovations that have allowed humans to evolve and flourish have come in these fields. The development of SSTO technology opens endless possibilities for the human race and would greatly expand the perceivable universe to humans. A breakthrough of that magnitude would certainly be one

of the most significant in modern history. The ability to access space frequently with the purpose of improving humanity is the pinnacle of human achievement. For this reason, advances in propulsion are fundamental to prolonged human presence in space.

For solar power technological energy resource example, the initial steps of commercializing space would either

involve energy or manufactured goods. The profitability and continuous demand for these would ensure a successful space business if the product could be transported to earth. SSTO propulsion would allow for the cheap and regular transportation of the final product and would greatly reduce the costs associated

with doing business in space. The commercialization of space is a critical element in the possibility of a space colony, because the only way human activity in space will increase enough is if there is a profit to be made.

Solar power arrays in space are a promising business opportunity and could be one of the first business venues involving energy. They are unique because, similar to satellites, they do not require a colony in space to be possible. Although the mining of Helium-3 would represent an extremely profitable and beneficial

source of energy, the labor source and supervision necessary would guarantee that a colony would need to be created to sustain such a long term operation. When studying commercialization as a step in the process

towards colonization, opportunities like this should not yet be considered.

● THE FINAL PROBLEM OF SAFE ENVIRONMENT LIVING CHALLANGE

WHAT IS SPACE ENVIRONMENT PROTECTION AND SAFETY ?

One of the greatest possibilities for humans in space is also one of their greatest obstacles.

It is the effect that being in space has on the human body and how humans can adapt to different environments. There are several naturally occurring reactions that take place within the human body when it is kept in space for extended periods of time. Although it is unknown if these are the body's adaptations to space or if space is causing the body to transform, this shows that some configurations of life work better in space. This offers great promise for bioengineering because after these transformations have been studied, scientists could engineer the human body to take on these desirable conditions. The body will need to react to different conditions quickly in order to become better suited for life in space. This research will greatly expand the possible lifetime of humanity as a whole, whether it is by staying on earth or by venturing into space permanently. Although bioengineering may not significantly speed up the race to colonize space, it will most assuredly make that colony possible and be a major factor in its success.

Within bioengineering and medical research in space there are a great deal of possible contributions to the improvement of humanity. First, the limiting factor in space travel now is the amount of time that the human body can survive in space. This is not only because of the issue of life-sustaining resources, but also the harmful effects of the space environment on the body. Aside from dieting and physical training, astronauts only protect themselves from the harmful effects of space while they are actually in space. They could go through a medical regimen before space travel that targeted the undesirable effects and would act as an initial barrier to limit any effects that were able to get by the in-space protection. Also, humans could be treated after they returned home to reduce the amount of harmful effects. Another possible way to protect humans while in space is a biological warning system. If the undesired effects of space are known then it is assumed that there also exists a way to measure them and determine how much the human body can safely withstand. For the example of radiation, something similar to a Geiger counter could be used to warn space travelers when they are nearing danger so that it could be avoided. After much data is gathered from such devices, safe routes through space could be mapped out so that travelers could avoid paths and locations that are substantially more harmful to them.

A key aspect of sustaining human life in space is creating an environment that is sustainable in space for long durations. The main reason why humans thrive on earth is because earth's

environment is very versatile and recycles nutrients and resources
so that life can flourish. Photosynthesis and plate tectonics are the two most
important contributors to this on earth and
similar processes would have to be adapted to a space colony to ensure that
life in space could be possible for a long period of time. An effective way
to conduct this type of research is to have a group of scientists that live in
space to perform
experiments in simulated environments. This will tell us more about how
biology reacts to a given set of living conditions.

Three types of environments that would be especially helpful for testing
are ones that models deep outer space, one that is
very similar to our environment on earth, and possible conditions that
could be created for a human colony in space. The final environment would
change slightly as more information is discovered because it would be
somewhere
in the middle of the other two. This set of conditions is what designers
would strive to replicate when establishing a colony
in space. The artificial environment would start out very close to the
conditions in a space ship and through refinements and iteration would
eventually be similar to those on earth.
Before starting a colony, numerous variations would have to be tested so
that an optimal set of conditions could be identified. This is a form of
evolution, but would have to be sped up so the humans in space would
not die out before achieving a successful balance between body and
environment.

In conclusion, despite the fact that the vacation industry would still
not be a profitable or enticing business opportunity, it is worth noting the
effect that a lower launch cost would have on the theoretical market. Once
commercialization and a possible colony have been fully implemented, the
costs will be reduced and the demand will skyrocket. Although orbital
hotels will not lead the charge for commercialization of space, they will
become a large industry generations after there is widespread human
activity in space. Hence, it explains that US government needs to solve
above these main challenges if it can not achieve space travelling
development aim in success, then it will feel more challenges to develop
space cities to let human to live in success, because development space
is one short term achievement aim, but developing space city mission is
absolute one long term achievement aim.

Developing space city tourism aim

Human needs to evaluate whether what are the actual benefits to bring to our future generation if space city is expected to develop to achieve. I feel that we needs to know why human needs to develop space city, e.g. what benefits it can bring benefit to human? Why does human needs to live space city?

Public spaces are holistic entry points by nature Through its multi-functional and multi-disciplinary nature, public space offers a holistic view of the city, including social inclusion, governance, legislation, health, safety, education, climate change, transport, energy and the urban economy. However, I feel that space city development may include these reasonable reasons as below:

Proposed Sustainable Development Goals

1. End poverty in all its forms everywhere

2. End hunger, achieve food security and improved nutrition, and promote sustainable agriculture

3. Ensure healthy lives and promote well-being for all at all ages

4. Ensure inclusive and equitable quality education and promote life-long learning opportunities for all

5. Achieve gender equality and empower all women and girls

6. Ensure availability and sustainable management of water and sanitation for all

7. Ensure access to affordable, reliable, sustainable, and modern energy for all

8. Promote sustained, inclusive and sustainable economic growth, full and productive employment and decent work for all

9. Build resilient infrastructure, promote inclusive and sustainable industrialization and foster
innovation

10. Reduce inequality within and among countries

11. Make cities and human settlements inclusive, safe, resilient and sustainable

12. Ensure sustainable consumption and production patterns

13. Take urgent action to combat climate change and its impacts

14. Conserve and sustainably use the oceans, seas and marine resources for sustainable
development

15. Protect, restore and promote sustainable use of terrestrial ecosystems, sustainably manage
forests, combat desertification, and halt and reverse land degradation and halt biodiversity loss

16. Promote peaceful and inclusive societies for sustainable development, provide access to justice for all and build effective, accountable and inclusive institutions at all levels

17. Strengthen the means of implementation and revitalize the global partnership for sustainable development

However, all these reasons are not actual needs to human, they are only estimated needs for human future possible needs. I shall indicate the clarification/debate points to enquire how space cities development is needed, the two clarification/debate views may include as below:

Issues for further clarification/debate
· Whether to aim for access and/or minimum spatial proportion ?
· Convergence/divergence of green/public space Indicator?
Hierarchy of Public Space indicators
BASIC: amount of public space (as % of total urban space) as the first, most basic, planning-level indicator.

MEDIUM: distance to (or area per cap of) that space that is green, as a higher-level, quality-of-life, management-level indicator.

HIGH: safety as a measure of what happens within that.

NASA were to disappear tomorrow, if we never put up another Hubble Space Telescope, never put another human being in space, people in this country would be profoundly distraught.
Americans would feel that we had lost something that matters, that our best days were behind us, and they would feel themselves somehow diminished. Yet I think most would be unable to say why.

The actual reasons that human hopes to live in space cities, they may include as below:

There are many good reasons to continue to explore space, which most Americans have undoubtedly heard. Some have been debated in public policy circles and evaluated on the basis of financial investment. In announcing his commitment to send the country back to the moon and, later, on to Mars, President Bush quite correctly said that we do it for purposes of scientific discovery, economic benefit, and national security. I've given speeches on each of those topics, and these reasons can be clearly shown to be true. And presidential science advisor Jack Marburger has said that questions about space exploration come down to whether we want to bring the solar system within mankind's sphere of economic influence. I think that is extraordinarily well put.

But these are not reasons that would make Americans miss our space program. They are merely the reasons we are most comfortable discussing. I think of them as "acceptable reasons" because they can be logically defended. When we contemplate committing large sums of money to a project, we tend

to dismiss reasons that are emotional or value-driven or can't be captured on a spreadsheet.

But in space exploration those are the reasons—what I think of as "real reasons"—that are the most important.

When Charles Lindbergh was asked why he crossed the Atlantic, he never once answered that he wanted to win the $25,000 that New York City hotel owner Raymond Orteig offered for the first nonstop aircraft flight between New York and Paris. Burt Rutan and his backer, Paul Allen, certainly didn't develop a private spacecraft to win the Ansari X-Prize for the $10 million

in prize money. They spent twice as much as they made. Sergei Korolev and the team that launched Sputnik were not tasked by their government to be the first to launch an artificial satellite; they had to fight for the honor and the resources to do it.

I think we all know why people strive to accomplish such things. They do so for reasons that are intuitive and compelling to all of us but that are not necessarily logical. They're exactly the opposite of acceptable reasons, which are eminently logical but neither intuitive nor emotionally compelling.

First, most of us want to be, both as individuals and as societies, the first or the best in some activity. We want to stand out. This behavior is rooted in our genes. We are today the descendants of people who survived by outperforming others. Without question that drive can be carried to an unhealthy extreme; we've all seen more wars than we like. But just because the trait can be taken too far doesn't mean

that we can do without it completely.

A second reason is curiosity. Who among us has not had the urge to know what's over the next hill? What child has not been drawn to explore beyond the familiar streets of the neighborhood?

A third reason, we humans have, since the earliest civilizations, built monuments. We want to leave something behind to show the next generation, or the generations after that, what we did with our time here. This is the impulse behind cathedrals and pyramids, art galleries and museums.

Cathedral builders would understand what I mean by real reasons. The monuments they erected to the awe and mystery of their God required a far greater percentage of their gross domestic product than we will ever put into the space business, but we look back across 600 or 800 years of time, and we are still awed by what the builders accomplished. Those buildings, therefore, also stand as monuments to the builders.

The final reason is a space land use aim. In land use planning, urban open space is open space areas for "parks," "green spaces," and other open areas. The landscape of urban open spaces can range from playing fields to highly maintained environments to relatively
natural landscapes. Generally considered open to the public, urban open spaces are sometimes privately owned, such as higher education campuses, neighborhood/community parks/gardens, and institutional or corporate grounds. Areas outside city boundaries, such as state and national parks as well as open space in the countryside, are not considered urban open space. Streets, piazzas, plazas and urban squares are not always defined as
urban open space in land use planning.

It has been suggested that Public open space be merged into this section. The terms "urban open space" can describe many types of open areas. One definition holds that, "As the counterpart of development, urban open space is a natural and cultural resource, synonymous with neither 'unused land' nor 'park and recreation areas." Another is "Open space is land and/or water area with its surface open to the sky, consciously acquired or publicly regulated to serve conservation and urban shaping function in addition to providing recreational opportunities." In almost all instances, the space referred
to by the term is, in fact, green space. However, there are examples of urban green space which, though not publicly owned/regulated, are still considered urban open space.

From another standpoint public space in general is defined as the meeting or gathering places that exist outside the home and workplace that are generally accessible by members of the public, and which foster resident interaction and opportunities for contact and proximity. This definition implies a higher

level of community interaction and places a focus on public involvement rather than public ownership or stewardship. A grassy area with tall trees leaving shadows from the sun above. In the distance are small row houses, and a street is at the right. The benefits that urban open space provides to citizens can be broken into three basic forms; recreation, ecology, and aesthetic value. Psychological benefits gained by visitors to urban green spaces increased with their biodiversity, indicating that 'green' alone is not sufficient; the quality of that green is important as well.

● Space tourism or living both recreational need aim

   Urban open space is often appreciated for the recreational opportunities it provides.

Recreation in urban open space may include active recreation (such as organized sports and individual exercise) or passive recreation, which may simply entail being in the open space. Research shows that when open

spaces are attractive and accessible, people are more likely to engage in physical activity.

Time spent in an urban open space for recreation offers a reprieve from the urban environment and a break from over-stimulation. Studies done on physically active adults middle aged and older show there are amplified benefits when the physical activities are coupled with green space environments. Such coupling leads to decreased levels of stress, lowers the risk for depression as well as increase the frequency of participation in exercise. Casual group walks in a green environment (nature walks)

increase one's positive attitude and lower stress levels as well as risk of depression.

● Space city living ecological need aim

   The conservation of nature in an urban environment has direct impact on people for another reason as well. A Toronto civic affairs bulletin entitled Urban Open Space: Luxury or Necessity makes the claim that "popular

awareness of the balance of nature, of natural processes and of man's place in and effect on nature – i.e., "ecological awareness" – is important. As humans live more and more in man-made surroundings – i.e., cities –

he risks harming himself by building and acting in ignorance of natural

processes." Beyond this man-nature benefit, urban open spaces also serve as islands of nature, promoting biodiversity and providing a home for natural species
in environments that are otherwise uninhabitable due to city development.

In a sense, by having the opportunity to be within a natural urban green space people gain a higher appreciation for the nature around them. As Bill McKibben mentions in his book The End of Nature, people will only truly understand
nature if they are immersed within it. He follows in Henry David Thoreau's footsteps when he isolated himself in the Adirondack Mountains in order to get away from society and the overwhelming ideals it carries. Even there he writes how society and human impact follows him as he sees airplanes buzzing overhead or hears the roar of motorboats
in the distance.

● Space living aesthetic need aim

The aesthetic value of urban open spaces is self-evident. People enjoy viewing nature,
especially when it is otherwise extensively deprived, as is the case in urban environments.

Therefore, open space offers the value of "substituting gray infrastructure. "One researcher states how attractive neighborhoods contribute to positive attitudes and social norms that encourage walking and community values. Properties near urban open space tend to have a higher value. One study was able to demonstrate that, "a pleasant view can lead to a considerable increase in house price, particularly if the house overlooks water (8–10%) or open space (6–12%)."Certain benefits may be derived from exposure to virtual versions of the natural environment, too. For example, people who were shown pictures of scenic, natural environments had increased brain activity in the region associated with recalling happy memories, compared to people that were shown pictures of urban landscapes.

` IN conclusion, before US government decides to develop space city mission, I feel that it needs have any methods to solve above any challenges as well as it also needs to know whether what it can bring what the actual aims and what the actual benefits to out next generation. Thus international partnerships and capacity-building missions are especially important for cities in the developing world, which stand to benefit the most from the global, accurate and cost-effective coverage provided by space technology.

CHAPTER FOUR

Computer tool useful leisure Consumer Behavior

Why China's computer manufacturing and product development industry will be global leader to compete US computer dominant market.

Nowadays, China's computer industry is the largetest hardware producer production and experts is dominated by Taiwanese firms. It is also the second largest personal computer (pc) market and domestic pc companies are top three sellers in global computer manufacturing and product development market. Forx example, Lenovo buys BM pc business in 2004 year. It implies US, IBM pc manufacturing leader can not dominate global computer market in possible in the future.

Reed Electronic Research, Yearbook Of World Electronic Data (2003) indicated that the leading computer producing countries of hardware production in US $millions and share share of total gogal production: The world region US was the global rank number one. In 1995 year, US had US $76,284 value, market value 26.5%. Then in 2000 year, US had increased up to US $ 90, 430 value, market share 24%. Till to 2003 year, US had fallen down to US $ 69,102 value, market share 21.7%. However, US hardware production was still the global rank number one , although its hardware production value had been falling down. But, the following second rank country, Japan and the third rank country, Singapore and the fourth rank country, Taiwan and the fifth rank county China which hardware production value could not exceed US till to 2003 year. However, although China had the lowest hardware production value US $5,600 to compare to among of these countries in 1995 year, but China had increased the value to US $65,000 and market share to 20.5%. Otherwise, Japan, Singapore and Taiwan value and market share had surprisingly fallen down below than

China value in 2003 year. Thus, it seemed that China will be a potential country to compete US hardware production industry after 2003 year.

Reed Electronic Research, Year book Of World Electronic Data (2003) also showed that these computer companies of China had these % of market share : Beijing Founder had 9.9%, Tsinghua Tongtang had 7.8%, dell had 7.2 % , IBM had 5.1% , HP had 4.8% of market share. Thus, it also seemed that China some computer companies will have impotant large market share percentage in global pc sale market. In the future, global hardware production and pc sale industry. China and Taiwan both countries will be one pc manufacturing and design and sale partner. The reason is that China and Taiwan had been the number one rank of markers of notebook pcs, motherboards, scanners, keyboards, add-on card optical drives, monitors and some network equipment etc. pc (personal computer) relative computer function products. It seems that these both countries had co-operated to research any computer relative products to sell to global computer market. They are also the original design manufacturers (DDMS) develop and manufacture over half the world's notebook pcs as well as their customers include all major branded pc vendors (OEMS).

Taiwan Minstry Of Economic Affairs (2003) indicated Taiwan's top notebook ODMS include: In 2003 year volume (thousands) Quanta had $8,500 sale volume thousands , for example, Quanta major OEM partners include Gateway, Dell, HP, IBM, Apple , Sharp, Sony, Fujitsu-Siemens (F/S). Compal had $6,000 sale volume (thousands) , Compal major OEM partners include Dell, HP, F/S, Toshiba, Acer. Thus, it also implied Taiwan had many small size and non famous brand of computer companies which choose to co-operate to be partners with some global large size and famous brand of computer companies to raise competitive effort in global computer market, such as Dell, IBM, HP, Gatway, Apple etc.

Thus, the future trend of computer new product manufacturing development will shift from US to Taiwan and SE Asia, then to China. However, what kind of knowledge work factors will be needed to China and Taiwan . In general, notebook manufacturing stages will include: The first process is design stage, it includes concept design, such as analyze need, create concept and set brand image as well as product planning, such as business case, specifications, industrial design and sourcing strategy. The second process is development stage, it includes design review steps, such as design review, such as mock-ups, electrical test as well as prototype build, such as commercial samples, integrated system test as well as pilot production, such as production process design, pilot. Final process is production stage, it includes mass production, such as ramp-up, volume production, production testing and global distribution as well as sustaining support, such as speed bump, component replacement, technical support and warranty support. Thus, I believe that China and Taiwan must own thee knowledge work skillful of computer design and development professionals who can assist these two countries how to innovate their future computer development to change global traditional computer model to be renew and innovate computer model in the future.

Due to computer industry's stages of development and manufacturing are closely linked , need manufacturability , testing of sample products, concept design and product planning stay together in lead markets and branded vendors, design and development can be separated organizationally and geographically. Thus, China and Taiwan choose to co-operate to exchange their different skill, such as either China has own more concept design and product planning skill or more development skill or more production skill. Then, China will choose either one of the most beneficial comparative advantage among of them. To bring this one of the most beneficial co-operative advantage to attract Taiwan to choose either one of the beneficial comparative advantage of skill, such as either design or development or producton to already co-operate to compete the Western developed country US together.

Thus, US won't be the global computer industry development leader if both US country famous and large employee number computer companies, such as IBM and Apple which choose to outsource their pc design and development and production skill to China and Taiwan both countries to help them to develop global computer design and development and production skill to be upgraded. Thus, I feel these both countries will plan how to co-operate to compete US to win the global computer industry leader position in the future.

Factors influence consumers' laptop purchases.
In the future, instead of global computer manufacters need to consider the design, development and production processes, who also need to consider what factors can influence consumers' laptop purchases. Because any consumers have much different computer model and brand to choose to make final decision to buy any computers. If the computer manufacturer can predict what factors will be whose weakness(es) to influence global computer consumers to change whose mind or attitude to choose to buy

other brands of computers, then it won't lose its many old computer customer numbers and reduces it market share in global computer market share.

Nowadays, in general computer has three kinds to provide to global consumers to choose to buy , such as laptop, notebook computers, desktops. it seems that laptop and notebook computers and desktops will have different factors to influence any consumers to choose to buy any brand of computer products. Thus, computer indsutry can divide three consumer groups, such as (stayers, satisfied switchers and dissatisfied switchers) of a computer company with respect to the factors influencing consumers' laptops or notebook computers or desktops purchases. However, I feel the factors can include such as core technicl features, post purchase services, prices and payment conditions, peripheral specification, physical appearance, value added features and connectivity and mobility seven main factors that are influencing consumers' laptop or notebook computer or desktop purchases in global computer industry market.

Ganesh et al., (2000) indicates the customer base of a company consists of three groups of consumers: stayers, satisfied switchers and dissatisfied switchers. Therefore, the consumers in this study replied to the question about whether the current brand that who were using was their first laptop brand or whether who had switched from a previous laptop brand. As a following question, consumers who had switched were asked to state the reason of why who switched from a previous laptop brand brand to their current brand. The options include overall dissatisfaction from the previous laptop brand and reasons other than dissatisfaction. Thus, computer companies need to know what factors influence either whose prior computer customers why who don't choose repeat to buy its any computer products or whose new potential computer customers why who don't choose to buy its any computer products in the first time choice. Thus, future computer manufacturers need to consider intangible salespeople service attitude or performance, such as salespeople current purchase and post purchase service, e.g. technical repair, model function explanation how to use the computer, instead of tangible product performance, e.g. computer appearance design , function , mobility and internet and document download speed connectivity function. Because salespeople and technicians' service performance can be represented to the computer image. If they can provide excellent service to let computer buyers to feel satisfactory, then they can help their computer company employer to build good image. So, staff service performance will be one important factor to influence computer consumers to make the final decision to choose to buy the brand of computer products more easily. Even, one famous brand computer company, such as IBM, Apple, Gateway, these any one of famous brand computer company must not attract any new (the first time) or repeat computer buyers to choose to buy their any kind of computer products , such as laptop, desktop or notebook more easily due to their famous brand. Althoug, these famous computer companies had built good image to let consumers have more confidence to buy any kind of their computer products. But, if these famous computer companies' salepeople or repair technicians can not provide excellent customer service or performance to satisfy their computer buyers' service need, e.g. explaining how to use the new computer, repair post purchase service etc. I believe these famous brands of computer consumers will not have more desire to prefer to chose to buy any one of these famous computer brand's products. Otherwise, if the other less famous computer companies' any kind of laptop, desktop or notebook sale price is higher than the famous brand of computer companies' products sale price, but their salepeople or technicians can provide more excellent service attitude or performance to satisfy their consumers' needs. It is possible that the new or first time computer buyers or repeat computer buyers will still choose to buy their computers. So, the famous or less famous computer brand is not one important factor to influence the computer buyer to decide either to buy the computer or not buy the computer. Otherwise, computer company's salepeople and repair technician whose service performance or attitude will be one important intangible factors to influence any first time (new) or repeat computer consumers to choose to buy any famous or less famous brand of computer company's product, instead of the tangible computer design appearance and reliable function and convenient mobility and long term durability etc. factors influences.

Can culture factor influence the computer consumer choice?

Durmza and Zengin, (2011:53) indicted marketers closely interested in this issue to know the family which changed and renewed in course in time. It provides an advantage for a marketer to know the family structure and its consumption characteristics. Nowadays, consumer behavior is influenced not only by consumer personalities and motivation, but also by the relationships within families. Family is a social group and it can be considered a crucial place in th perception of marketing (Durmaz, Yakup,

CELLK, Mucahit and ORUC, Reyhan, (2011).
The consumer buying behaviors examined through an empirical study. Then, it brings this question: Whether cultural factors will influnece the computer consumer choice. Choice and include computer brand choice, computer price choice, computer model choice, computer design choice, laptop or desktop or notebook product choice, new or second-hand old computer choice, the computer of manufacturing country choice, computer package choice etc. So, any consumer will consider to choose any one of these to decide to buy which kind of computer.

Every country computer consumers had different culture to influence their computer shopping choice. I feel culture can be explained how to influence to computer shopping such as: How do the country computer consumers buy and use their computer products habitually ? How do the country computer consumers react to th computer price changes, attractive advertising methods to satisfy whose needs and computer company store interiors? What underlying mechanisms operate to produce any one of the country computer consumers' responses? If computer marketers have answers to such these questions, who can make better managerial decisions how to adopt which computer target country (countries) consumers' culture.

Consumer behavior deals with many other issues, for instance (Priest, Carter and Statt, 2013: 19). How do we get information about products? How do we assess alternative products? How do different people choose or use different products? How do we decide on value for money ? How much risk do we take with what products? Who influences our buying decisions and our use of the product? How are brand loyalties formed and changed? For computer industry, it means that how computer consumers get information about computer products, how computer consumers assess alternative notebook, desktop, laptop computer products, how different age, country, culture, sex, student or working people or retired people computer consumers choose or use different kind of computer products, such as notebook, desktop, laptop computer products, how much risk computer consumers take with notebook, desktop, laptop computer products, the computer consumers' buying decisons and their use of the desktop or notebook or laptop computer products will be influenced by whom, e.g. family, friends, teacher, employer, computer salepeople, advertisement marketer etc. , computer company brands how are formed and changed by whom, e.g. computer consumers, computer company competitors, marketers, different countries' culture etc.

Durmaz and Jablonski, (2012:56) also explained culture is the essential character of a society that distinguishes it from other cultural groups. The underlying elements of every culture are the values, language, myths, customs, laws and the artifacts or products that are transmitted from one generation to the next (Lamb, Hair and Deniel, 2011: 371). Culture is the most fundamental determinant of a person's wants and behavior. Whereas, lower creatives are governed by instinct, human behavior is largely learned. The child growing up in a society leans a basic set of values, perceptions, preferences and behaviors through a process of socialization involving the family and other social roles. So, I feel different country have different culture to influence as well as different country computer consumers who have different computer purchase and consume habitually. So, computer manufacturers ought focus on manufacturing the unique need and characteristics to satisfy any country's consumers' needs.

What is my idea about future global computer competition and factors influence computer consumer behavior ?

In conclusion, future computer industry development will trend that computer manufacturers need to consider every country's computer comsumer culture. Because every country computer consumers who will have different computer consumption habitually if who can predict what the country most computer consumers culture, then they can have more confidence to sell their computers to different country markets. Moreover, US computer manufacturers need to consider China and Taiwan computer manufacturing technology because it is possible that these both countries will be its main competitor among different computer manufacuring countries. Because thess both countries will cooperate to research new model of different computers to attract global computer consumers to choose to buy their new model of computer products in the future. Finally, computer manufacturers need to consider salepspeople and repair technicians service performance because computer consumers will consider intangible service performance , instead of tangible computer quality and price and style etc. factors . The main reason is that any computer have chance to be needed to repair and salespeople' skill will influence the computer consumer to make final decision to choose to buy the brand of computer. Thus, these factors will influence global computer development and trend in the future.

● Computer industry related service market development

What kinds of technologies innovation products will impact our future lives.

Europe in the 21 St Century is a technological society, how today technological trends could impact upon society in ways to be fully considered by clients' needs. What technological advancement products which can carry trend with it the promise of saving time, or assisting business or manufacturer industry clients to do more in the same amount of time.

In our clients buying choice view point, who ought hope any technological innovation products which can offer them that the opportunity to do things more efficiently. I shall suppose that technological innovation will be the main factor which can attract future many clients' purchase choice from the owned technological innovation product seller. For example, mobility, resource security , electronic government technological innovation products will be popular trend in future technological innovation product market.

● Autonomous automatic vehicle

Can autonomous vehicles be popular in the future driving market? Will your child soon be driving you to work? The autonomous vehicles (artificial intelligent vehicles) will change the responsible driver concept. Why does autonomous vehicles will be future popular driving tools?

In fact, autonomous vehicles have these feature characteristics to differ to compare our common traditional driving tools. Their characteristics, such as real-time human control option, advantage of the large amount of high -quality mapping data of possesses to programing travel routes, exploring ways in which autonomous vehicle technology can be integrated with existing parking infrastructure to produce " driverless parking systems" accessible via existing personal electronic devices, e.g. smartphones is demonstrating the use of fully automated road transport systems in Europe and developing guidelines to design and implement such systems.

With some analysts predicting that by 2022 year , there will be around 1.8 billion automotive machine -to-machine connection its is clear that a large amount of data will be generated by vehicle in the future. Thus, this level of communication between automated vehicles should make to possible for such vehicles to navigate to destinations and interact with other vehicles and objects most effectively than a human brain. Moreover, they believe the chance of automatic vehicles' highway accidents occurrence will be less than traditional human driving vehicles.

Thus, the increased connectivity required to facilitate automation of vehicles would significantly improve the degree of monitoring of the performance of such vehicles. Individual owners would be able to better maintain and enhance their vehicles with improvements in fuel efficiency and lesser fuel spending and safety. This could also provide further benefits, such as terms of reducing traffic jams, reduced pedestrian exposure to pollution and lower risk of road-traffic and pedestrian incidents occurring, particularly in urban areas.

The rise of autonomous vehicles is also likely to combine with continuing electrification of vehicles as telecommunications software and hardware and further integrated into vehicles. Thus, the rental-orientated and purchase-orientated automatic vehicle business both models will have chance to be raised in future global driving market.

It causes the responsibility tends to lie with human drivers of vehicles will be decreased. A new set of IT skills in addition to a practical ability to drive and operate a more digital type of driving machine as well as it might impact upon existing vehicle users in terms of requiring re-training, particularly those less able to learn. Even, future public transport will have possible to be changed from non-human driving and change to automatic vehicle market will be individual and business both client markets in possible.

In conclusion, to success to sell non manual driving tools. The non manual driving sellers need to know how to solve these two artificial intelligent vehicles innovation questions: Could our future living habits change as a direct segment of changing transport behaviors? Will autonomous transport simply become and essential transportation tools for our homes and workplaces? Thus, if manufacturers want artificial intelligent vehicles sale number increases, which needs to influence future whose clients to accept this kind of non -human driving tools can be satisfy to change their traditional driving living habits for their new habit of non -manual driving method to substitute traditional manual driving tools.

● 3 D printer

Can 3 D printer be popular sale to manufacturing industry clients? What could be the effects to the physical environment and human health of such application 3D printer to copy to manufacture any productions? For example, medical equipment products, car keys, guns, furniture etc. different heavy or light weight manufacturing products.

The benefits to 3 D printer include: less production time, reducing purchase bulk or materials to produce any products, reducing to employ worker number to produce products, workers can learn to use 3D printer to copy to manufacture any products easily, to avoid air or water pollution to pollute working environment to influence worker health and safe production in factories, employers can pay less wages to employ less workers, workers can also raise more efficient during using 3 D printers to manufacture any products.

Thus, in the future 3 D printers can be popular to be used to copy to manufacture for these any products, e.g. jewelry or weapon industry products. In fact, 3 D printer is an additive manufacturing technology for making three- dimensional object, of almost one sharp using a digital model. Such as jewelry manufacturers apply it to copy to manufacture new kind of jewelry, hospitals can apply it to copy to manufacture any new medical equipment, weapon manufacturers can apply it to copy to manufacture any new gun weapons, aerospace or air plan manufacturers can apply it to manufacture new air plane engineering equipment or space exploration equipment or transportation tools. Thus, 3 D printer application will be popular to different aspects of manufacturing industry.

Future expected impacts and development for 3 D printer development. A macro economy level impact of 3 D printing will be considered to manufacturing industry business consumer-based economy and the societal behavioral acceptance in factories and offices manufacturing environment.

However, buying habits as individuals are able to print their own products, in comfort of their own home. Activity would be changed from traditional shopping methods to purchase 3 D printer to copy to manufacture own same products at home. Consumers can also choose how to design to print the product, rather than the manufacturing process itself is what consumers will be paying for and thus these is the potential for a design -lead choice behavior. Manufacturers don't need to buy many materials to manufacture products, they can use 3D printer , such as individual manufacturing machine parts, which could drastically improve their ability to design and manufacture more effective machine and components.

In conclusion, how to sell 3 d printer successfully. 3 D printer sellers need to know what advantages can give to 3 D individual consumption buyer and business buyer to let them to know to aim to let them to accept to change their buying behavior and manufacturing behavior for some products. There are some questions for consumers to attempt to answers:

What will the implications be the level of personal interactions between individuals in society of all of our products were to be manufacturing at home?

How would this change our typical buying habits and what would be the impact on our economy?

Would an increased use of 3D printing technology in the home or factory accelerate this process and what would be the implications for local high streets?

Would economies change being-focused will digital design skills having a greater benefits than traditional manufacturing methods?

If the ability to print everyday items at home becomes a reality , who is society would have the greatest access to such technology?

If a particular demographic section (age, gender, race, income levels can be in factor to influence 3D printer consumer group, e.g. the 3 D printer buyer needs skills to manufacture any products, it seems only represented in a younger demographic. Could this mean that older members of society would not be able to benefit from 3 d printed projects?

In micro economy view point, although 3 D printer has benefits to individual and manufacturing consumers to reduce that their shopping or manufacturing expenditure, more design choice, raising worker individual skill and work performance. However, in macro economy view point, it also bring disadvantages to society. For example, if some members of society could not work move quickly, as a result than others, then what might be the impact upon their employability , e.g. causing unemployment of the 3D printer skillful learners who can not upgrade their working skill. Then, their employers will choose to dismiss these low skillful level 3 D printing learning skillful workers. Consequently, it will cause these member group of worker unemployment in the future society in possible. In conclusion, employers can not neglect how to train workers to learn how to apply 3 D printing skills to copy to manufacture any products.

● Massive open online course education

Will online education change traditional education? Basically, the students who choose to study from online channel, who must need have personal computers at home or school and often use internet from online platforms. In contrast to traditional methods of teaching with much small class size because every student can learn from online course at home. It means one teacher can choose to teach only one student from online channel. So, the teacher can stay at home or school as well as the student can stay at home , both of them can teach and learn from online teaching platform at the same time.

Whether the primary school, high school and university students who can accept to choose their learning habit to learn from this kind of online learning method more easily. In fact, online education will resultant impact on any teaching competitiveness. Due to , it is attempted to develop one kind of new technological education method to replace the traditional classroom by face -to-face teaching method between teacher and students contact.

However, it is not all course are suitable to adopt online teaching method and some courses re pointedly directed towards areas of interest that help education providers to also sell other online course products what other simply promote passive learning. For example, music, art, history, math, commerce courses which can be taught by teacher from online channel more easily. Because they do not need students to go to laboratory to do any experiments. Otherwise, engineering, food science, space science, medicine , doctor courses which need students go to laboratory to do experiments often. Thus, they are not suitable to be taught by teacher from online channel. Classroom teaching is more suitable to them.

Although, online teaching is low cost , due to that schools do not need many classrooms, even employ many teachers. So, they only buy computers and provide online education and less teachers are employed to teach whose students. So, it brings this question: Simply coursing cost barriers of success to education would not necessarily result in automatic take-up by young student consumers. May also need to think about best to education market, particularly to disadvantaged groups , such as older generations with lower computer and internet skills.

Who would be the winners and losers of an education market based upon such stronger principles of knowledge sharing and how can the institutions employing the use of such online or classroom or distance learning education methods be appropriately supported to maintain the high quality of further education? It seems to persuade students to choose online learning, the only method is that to let students feel online education can provide higher teaching quality level to compare traditional classroom learning method.

Other potential impacts of education market method relates more to education going online and a shift away from the more traditional forms of campus-based teaching in highest education . Would improving access to online education have the effect of increasing online students number. Due to who accept to choose online learning from traditional classroom learning habits . Thus, this is one learning habit change challenge for the traditional classroom learning students to adopt the online learning habit change.

In conclusion, for online education providers who need to consider how to change traditional classroom learning and teaching habit to adapt new online learning and teaching habit, as well as how to provide online teaching quality is higher level to compare to traditional teaching quality if who want their online education service businesses are successful.

● Future computer innovative and sustainable food source market

Future human considers health , so whose demand will high for quality of foods, farming of fish, typically freshwater with the cultivation of plants. It is simple future food source needs high health quality to provide to human to eat. If the food manufacture can have method to innovate any food quality to be more health to reduce poor health risk to influence human to eat. Thus, the food manufacturing process will be one important factor to attract consumers to choose to buy the food manufacturer's food supply. So, health food source market must attract many consumers to choose to buy to eat.

Computer technology can bring health foods supply method. Aquaponic system will be one health food manufacturing method. Aquaponic systems combine the farming of fish, typically freshwater, with the cultivation of plants. This takes place within a closed -loop aquaculture system, whereby fish are fed nutrients and their excrements one need as fertilizer directly into the water in which they are being loop. The water then feeds plants which use it for growth and filter the water , so it is suitable for re-use with the fish in the system. Such a system can be said to be closed-loop and hence a significant emphasis is placed upon the environmental and economic sustainability characteristics of acquaponic systems are only small-scale and therefore incur high costs of production relative to current methods of large-scale-farming.

However, in the future, due to human ought consider health, so who we need any food have good health quality to avoid any illness, e.g. cancer, even death causing risk from bad health foods source. In conclusion, food manufacturers need to consider any new food manufacturing methods to achieve how to manufacture foods to keep fresh and health level if they hope their food products can be attractive to consumers to choose to buy to eat.

Hence, future any new technological invention to manufacture health food will be one important factor to influence global food industry development. Also, it implies any food manufacturers need to consider how to manufacture any health foods in whose food manufacturing process. In conclusion, future foods and agriculture development will be trend to agriculture health productivity, avoidance from pests and diseases influence to food manufacturing process, avoidance food supply inequality and insecurity, more nutrition and health, changing food source manufacturing process system, reducing food losses and waste during food manufacturing process, making food systems more efficient, building resilience to protracted arises, disasters and conflicts, preventing transboundary and emerging agriculture and food system threats.

Future computer industry related service business strategy trends

● Government (public) and private partnership property development strategy

In future some business, public and private partnership method is more suitable to compare the private entrepreneur sole operation. For example, property development, construction industry example, building and rebuilding cities and new communities is a complex challenge, it requires public and private interests and resources. However, the traditional process of urban and suburban can be developed between the local government and private property developer, which will win distinctly different benefits if they decide to cooperate together.

The need to rebuild and revitalize older portions of urban areas , the public need to monetize underused assets have dramatically changes. In fact, private sole property developer's disadvantages is that it has no longer can private capital be relied on to pay the high price of assembling and preparing appropriate sites for redevelopment. Also, it has no longer can local governments bear the full burden of paying the costs of public infrastructure and facilities. If public housing department and private property developer can cooperate to achieve shared goals and objectives, this process can require applying far more effort and skill to weighing, and then balancing, public and private interests and minimizing conflicts.

For another public and private partnership example, such as health care providers and education institutions, non profit associations, such as community based organizations and business improvement district organization , these organizations are very suitable to choose to cooperate with government (public organization) to do their businesses together in the future global business environment trend.

However, the property development industry will have more benefits and needs to choose public and private partnership to compare these above industry. The main reason is that this industry will much capital to invest to any building business and it is long term tangible fixed property development business. Thus, the public and private property development partnership can implement a range of pursuits from projects to long term-plans for land use and economic growth. Partnerships have completed real estate projects, such as mixed-use developments, urban renewal through land and property assembly, public facilities, such as convention centers and airports and public services , such as affordable and military housing.

However, each public and private property development partnership is the best to share common stages with each development process as below:

In the first stage, conceptualization and initiation, stakeholders' opinions of the vision and surveyed and partners are selected through a competitive process.

In the second phase, entities document the partnership and begin to define project elements, roles and responsibilities, risks and rewards and the decision and implementation process.

In the third phase, the partnership attempts to obtain support from all stakeholders, including civil groups, local government (through entitlement), and project team members.

Finally, in the fourth phase, the partnership begins construction, leasing and occupancy and property and asset management.

However, the process is repetitions and can continue beyond the final phase when partners manage properties or initiate new projects.

For US one successful public and private property development partnership example, the contributing major benefits to the citizens of Washington, D.C. The James Foyster School Henry Adams House, a public elementary school and 211 unit residential apartment complex was constructed as a result of a partnership among the District Of Columbia Public Schools.

● Online tourism service partnership

Another a major public and private partnership is tourism industry. Will public and private partnership to tourism be better than sole travel agent business operation? I believe it is better to any travel agent to choose public and private partnership strategy, the reasons include as below:

● Public tourism partnership goal, to provide the countries' different tourism destinations and tourism features to consider any country tourism information to assist travelers in understanding the travel problem, alternatives, opportunities and/or solutions to adapt every traveler individual travelling need.

● To obtain public travelling feedback on analysis, alternatives and/or travelling decisions, to work directly with the public throughout the travel public promotion process to ensure that public concerns and aspirations are consistent understood and considered, to partner with the public in each aspect of any tourism tickets comparison, tourism destinations, tourism entertainment, and transportation of the decision information , including the different tourism destinations development of alternatives and the identification of the preferred solution to place final decision -makings in the hands of the public.

● Every travel agent and public organization will keep every traveler's informed, listen and knowledge concerns and provide feedback on how public input influenced every tourism decision to every individual traveler considerately.

● Tourism techniques will consider fact sheet, web sites, open houses, public comment, focus tourism groups, surveys, public meetings, workshops, deliberate polling.

In conclusion, public and private partnership will be future trend to develop because capital can be shared, reduces sole business operation risks, promotes business information efficiently and easily when public organization can participate to assist these private business organization to cooperate to develop their businesses together.

● Higher education marketing, enrollment, branding and recruitment strategy

Future the most important tools for social and online education marketing will be an effective university website promotion tool to build ultimate brand for any university organization. Websites often feature elements and highlight content, including navigation, bars, engaging visuals, such as slideshows, and prominent " call to action" buttons that encourage students to apply. For example, radio ads., asking current students or for applicant referrals and online college fairs were deemed least effective, when the most effective methods of outreach open houses and campuses visit days for high school students.

Online education courses will be popular, due to adaptive learning technology has also enjoyed. So, successful branding can help increasing enrollment, expanding fundraising capabilities and other outcomes. Today, effective strategy planning and brand management require more than traditional advertising. Education institutions present and manage brand message, experience and environment achieve a competitive advantage in recruiting, building royalty among their students, parents , staff , faculty and donors.

In conclusion, how to do effective website advertising to promote university courses, website enrollment method? I shall recommend these methods as below:

Firstly, design responsive website, education institutions are placing more emphasis on responsive web design to create intuitive and easy to navigate websites that can be viewed on multiple, devices and platform.

Secondly, university administrators want their education institutions to receive a spot in search engine result particularly Google website. Especially for education institutions that offer niche programs , it is increasingly important to ensure that search results, including the programs at the top.

Thirdly, how to use of web analytics, colleges and universities are relying on data-driven analytic to determine who, whom and where they are reaching their audiences. The use of analytics software is increasing as the higher education web ecosystem is becoming complex, e.g. domains, subdomains etc.

Fourthly, getting a better handle of this data is a new area of concentration for colleges and universities strategic social media, when recent polls indicate nearly every education institutes of higher education use some form of social media, e.g. face book or twitter account, these trends are explored.

Fifthly, the rise of mobile development and connected decides to colleges and universities for a greater amount of course content of mobile versions of websites to promote to every student to know from whose every mobile, CRM systems are heavily on content management and customer relation systems for admission for prospective students service in the future mobile promotion technology.

Bibliography

Durmaz, Yaleup and Jablonski, Sabastian, (2012): Integrated Approach To Factors Affecting Consumers Purchase Behavior In Poland And An Empirical Study. Global Journal of management and business research (GJMBR), volume 12 issue 15.

Ganesh, J., Arnold, M. and reynolds, K.E. (2000) ." Understanding The Customer Base Of Service Provides: An Examination Of The Differences Between Switchers And Stayers" , Journal of marketing, 64 (3), 65-88.

Journal of business and social science (IJBSS). volume 2, no 5, p: 105110, radford USA. http://www.ijbssnet.com /journals/vol._2 _no._5 1 special_issue_March_2011J/13,pdf

Lamb, C.W. Hair, J. F. and Mc Daniel, C. (2011): " MKTD student edition". South Western , Mason.

Priest, J., Carter, S. And Stat , D. (2013) : Consumer Behavior, Edinburgh Business School Press, United Kingdom.

Further resources.

Reed Electronic Research, Yearbook Of World Electronic Data (2003)

Taiwan Minstry Of Economic Affairs (2003)

Internet market development trend

What is Internet entertainment function

The internet is one of the most used platforms in the world today particularly because of its limitless access to information from different subjects and times in history. The internet and its uses play a very critical role in the life of each and every individual, especially the literate ones and can most be appreciated in the 21st Century.

Will future internet be main entertainment need?

I believe future the internet is used for research purposes mainly because it has unrestricted access to a vast amount of data from all parts of the world and over. Moreover, internet is also used for communication purposes through protocols such as email and many more in that it provides a platform through which information can be sent hence bridges geographical gap. For example, download and upload of files is also another significant use of the internet, where the subject is able to access different files due to the permission the internet has, as well as send information. It does not matter where the files were uploaded from.

In internet entertainment function aspect, video game players can also achieve conduction of interactive games as well as discussion groups over the internet regardless of the groups' geographical position in that all of you could b at different corners of the world. In Education and self-improvement aspect, teachers can also be done over the internet by making reference to multiple educational materials available over the internet. Electronic newspapers and magazines fall here. It is also possible to make friends and even date over the internet by provisions such as chatting and even making video calls.

Is internet one popular tool useful to future communication aspect? Internet has these different unique characteristics:

● Internet has made almost unlimited amounts of information available to everyone.

● Since many official procedures are available online, internet has dramatically reduced the processing time for them such as registration of a business, application for a passport etc.

● Critical information, such as the traffic situation on road or air etc. is easily available avoiding many harassing situations for passengers.

● Internet has made commerce very easy. People can browse the online shops virtually and make payments for shopping online.

● Learning has become easier due to the information and learning material that is available online.

● Many courses can be conducted online thus making distance learning much more feasible.

● Internet banking has made transfer of funds much easier. One doesn't have to carry around cash in large amounts.

● Because of internet the availability of jobs also goes up as online jobs with no location restriction become easier.

● Quality of work of all kinds improves since the candidate pool for any job is bigger.

● For readers, all kind of books available at one's finger tips, many of them free of cost, online.

● Internet also makes it easy for people to connect on issues close to their hearts. Parents from across the globe and discuss children's issues etc., which works as a support group.

● Entertainment has become easily available through internet media such as YouTube.

● Internet has made social contacts much easier to maintain.

● Crime can be reduced if social media is used as an awareness tool.

● Internet has also made medical issues easier to handle by sharing the reports and diagnosis of a patient through email etc.

● Pictures and videos can be easily shared over the internet.

● Video apps on the internet have made video calls not just possible but also common getting people closer.

● Paying bills etc. is also much easier due to internet making life much simpler especially for the elderly.

● A young mother can watch her toddler in a day care while she works through the CCTV connected to the internet.

● Internet makes it easier to reach out to the experts across the globe for consultations if necessary because of the internet.

The media is analyzed in two ways here as an informative aspect as well as a form of entertainment.Freedom of expression is usually questioned in the media, how 'free' is the media allowed to be? Isn't the media always controlled? What is the role of media in society, for entertainment aim, I shall explain the reasons internet will not be the suitable entertainment media aim as below:

Is everyone in society treated equally in the media, when being reported on from internet channel? It is often a belief that the media is a rather powerful tool, one that gets blamed for all the wrong that occurs in society. What we read in the papers and view on television is usually what we believe.

What is functionalism to internet entertainment aim?:

Functionalism refers to a system, a belief in function over form. Functionalism with regard to the media – refers to how the media operates as a whole 'system' in society to help create a balance in society. Society as an integrated, harmonious and cohesive whole. Different social systems function to maintain equilibrium, consensus and social order. Media as a powerful socialization instrument should contribute towards integration, harmony and cohesion through information, entertainment and education.

Functions of the internet entertainment media:

Main functions of the media are – to inform and entertain, this allows the media to contribute manifestly or latently to cultural growth for individuals and society. Though its rather a simplistic model especially when it comes to the political functions of the media

Objections (Short comings) to internet entertainment aim functionalism:

Functionalism takes for granted that agreement prevails over, and disregards conflict in society. The media will not have the same functions for all the people in society. Interpreted differently by individuals. Cultural barriers could arise when interpreting different media Functionalism does not account for social change well established democratic societies Vs societies in the process of transformation. Neglects to provide for feedback (seeing that feedback modifies both the message and the context)

If future internet can bring entertainment aim to provide information about events and conditions in society and the world, facilitate innovation, adaptation and progress for human entertainment aim, it will be worth technological tool. e.g. express the dominant culture and recognize subcultures and new cultural developments provide amusement, diversion and the means of relaxation entertainment aim, reduce social tension and provide social objectivity in issues such as war and politics and economic development.

Future internet will need to be one fun entertainment media should exist in various forms such as radio, television, and print among other forms catering for all of society. Think of DSTV as an example does a wide range of channels mean a wider range of program content? Are more groups of people catered for with the diversity of channels? To criticize political developments and decisions. Internet entertainment media policy ensures media pluralism (the existence of different media: various newspapers, radio stations, television stations, magazines, films and so on.Internet needs to provide these entertainment message, e.g. differences within the information and entertainment content of newspapers, radio and television stations ® should be balanced, offer different opinions etc. differences between different newspapers, radio and television stations. Concerns all the media, regardless of category, available in a society; the variety of choices.

Internet entertainment media should be able to publish what they see fit, the media is also allowed to publish information against the ruling power and society should interpret the messages accordingly. People are rational beings capable of distinguishing between truth and falsehood, and between good and evil. Give them all factual information and let them decide. Its the responsibility of the internet media to keep the citizens of a country duly informed of the actions of its government. Internet entertainment media needs to be basic on these assumptions as below:

The media is a source of information.

The media is a platform for expression of divergent opinions.

Free from government control.

Media should be free from external censorship.

Should be accessible to any individual or group.

Editorial attacks should not be punishable.

No coercion to publish anything.

No restrictions on the acquisition of information.

No restrictions on import and export of information across borders

The media should be free from censorship that is external from it, so that certain officials from a political party can't restrict or delete certain remarks that were made to the public because they would want to dictate what the public reads and what not.

– Publication should be free without a licence for the people reading the material. There are no restrictions like this in South Africa currently.

– If there are any "editorial attacks" on government it should not be punishable; this paves the way for free speech like the article of Boyle, giving his opinion and informing the public.

– There should be no compulsion to publish anything as this will give an unjust and skew view of what is happening in South Africa. With parties exerting their power to help their own cause.

– The "acquisition of information" should not be restricted if they are obtained through legal channels. For instance the number of South African Police Service members that were suspended because of corruption – those are available thus it can be published if the journalist wishes and to inform the public.

– There should be no restriction so that information about the country may or may not be imported or exported.

Social responsibility theory:

Internet entertainment Media should be equal and fair in its reporting of incidents and issues. It must be diverse and responsible towards society. The social responsibility to internet entertainment media may include: Reconcile the ideas of freedom and independence with responsibility towards society, media should support democratic political principles, create a form for different viewpoints and should meet certain standards.

Internet entertainment media should accept responsibility towards society. They include as below:

Set professional standards (truth, accuracy, objectivity, balance)

Avoid information that could lead to crime, violence or social disruption.

Not offend ethnic or religious minorities.

Be representative of all social groups. Reflect the diversity of society.

Intervention if the media fail to meet these standards.

Media must work and be owned by the working class.

Main assumptions:

Act in the interest of, and be controlled by the working class.

Media should not be privately owned.

Socialization, education, information, motivation, mobilization.

Media should respond to needs of recipients.

Society can use censorship.

Marxist-Leninist view of society must be reflected in programming.

Supporting progressive (communist) movements.

Individuals as well as minority groups must be catered for by the media.

Basic assumptions:

Media should make a positive contribution to the national development process.

Economic development and society should be more important than press freedom.

National, cultural and language issues should be high on the media's agenda.

Media should give preference to information about other developing countries that are geographically, culturally and politically akin to each other

Journalists have both responsibilities and liberties in obtaining and distributing information

State has the right to intervene by restricting and censoring the media. State subsidiaries and direct control is justifiable

Reaction against commercialization and monopolies

Against centralization and bureaucracies in public broadcasting

Developed societies

Internet future entertainment function

Much of the media produced today serves for the purpose of entertainment. Inform and educates on a latent and manifest level. The five internet entertainment aim and characteristic, it needs to own as below:

identity means entertainment focuses on human relations

ability means gives problem-solving possibilities

survival means awareness of eternal values (freeing from anxiety about destruction and death)

understanding means of reality and knowledge. shedding new light on reality (you're not alone)

From a rhetorical perspective the individual determines their interpretation of entertainment ,according to identity, social relation You can consider family series, police and action dramas or situation comedies, soap operas, game shows. From a behavioral perspective, entertainment is associated with the human ability to identify with others project and introject feelings but also with distancing from others.

Internet entertainment also makes a visual impact on the viewer, viewers become outsiders (not participants). Entertainment content (like any form of play) is always voluntary. The two parties on internet entertainment players may include: Introjection means viewer adopts feelings of other party. Projection = viewer projects feelings on other party (actors, characters) People are entertained when they produce their own opinions on these internet media situations.

Importance of understanding internet entertainment media effects:

Strategic importance: to understand that messages – specific response – certain circumstance = strategically important in political, social awareness, marketing and advertising campaigns.

Scientific importance: contributes to the beneficial use of the media for the improvement of people's circumstance and society in general

Ethical importance: Responsibility of communication workers to know about the possible consequences of their work on the lives of people and society

Effects studies seek to discover describe and explain the internet entertainment media's specific effects on our behavior and thinking in a specific way. For example, the impact of pornography, violence and / or crime portrayed in and by the media on people's behavior. Internet can make use of mainly quantitative research techniques such as content analysis, survey research for entertainment aim.

CATEGORISING MEDIA AFFECTS:

Internet entertainment media ought not need to brings these message. They include: Media messages can affect our knowledge and thinking about something (e.g. thinking about racism), media messages can affect our feelings about something (e.g. child abuse, terrorism, violence.), media messages can affect our behavior towards something or someone (e.g. contribute to political rising against a government, org or group)

Internet entertainment media ought bring these message, such as , may have been planned to achieve a specific effect (e.g. HIV awareness campaign may be intended to warn people against disease) or not planned or intended (e.g. May teach certain people how to spread the disease, short term message exposure to single message like one program – after that person forgets about it or intermediate message exposur to a series of related messages like a series on TV – (e.g. product campaign, stopping smoking) or long term exposure. Many exposures to related messages over time (e.g. media violence, pornography or awareness of environmental issues) may change our response or behavior over a long time.

An ongoing campaign to influence people's minds by focusing on negative aspects of an opponent / topic. Withholding positive or objective information Internet entertainment media campaigns ought include these elements, such as: An advertising campaign to promote a specific product or educational development. E.g. Topic people knew initially little or nothing about like global warming and its effects. Knowledge distribution concerns the media's contribution to cultural change, the media's contribution to Socialization.

● Reality defining – the media's interpretations of the realities of daily life and how we should understand them and avoiding Media violence – if the film or TV program causes violent behavior in an individual or amongst group.

Future internet entertainment media needs to bring these long-term benefits to internet players. They may include as below:

Media focus (a newspaper or different newspapers by example)– repeatedly and consistent and over a long period, focus on a specific topic equals to changes in beliefs, attitudes and behavior. Focus attention and produce messages on specific problems or issues (E.g. race, discrimination, the environment, social habits, crime, divorce, style, sex, politics). Over extended period of time focus stays and presentation corroborate each other. Individuals become aware of these messages, and a growing.

In general, children will apply internet to play online games. However, online games will bring both advantages and disadvantages as below:

The Internet has been a gaming medium for almost as long as it has existed, as early users quickly adapted email and newsgroup technology to create online versions of classic board games or roleplaying games. Since the early 2000s, the growth of broadband Internet has brought new generations of gamers online; in fact, you can't play some modern games such as Titanfall offline at all. While there are a lot of advantages to online gaming, it does have a seedy underbelly.

Internet can help children to make friend when they entertain from internet. More than anything else, online games have brought players together, forging people with a shared interest into a community. Whether cooperative or competitive, online gaming makes it much easier for gamers to play with their friends or make new ones. Guildmates can play together in an online role-playing game or sports rivals test their skills even though they live thousands of miles apart. Friendships can develop in online games between people who would never have met otherwise. Recent research even shows that children who play online games are more likely to develop positive attitudes toward people from other countries and cultures.

But, internet can also encourage bad behavior

Game makers and community moderators do their best to limit this kind of behavior, but it still plagues some online communities. Luckily, most games offer a way to ignore or mute other players if you are encountering a barrage of insults.

Connection Problems

Modern online gaming is usually a very smooth experience, but the technology still has its limits. Small delays in internet connections can result in "lag," a delay between when you press a button and the action occurs in the game. In input-sensitive games like first-person shooters or fighting games, this small delay is the difference between victory and defeat.

Cost

Internet connection charges can quickly add up when playing online: Gamers whose ISPs impose data caps may find themselves using up their bandwidth quickly. Players may also have to pay monthly for online accounts or spend money per item on in-game purchases, and the costs can add up quickly for unsuspecting players.

Competitive Communities

Competitive gamers are among the biggest beneficiaries of online gaming. Previously, most players' knowledge of the competitive scene was limited to a local group such as an arcade or a university gaming club. Online gaming -- aided by other online tools such as Twitch and YouTube -- has made it possible for competitive players to share strategies and analyze gameplay like never before, raising the standard of play to a new level and creating an entirely new industry of professional competitive gaming. However, there is a downside to this boom, as new players can often find the high level of play demanded by competitive gamers intimidating, and may not even attempt to play online.

Thus, future internet entertainment ought not need concern on playing games aspect, it ought apply to entertainment media knowledge or message aspect, if our society can expect our generation develop successfully, because when they apply internet to learn new and useful knowledge for entertainment aim more than playing games to waste time aim. Then, we shall have many internet new knowledge young people who can apply their new knowledge from internet learning to attribute our society.

What is Internet learning function

The Services are used by the people to get information, do online works, discussions, e-mailing, video chatting, voice calling, social activities, news channels, online booking and many other hundred and thousand terms that we use with the help of internet. In every country there are many companies that provide the services of net in different rates. There get benefits from full functions you need to have a laptop, mobile or PC. All above these which will need any internet users to learn in order to achieve their consumption or playing or entertainment or learning aim.

Advantages / Merits / Uses / Benefits of Internet

● Online Shopping

Now today's the trend of online shopping is growing up very fast. Users have now the facility of shop everything what they want without going outside to stores and super markets.

Benefits for Students Studies

You are a student and you miss the lecture. Don't worry internet helps students to find notes, essay, lectures, guidelines and more than points related to your subject are available in your books.

Book Tickets online

In the race of technology and companies are giving best services to their users. And almost all the airlines are providing advantages to their customer to buy the tickets online on internet. So people are no need to go to the agency or airline office.

Learn Online From Videos

Internet is the solution of many problems. If you face any problem in your mobile, laptop, cars, television etc. You can easily find the solution on the screen with the help of video providing website. Mostly used websites for videos upload and downloads are YouTube, Dailymotion, tunepk, viemo and etc.

Play Online Games

People fond of video games are easily access to download multiple games. Also can play online games with the help of internet connection. Without it you can't play online either can't download.

Entertainment

Every day new movies and music lunched in every country almost. People how are fond to watch movies or listen music. They can easily find latest music and movies on Internet and can download it and also watch it online.

E-mailing

Government Departments, Private Organization, Businesses, NGOs, School, Colleges and Universities etc. And many other departments and peoples are using the e-mail services. And I'll say that without e-mail conversation half of word would be stop work. Because big projects, secret information and files are shared through e-mails and this service is not possible without Internet Connection.

Results and Roll No

Students of Universities and Colleges now even the students of Schools are easily see their results on internet. To access to the result you must need to put the right roll no in the search bar of school or college website.

Jobs

Hundreds of mobile application, and thousands of website in every country. In their national language provide the services to the jobless peoples to find the jobs on Internet related to their experience and criteria.

Bank Accounts

Money in your bank account is now same like money in your pocket. Yes you can login to your account and make online transactions either bank is open or close.

Buy and Sell

If you have second hand or new bike, car, clothes, shoes, jewelry, mobile or laptop etc. You can place an add to website and easily can sell on reasonable price as compare to market. You can also buy same like this by contacting the selling person.

Earn Money On Internet

Create a professional website or create a channel on video website. Run for little time and place an advertisement on your website or channel and earn money through net. You can also earn money by affiliate marketing.

Hire Peoples for Work

Hire online people to get advantages to complete your assignments, petty works, designs, data entry works etc. there are several famous website where you can easily hire a person for your work. Fiver and Upwork are good example of it.

However, online learning may bring these disadvantage to influence student individual learning attitude or learning emotion, I shall indicate reasons as below:

In recent years, internet addiction has been a world-wide problem among the youth. Many of them may sit in front of the computer to play online game; chat with others for the whole day without resting. Those prolonged activities bring a lot of destructive effect to them both. They apply internet to play more than apply this high technological media tool for learning aim usually. Internet can be very constructive, but we must be conscious how much time we spend on it on a daily basis. People are addicted to the internet since they do not control the amount of time they spend on it. It is important to have other interests apart from the internet.

Today, surfing the Web has become a hobby as social and marketable as bar hopping or going to the movies. As the web has become a part of mainstream life, some mental health professionals have noted that a percentage of people using the web do so in a compulsive and out-of-control manner. In Japan (Aril 2010), a 30-year-old man who is addicted to internet killed his father and his 1 year-old niece because of his father terminated the contract of internet broadband. He then set up a fire and burnt his house. In this case, 2 people died and 3 people injured. This phenomenon of obsessive Internet use has been termed 'Internet Addiction' based on its similarity to common addictions such as smoking, drinking, and gambling. Internet Addiction has even been championed as an actual disorder, notably by some psychologists. Nevertheless, at this time the true nature of Internet Addiction is not yet determined.

Because the Internet is used by many people as a normal part of their career or education, knowing how to separate excessive from normal use becomes difficult and cannot using simple measures such as amount of time spent online in a given period. Most fundamental in distinguishing normal from problem Internet use is the experience of compulsion to use the net. Normal users, no matter how heavy their usage, do not need to get online and do not neglect their occupational duties or their relationships with family and friends to get online.

Mental health professionals are split as to whether Internet addiction is real or not. No one disputes that some people use the Internet in an obsessive manner even to a point where it interferes with their ability to function at work and in social relationships. What is doubtful is whether people can become addicted to the Internet itself, or rather to the stimulation and information that the web provides. The argument surrounding Internet Addiction is precisely whether people become addicted to the net itself, or to the stimulation to be had via the net, such as online gambling, pornography or even simple communication with others via chat and blogs. Some psychologists do not consider in addiction to the Internet itself, but rather in addiction to stimulation that the Internet provides. They propose that new Internet users often show an initial fascination with the innovation of the Web, but eventually lose interest and reduce their time spent online back to a normal, healthy amount. Those abuser who do go on to show obsessive Internet utilization, for the most part become compulsive only with considering to particular types of information to be had online, mainly often gambling, pornography, chat room or shopping sites. This is not an addiction to the Internet itself, but rather to risk-taking, sex, socializing or shopping. In real meaning, the main addictive characteristic of the Internet is its capability to enable instant and relatively social stimulation. "Addicted" Internet users are addicted to a favored kind of social stimulation and not to the Internet itself, although it is also true that the Internet has made it easier and more convenient for someone to develop such a compulsion.

Why peoples especially youth have internet addition? There are some reasons to explain it. By Internal Factors-The background of growth, the family is believed to have a fundamental influence on the developing child. A caregiver who is emotionally and physically available is essential for healthy child and adolescent development. Besides, dysfunctional caregiving, lack of positive parenting skills, and poor family management are strongly associated with substance use and delinquency in youth. Therefore, the youth growth up in poor family will seek alternative to fulfil their psychological needs, it is compensation. The level of compensation is depending on the individual factors such as the degree of self control, emotional control, ability of problem solving, anxiety management. When over compensation, addition will occur. There are some reasons that people choose internet for compensation. From social learning, when adolescents' strong developmental needs, such as personal identity, autonomy, and relationships with peers may not be fulfilled through physical activities, they may then shed social inhibitions, also when they are dissatisfied with their leisure time, they may be motivated to seek excitement and pleasure from cyberspace and therefore raise their level of Internet addiction. Besides, encourage of society and the common use of Internet activities raise the level of Internet addiction. Furthermore, the traditional activities are perceived to be boring and fails to satisfy expected optimal experience, the youth may be motivated to seek another alternative-the Internet. Internet not only fulfills youth's psychological needs but also entertainment needs. Lastly, Internet dependency was burden and the youth become habituated by using.

Internet addiction is not recognized as a formal mental health disorder. However, mental health professionals who have written about the subject note symptoms or behaviors that, when present in sufficient numbers, may indicate problematic use. These include:

Obsession with the Internet: User often thinks about the Internet while he or she is offline.

Loss of control: Addicted users feel unable or unwilling to get up from the computer and walk away. They sit down to check e-mail or look up a bit of information, and end up staying online for hours.

Inexplicable sadness or moodiness when not online: Reliance on any substance often causes mood-altering side effects when the addicted user is separated from the substance on which he or she depends.

Distraction (Using the Internet as an anti-depressant): One common symptom of many Internet addicts is the compulsion to cheer one's self up by surfing the Web.

Dishonesty in regard to Internet use: Addicts may end up lying to employers or family members about the amount of time they spend online, or find other ways to conceal the depth of their involvement with the Internet.

Loss of boundaries or inhibitions: While this often pertains to romantic or sexual boundaries, such as sharing sexual fantasies online or participating in cyber sex, inhibitions can also be financial or social. Online gambling sites can cause addicts to blow more money than they would in a real-life casino because users never actually see their money won or lost, so it is easier to believe the money is not real. Chat rooms can incite users to reveal secrets they would not reveal in face-to-face or phone conversations because of the same separation from reality. Also, addicted users are much more likely to commit crimes while online (e.g., 'hacking') than non-addicts. Creation of virtual intimate relationships with other Internet users: Web-based relationships often cause those involved to spend excessive amounts of time online, attempting to make connections and date around the Net. Loss of a significant relationship due to Internet use: When users spend too much time on the Web, they often neglect their personal relationships. Over time, such relationships may fail as partners simply refuse to be treated badly and break off from relations with the addicted individual.

Internet Addiction is not an official disorder, and many mental health professionals are not certain if it ever should be considered a real disorder. Nevertheless, compulsive Internet use is a serious problem for some people, and there are methods that can be helpful in alleviating this problem. Discussion below will describe some of these methods. Internet addiction is a problem of compulsive stimulation, much like drug addiction. Because of this similarity, well studied treatment procedures known to be useful for helping drug addicts towards recovery are adapted for use with Internet addicts when the need arises. The techniques we describe below are drawn from a popular school of therapy known as 'cognitive-behavioral' therapy. Cognitive behavioral forms of therapy are well studied and known to be helpful as applied to many different mental and behavioral difficulties. They are also very practical and focus directly on reducing out of control 'addict' behaviors, and preventing relapse. They are not the only valid forms of therapy, however.

In treating drug addiction, frequently the goal of therapy is abstainence. An alcoholic, for example, is often best off if he or she ceases to drink alcohol entirely and to maintain a sober lifestyle. While this makes sense for a drug like alcohol which we might argue is a at best a luxury recreational indulgence and not a necessity, but it doesn't necessarily make sense for Internet over-usage. Much like the telephone, the Internet has become an essential part of modern business. To ask people to not use the Internet at all could be a significant burden for them. Instead of abstainence, then, a reasonable goal for Internet addiction therapy is a reduction in total use of the net. Because Internet addicts by definition will have difficulty moderating their use on their own, therapy techniques can be employed to help them to become more motivated to reduce their use, and to become more conscious of how they get into trouble with the Internet.

Motivational Interviewing may be employed to assess how motivated Internet addict may be to change their behavior and to help addicts to increase their motivation to make a lasting change. To accomplish the latter, a therapist may help addicts to develop genuine empathy for the people who are hurt by their addiction (e.g., family and friends, employers, etc.). By helping addicts to see how their actions affect others they care about or are dependent on economically, therapists can help increase addicts motivation to change.

Setting up (healthy) rewards that patients can earn when goals have been met for an agreed upon amount of time. Since one of the main draws of the Internet is the secrecy it appears to give, sharing online experiences in the context of offline relationships may discourages a user from 'hiding' in the Internet. Sharing progress in a group therapy session, with a therapist, or with a family member can help motivation to cut back on Internet time.

With regard to Internet addiction, it is possible to install computer programs designed to monitor where someone surfs and how long they spend there to provide an accurate and objective report of someone's surfing behavior. PC software will monitor the kinds and number of websites a person uses and the amount of time spent Web surfing or checking e-mail. Such programs can help compulsive Internet users supervise their own Internet use, but only if they are installed so as to be hard to tamper with.

What Are The Advantages And Disadvantages Of Online Learning?

Learning is often considered to be a normal part of working and personal life. Both learning for achieving a job as well as for achieving knowledge should not be neglected. Online environment is changing continuously and it represents a great opportunity for learning. It is very important to discover how to learn using all available communication channels and choosing the ones that best suit a person's style of filtering the information. Nowadays, online learning turns out to be more and more practiced. Many traditional universities started to share their courses online for free. It represents an easy and comfortable method to achieve knowledge in almost every field, from law and accounting, to human sciences, such as psychology and sociology or history. Online learning is a great alternative to traditional universities, especially for people who can't afford the time and money to take real courses. But what are the advantages and disadvantages of online learning?

Advantages Of Online Learning

Although many people still consider traditional universities as the best way to achieve knowledge and get a diploma, online learning proves to be a great alternative. Students have the chance to study in their own time and especially for free. It represents a great way to study many fields and to boost the level of self-motivation. Online learning is so effective because students can finish their homework quickly, and there is more time left for hobbies or for finding a job. An access to all resources of a traditional course helps participants learn wherever they are, leaving them the freedom to choose the time for study. With basically an Internet connection, a person can attend different courses. Among the advantages of online learning there are the responsibility and self-discipline of students.

Disadvantages Of Online Learning

Only in a small group a person can develop properly. At school, students learn how to make friends, be patient, get rid of disappointment, and especially to compete. Competition between colleagues can be very stimulating and students will only benefit from it. Online learning cannot offer human interaction. Another disadvantage refers to the fact that online courses cannot cope with thousands of students that try to join discussions. Also, online learning can be difficult, if it is meant for disciplines that involve practice.

In conclusion, online learning should be seen as a complement and extension of classical forms of learning. Not even the best online course can fully replace the personal contact with a teacher, or the human relationships that develop in a group. So, traditional classes shouldn't be replaced with online

What is internet for searching information function

The Internet is important for a huge variety of reasons, and it affects and facilitates nearly every aspect of modern life. The Internet is extremely important in many fields, from education and healthcare to business and government. The Internet has had an enormous impact on education, streamlining access to information and making it easier for individuals to engage in online learning. Distance education programs make it easier for students from a variety of backgrounds to attend classes remotely, cutting down the need for travel and reducing the resources required for education. The Internet has also made access to information and communication far easier. Rather than searching the library, users can access vast amounts of information from home computers. Internet access has a huge impact on businesses, allowing employees to work remotely from home and communicate more efficiently. Healthcare is another field greatly affected by the advent of the Internet. Improvements in online connectivity and communication technology allow physicians much greater access to medical resources. Doctors in rural areas can also use the Internet to communicate with experts all over the world, improving the quality of patients' diagnoses and treatments. Politics and government are another area in which the Internet is important. Government organizations use the Internet to improve organization and communication, and voters can go online to gain more information about current issues. According to Web Junction, 54 percent of adults went online to get information about the 2010 U.S. midterm elections.

Most information is found on the Internet by utilizing search engines. A search engine is a web service that uses web robots to query millions of pages on the Internet and creates an index of those web pages. Internet users can then use these services to find information on the Internet. When searching for information on the Internet, keep the below things in mind. If you are searching for multiple common words, such as computer and help, it is a good idea to place quotes around the full search to get better results. For example, type "computer help" as your search criteria. This trick can also be used in parts of your search query. For example, Microsoft "computer help" would search for anything containing 'Microsoft' and that also has "computer help" together. Finally, you can also do multiple words surrounded in quotes. For example, "Microsoft Windows" and "computer help" would refine your results even more. Many search engines will strip out common words they refer to as stop words for each search that is performed. For example, instead of searching for why does my computer not boot, the search engine would search for computer and boot. To help prevent these stop words from being stripped out, surround the search with quotes.

The Internet is a very powerful worldwide instrument, which serves as a good source for research work and learning. It generates current information, facts-finding, and is the most outstanding invention in the area of communication in the history of human race. The Internet has been very useful to mankind in the aspect of learning and research development. In due course, this essay emphasizes on details of advantages and disadvantages of the Internet in relation to research work.

In conclusion, internet can bring searching information advantages and disadvantages to compare other channels as below:

Advantages:

The Internet eases of communication to the researchers; because it serves as a guidance and original source of information. It is very easy to access and at the same time saves time thereby allowing an individual to manager his/her resources better and effectively. Additionally, the Internet is very convenient because an individual can easily carry out a research work at home with much comfort and convenience. The internet is a valuable search tool and has been informative for academic research, as it helps significantly to improve research skills, and makes learning visual and easy to follow.

Comparatively Inexpensive and Quick Dispersion of Information:

The Internet creates a comparatively inexpensive avenue for releasing information and articles. Subsequently, several organizations and individuals can now circulate information to millions of users. In due course, researchers could assess and make use of this circulated information and articles for their work, thereby giving them a broader idea and knowledge in their work.

Additionally, there is a spontaneous dispersion of information to various users of the internet when such information is being added to a web site. As regards this, millions of users including researchers would browse through these information and subsequently use them for their work. Hence the web is then regarded as a paragon medium for disseminating information because it removes the time wasting in between publishing content and making it available to users.

Wealth of Information:

Furthermore, the Internet is a wealth of information and very advantageous in various reasons; students delve into the Internet to gather lots of very useful academic information for research purposes; and the information contained on the Internet can be useful for academic research. It is a potential research tool and opens up a new and comprehensive source of information.

In another development, information is probably the biggest advantage internet is offering to the users. The Internet is an apparent treasure trove of information. Any kind of information on any topic under the sun is available on the Internet.

Sending E-mail Messages and Receiving Feedbacks:

With the help of the Internet the user could send e-mails to colleagues, friends, co-workers etc, either to get more information from them or pass on the acquired information to them. In view of this the Internet could be regarded as a powerful content publishing tool because there are some application software embedded in the Internet that enable such transmission and transfer of information from one user to another. Consequently, these applications will allow and assist the researcher to develop content for the World Wide Web by simply saving as an HTML file.

Disadvantages:

Having discussed the advantages of the Internet for academic research it is worthy to mention some of its disadvantages. One of the disadvantages of the Internet is that it provides a huge amount of information thereby causing information overload. In due course, one can easily get confused with this infinite amount of titles, texts and abstracts. And because of the overwhelming information available on the Internet, one must be cautious about information obtained.

There are no standards, that is, no process to check information accurately. Most information in the Internet does not go through a review process. Anyone can publish on the web, without passing the content through an editor. Pages might be written by an expert on the topic, or even a child, or a disgruntled contributor. Therefore, getting information from book or from various other printed sources in the library can guarantee that it is of high standard and peer reviewed.

Additionally, it can be observed that with a large amount of information freely available on the internet, theft of personal information and misuse of this information is in abundance. In this regard from time to time people use someone's information and research materials and pass it off as their own work. Also, Spamming, which is the process of sending unwanted or junk e-mails in bulk, which provide no purpose and consequently hinder the entire system. This in due course is regarded as an illegal activity resulting to frustrate people. As regards this, a researcher could check his e-mail to obtain some materials for his work; only to get disappointed when noticed that the e-mail was a junk. The issue of spamming extends to commercial advertising, frequently for dubious products, get-rich-quick, or semi-legal services.

Furthermore, another disadvantage of the Internet is virus threat. In this regard, Virus is a program that interrupts the normal functioning of the computer systems. Computers that are attached to internet are more likely to be attacked by virus. In due course, this attack could result to hard disk crashing, thereby causing a big disaster on the computer. On the other hand, some unprincipled individuals have been successful in creating viruses and links that once clicked can automatically transmit ones personal e-mail addresses and other details to certain parties and even the person's bank account details in some extreme cases.

Additionally, another disadvantage of the Internet for academic research is that, it is not arranged according to system and no index format. Information on the Internet is not organized; for example too many web pages for any single directory services and fees are often charged for access to specialized information.

In conclusion, irrespective of the fact that the Internet has some numerous disadvantages, it can be understood that it is still very useful to mankind as in helps in medical research works and subsequent inventions, as well as produce some good interactive entertainment and multimedia. Hence, man needs the Internet to keep life going. Man asserts that, the Internet is considered not simply as a technological tool, but as a wholly new constructed environment with its own codes of practice.

Information security threats

New security threats are emerging every day from malware programs that can be inadvertently installed on a user's machine, to phishing attempts that deceive employees into giving up confidential information, to viruses, worms, and strategic identity theft attempts. Sometimes the threat that attacks the information in organizations is difficult to handles. It is because the protection programs that installed in the computer system to protect the data are not appropriately function or not good enough.

Difficulties in manage information security because of do not the proper qualification in information security.

Sometimes organizations do not take seriously about hiring employees based on their qualification. This is because there are organizations that hiring employees for the information security manager but it is doesn't match with his qualification or skill that he have about information security. So, it is difficult for that staff to protect the organizations data with proper protection. This will makes other attackers easier to attacks and stole the information if the employees don't have skill or knowledge on how to protect the confidential data.

Conclusion

Information security is crucial in organization. All information stored in the organization should be kept secure. Information security will be defined as the protection of data from any threats of virus. The information security in important in the organization because it can protect the confidential information, enables the organization function, also enables the safe operation of application implemented on the organization's Information Technology system, and information is an asset for an organization. Even thought the information is important in organization, there are several challenges to protect and manages the information as well. One of challenges faced in an organization is the lack of understanding on important of information security. When employees is lack of information security knowledge in term of keeping their information, the organization is easy to being attacks by hackers or another threats that try to stole or get the organization confidential information. So it is crucial and important to all staff in an organization to have knowledge and understanding about the importance information security practice in an organization to protect the confidential data when they need to gather any information from internet channel.

What is internet for online office function

There are lots of compelling reasons to work remotely — but some business leaders and employment experts argue that it's better to work onsite. So, online working mode is same to virtual teams — geographically scattered colleagues who use high-tech communication — are now common in many organizations. Some of those team members are remote workers and some still work onsite, in the traditional office. But if remote work is indeed going to kill office work, get ready for a tough time. Remote work can be hard, both for workers and their managers. Even if the employer has a good flexible working policy and the employee has the right skills for remote work, there are downsides to working from home.

Why all the office jobs will disappear in possible? Here are examples of how onsite work is replaced by remote work. They include :

1: Working onsite fosters innovation

It's all very well offering flexible working improvements like remote work to employees. Online working can bring these working benefits , such as Some of the best decisions and insights come from hallway and cafeteria discussions, meeting new people, and impromptu team meetings, they can finish from internet channel.

2: Onsite workers are easier to manage

In addition to the regular employee management that a team leader deals with, remote workers carry plenty of extra baggage that needs managing. Having remote workers, "creates a potential problem for managers used to having their team in the same room as them," said Jonathan Swan, of work/ life balance charity Working Families.

3: Some employees can telecommute

Some employees can learn certain combination of skills to successfully work from home easily. Also, remote workers must show better discipline, communication skills, and punctuality than their office-bound colleagues. In other words, they have to run faster just to keep up.

4: Communication is easier in the online environment

Some employees can feel easy to communicate in a video conference? Can you share donuts using Windows Messenger? And what happens when you communicate less effectively with your peers? They trust you less. Remote workers must be even more contactable than their office-based colleagues or trust goes out the window.

5: Office work is bore and some jobs can be done remotely

It is important for young people to have a sense of belonging and that they needed to know the rules and boundaries between work and play before taking advantage of remote working. In Europe, where many employees have a legal right to be considered for flexible work, only 18% actually telework (telework is defined as remote work using IT). In Germany it's 12% —and those workers are mainly highly qualified, such as managers, academics, lawyers, journalists, engineers and teachers.

6: Flexible hours are popular with businesses to remote work

A CBI (Confederation of British Industry) employment trends survey said, "Five years ago, just 13% of firms offered teleworking for employees in at least certain roles some of the time, but now nearly six in ten (59%) do so." Sounds like a lot, right? But just because remote work options are available doesn't mean that's the type of flexible working all the cool companies are doing. Andy Lake, editor of flexible work resource Flexibility, said that more than 90% of companies offered flexible working of some kind, but that this was mostly flexible hours and part-time working.

Future online working model brings traditional office working model to be reformed

Office work is alive, well, and adapted to the needs of modern organizations. Traditional onsite working is going nowhere.

Pros and Cons of working from home vs. working from the office

If your job offered you an option of working from home or working in the office – would you take it? Would you be more productive working in sweatpants vs your usual business casual? Would you have more time for you family if you do not have to spend two hours commuting every day? Would you miss the corporate environment or would you enjoy solitude? Can video conferences, phone calls and remote access really make you feel like you are part of the office when you are not physically present? If you are confused about what option is right for you – here are a few things to think about.

The positive side of working from home

It can bring time saved , it means that the online working can do more himself time at home. The biggest advantage of working from home is that you save a lot of time commuting back and forth to work. This may mean some extra shuteye or the opportunity to not skip breakfast in the morning. You can spend extra time with your children or spouse, read the newspaper instead of sitting in traffic. Start off your day in a calm fashion instead of being stressed and rushed to get to the office. Taking time for yourself is often very difficult, you may find that having extra me time in the mornings will make you happy and therefore a more productive employee.

You are in control of your working environment

Another benefit of working from home is that you have the ability to create your working environment. With no cubical walls defining your space you have the freedom to choose your office location, the perfect corner office perhaps?

You define your hours

With no time clock, you can start and stop your day as you please. You can get started a little earlier or take a few extra minutes during lunch. As long as you work your required hours and get your job done there is no harm is shifting your schedule a bit. For example, Video conferences only show you from the waste up. If the mood felt right you could wear a suit shirt and shorts or pajama bottoms. And what about days when you don't have to video chat with anyone from your office. Working in sweatpants and pajamas becomes completely possible.

The negative side of working from home

Solitary confinement?

Many people find that working from home is like solitary confinement. We all crave human interactions and sometimes video conferences and phone calls wont satisfy this need. Even though you can get in touch with your office, you no longer have the constant support of your colleagues and supervisors.

Technical issues

Sure, when everything works – it is fantastic, but if your Internet cuts out or you loose access to your company's intranet, you may be unable to do your job. Most companies have tech support designed to handle off-site employees, but you will never receive the same level of support as you would in an office setting.

How disciplined are you?

Have you ever thought that working from home also takes discipline? It is very easy to switch to surfing the web or home chores that need to be done. When you work from home you may actually find it harder to focus and get your work done. When you work from home your work day never ends. Since it starts and stops in the same place you may find yourself working later into the evening not realizing what time it is. Some people find that when they work from home that their jobs starts to bleed into their personal life. That while they assumed working from home would give them more freedom that it in fact has caused them to work longer hours and sometimes on the weekends.

The positive side of working in an office

So are you asking yourself, if I don't have to get dressed and spend an hour commuting back and forth everyday why would I want to? Well, have you ever thought how positive and rewarding working in an office can be?

Motivation for career growth

When you work in an office environment, you have supervision and restrictions, but you also have knowledge and support from your bosses and colleagues. Being around intelligent people might motivate you. A competitive environment might encourage you to preform better, helping you to excel in your field and ultimately your place in the company.

Immediate feedback

If you are in an office and you have a question – you can stand up and walk over to someones desk and ask them. You can bring them to your desk to show them something on your computer screen. You can have a meeting that doesn't involve videoconferencing. You can collaborate with your colleagues on a project without a digital whiteboard, you can use an actual whiteboard.

Social network

You may find that you benefit personally from being in an office. Having a social life is very important and for many their coworkers are their social network. Having lunch with your coworkers, catching up with one another, going out for happy hour, these are all positive and rewarding activities. Again, when you are happy and satisfied you are a more productive employee.

The negative side of working in an office the commute

One of the biggest advantages of working from home is in turn the biggest disadvantage of working in an office. You can spend upwards of three hours commuting back and forth to work everyday. Traffic, congestion and wasted time all add up to stress. Have you ever found yourself running to work flustered that your boss would be angry with you for being late, even if the circumstances were out of your control? Have you ever had to leave work early to make it to your child's soccer game, dance recital or a PTA meeting? The extra time it takes to get to and from work is time wasted that could be spent in a much more productive manner. If your office is like most offices it consists of a few corner offices, a wall of windows, and a sea of cubicles. It is very possible that you may not be able to tell the weather or if it is day or night from where you sit in the office. Sun light increases happiness and indirectly your productivity. It is an essential part of life. You wouldn't choose to live in a home with no windows would you?

Some people are happier working in an office and some people are happier working from home. You have to weigh your options and decide what is best for you. Can you be disciplined enough to work from home? Will you be happy without the daily support of your co-workers? Both options have their advantages and disadvantages. Only you can decide what is the best option for you. Otherwise, some online working people give their opinions, they indicate that they work from home every day, as my employer mandates it for all paid staff due to financial reasons. Great for work life balance and saves on commute time, road tolls and petrol. But it does feel isolating at times and I miss the collaboration with the rest of my team, though we have our monthly team meetings back at our headquarters! And yes, on those rare occasions when my computer or internet connection is not cooperating with me, it can be depressing as we don't have easy access to IT support. On those days when I feel like working from home is doing my head in and I start feeling the loneliness creep in, I head to any of my local cafes with good Wifi connection, or even my local library. They agree – it's not for everyone, but as long as the work gets done, I don't see any issues with it.

That's what facilities managers and office managers around the world are asking themselves about the office spaces they're responsible for organizing. How can they set up a space that's not just a place to shelter all your employees, but one that's a strategic tool for productivity, collaboration, and growth?cWhat makes an office environment great is different for every company. A lot of it has to do with a company's culture and how employees there like to work. And the right office environment can set employees up with the right situation and motivation to tackle big, important projects (like getting inbound certified, perhaps?)Want to get inspired by examples of what your workplace could look like?

Why are changing the Workplace when online office working model will be popular ?

Thanks to wireless internet, laptops, and tablets, employees are finding they don't necessarily need to be chained to a single desk. Instead, they can move around their space more, technology in tow. And some companies have taken this to the next level by eliminating personal desks and opting for a configuration called "hot desking." Hot desking simply means no one in the office has an assigned desk or seating area. Instead, when you come in to work in the morning, you can sit anywhere you please -- from open tables or desks set up with cables and monitors, to more public spaces like couches and chairs. For this to work, a company should take special care to create spaces in the office that can easily be reconfigured for different tasks and evolving teams.

Some companies CEO believe that they don't want our employees sitting in one chair all day, because that's not good for them and it's not good for collaboration. We just get these really great intersections of people and ideas ... Suddenly and randomly, we'll have these conversations with people from finance, legal, design, and you get these collaborations that wouldn't otherwise occur. They love how flexible it is, and that there are always different people sitting at my desk. It makes me feel more in touch with my co-workers and what's going on in the company."

But be aware that hot desking may not be an effective way to create movement in the office. One study found that when people didn't have an assigned desk, they didn't move around more; instead, they would find a place to work and then stay there for the rest of the day. So, while interaction among employees did increase by 17% in the study, the number of individuals' encounters during the day actually dropped by an average of 14%. As a result, team communication actually dropped by 45%. If you like the idea of creating movement in your office but don't want to eliminate assigned seating altogether, you might try playing "musical chairs" every few months, where you keep teams together but change their assigned seating area every few months.

For international office in Zurich, Switzerland, and use desks that can be reconfigured to work individually or collaboratively. Desks there fit together like puzzle pieces and can be moved, reworked, and reattached as employees see fit -- a nod to the values of modern office design, which include mobility, flexibility, and collaboration.

Another alternative to help encourage spontaneous collaboration among your employees is designing your space to allow for "overlap zones," which make it more likely your employees will run into each other. How do your employees move throughout the day? Where do they go? What kind of spaces would cause them to run into each other more frequently?

Research from the University of Michigan showed that when scientists worked in a space where they ran into one another -- in areas known as "zonal overlap" -- they were more likely to collaborate. The data suggests that creating opportunities for unplanned interactions among employees both inside and outside the organization actually improves performance.

Music Rooms innovation

One way to boost employee productivity at the office is to foster a positive company culture. To give employees a place to blow off steam at work, why not add a music room to the mix? For the musically inclined, going into the company music room to playing music alone or with coworkers is one way to do it. (And for the non-musically inclined, let's hope that music room is super soundproofed.)

A "Superdesk" innovation

Designing an office space around the "open office" concept is one thing. But what about creating a shared desk for your company's entire staff? For employees who want to work in a quieter space or have more private discussions, the desk lifts into large arches that have seats built underneath them.

Researchers have found that adding plants and greenery in an office can help increase employee productivity by 15%. "A green office communicates to employees that their employer cares about them and their welfare," said Psychology Professor Alex Haslam, who co-authored the study. "Office landscaping helps the workplace become a more enjoyable, comfortable and profitable place to be." Some companies have even started investing in installing plants and greenery around the office help make their employees happier and healthier (and boosting productivity at the same time). For example, Google's office in Tel Aviv, Israel has an indoor orange grove that turns an otherwise normal, collaborative space into a relaxing area that makes you feel like you're sitting outside on a park bench.

Thus, online communication systems are emerging as real-time communication tools for individuals, students and business professionals and it can bring above innovations to traditional office working designing environment change. These systems are a perfect blend of video, audio and computer technology that allows people to connect in real time irrespective of their geographical locations and time zones.

Undoubtedly, digital conferencing makes interaction exciting for users at different physical locations by providing them access to high-quality sound and full-motion video effects. However, research shows a two-sided report of the impact of these online communication systems.

Top Benefits of Online Communication can include as below:

1. Cost effective compared to physical meeting

Web conference services are cost effective in every possible angle, as the services would be in need of a computer or a mobile along with internet connectivity. To a physical conference, you have to spare time, money to travel, cost to stay and so on. A digital connectivity has given huge benefits regarding using web conference option on a regular basis.

2. Easy connectivity from every place in the world

online conferencing is not a baby technology anymore, where the connection was never stable. The web conferencing technology has improved to a great extent and provides flawless connectivity from any part of the world. You can use the online conferencing services for both official and personal purposes, as there are multiple numbers of applications that you can use to initiate a virtual meeting.

3. Best to use in different devices and gadgets

You can do online conferencing both on the computer and on mobile phones. Most of the smartphones give out an option for users to have a web meeting on a regular basis without paying any cost. As technology is advancing at a rapid speed, some of the applications are available free of cost both in mobile and in the computer, which can be used to make long distance calls without paying a dime.

4. Increase productivity and efficiency

The efficiency of a business house depends more or less on the ease of communication and smooth flow of information between employees working at different levels. Though interaction mostly takes place via e-mail, phone or instant messaging system but visually interactive video-conferencing is providing a better alternative. It gives vital visual images that enable employees and customers to interpret and collaborate properly over a long distance. As a result, decisions are taken faster, projects execute on-time and productivity increases.

5. Long-term competitive advantage

Video-conferencing gives users multiple options for securing competitive advantage. When employees or business associates interact over video, they can share messages more rapidly resulting in more wise decisions that minimize both the time and price required to promote new services and products. Through the technical support of the videoconferencing company, business owners get an opportunity to leverage video effects and create more valuable and personal bonding with the customers and build up a loyalty which is far beyond the capacities of traditional phone conferencing system.

6. Ultimate support for environmental protection

Since the videoconferencing system works on green technology, business organizations can be prevented from emitting energy and increasing the level of carbon in the environment. Thus, interaction over video has made every small and medium sized business organization environment conscious and urged them to stick to environment-friendly communication methods. With wide scale availability of tools that make on-demand production of live video footages possible anywhere in the world, students, customers, and employees get a chance to become part of an environmental initiative.

However, web conferences can also bring this disadvantages as below:

1. Time-consuming and costly

One of the major disadvantages of web conference call is that detail planning is essential for its success. The people engaged in the conference call need to have high discipline and high level of concentration. For an effective conference call the web cam, microphone and other gadgets need to be in proper position and in good working condition. Failure in any one of the key gadgets can lead to the total failure of the conference call.

2. Ineffective

There are some human ways of communicating that do not translate very well over a distance, such as an eye contact. When you sit in the same room with someone and listen to a speech or presentation you will make eye contact and they will judge who is paying attention by looking around the room. Much of this contact is not easily delivered through a webcam.

In conclusion, the advantages and disadvantages of video conferencing have to be weighed against your purpose and whether there will be something valuable lost through this technology that you don't want to give up. ezTalks is a one-stop video and audio conferencing solution provider offering a wide range of quality online communication services. The company offers cost effective call solutions which will require an IP or ISDN network connection, conference equipment (camera, microphone, monitor, and speakers), a codec and an audio system for being functional. The recent developments in audio and video conferencing technology have made it far more productive and engaging than conventional teleconferencing.

Cross-team collaboration in the workplace is a critical aspect when it comes to performance and productivity on any project. It not only inspires innovative approaches to a project but also leads to quick decision making. With the growth of video conferencing systems and software, employees can now collaborate from anywhere at any time using minimal resources.

The use of such video conference software as ezTalks Cloud Meeting has really revolutionized the way businesses collaborate online. But just like any other office process out there, online collaboration comes with a set of advantages and disadvantages. Determining these pros and cons can help a business to draw an action plan to overcome the challenges and hurdles that may come up along the way.

Advantages of Online Collaboration

1. Convenience in Organizing Meetings

One of the key advantages of online collaboration is that it makes it easier for people who aren't in the same location to work together. Most companies have branches and/or offices in multiple cities and countries. And to ensure those working on a given project are informed and engaged, the use of online collaboration software is important. For instance, ezTalks Cloud Meeting can allow up to 500 participants to join in a meeting and listen to the presenter at once. With such a huge meeting capacity, company employees can effectively call for a meeting and collaborate with one another, regardless of their geographical differences.

2. Easier Management of Projects

With the ability to convene a meeting at anytime from anywhere, online collaboration makes it easier to manage team projects. For instance, when introducing or analyzing a new company product, the production team may need to work with other departments like Research & Development (RD), marketing and sales. Online collaboration software provides an ideal platform for all these players to engage in meaningful discussions about the proposed product. That means the person in charge of the product department can generate a report quite seamlessly and submit it to the bosses within the set timelines.

3. Faster Completion of Projects

When different stakeholders are involved in a given project, each of them is likely to give the best input in terms of expertise. A collaborative team that recognizes its synergies can have excellent viable solutions shared quickly and decisions reached in time. Once the conclusions have been tabled, presented to the bosses and approved, the next phase will obviously be implementation. Online collaboration can particularly fuel faster completion of projects since project stakeholders can meet and interact online without experiencing time constraints and inconveniences.

4. Significant Cost Savings

If those participating in a meeting are many, it can sometimes be a challenge to find a physical space that can accommodate everyone. Online collaboration software allows businesses to host online meetings in real time with hundreds of participants interacting simultaneously. Employees can actually call for urgent meetings and discuss important project issues using the minimal resources. It doesn't really matter whether one is at home, on the road or in the office. EzTalks Cloud Meeting provides users with innovative whiteboards and screen sharing options that make collaborative sessions even more engaging. The use of telepresence video conferencing particularly simulates the real-life meeting rooms, which makes mastering facial expressions and body language easy. With such robust online collaboration solutions, there's no need to book flights, hotel rooms or meeting spaces. Online meetings can simply be organized and disseminated instantly over a virtual meeting room. In the long run, a business utilizing online collaboration will experience improved performance and productivity while enjoying significant cost savings on communication.

Disadvantages of Online Collaboration

1. Lack of Face-To-Face Interaction

While online collaboration through video conferencing provides real-time communication between people, it lacks the aspect of face-to-face interaction. For instance, meeting participants cannot argue with one another simultaneously over the online platform because of longer lag times. That may sometimes limit the level of engagement of the employees in an online meeting. And when the quality of video stream is poor, it's difficult for meeting attendees to decipher facial expressions and body language of the presenter.

2. Possibility of Network Failure and Equipment Breakdown

Online collaboration might provide a range convenient and efficient meeting options but network failure and equipment breakdown might limit its use. Participating in online collaboration meetings through video conference also requires the use of huge data bundles, which can be limiting to some attendees. Running out of data bundles leads to disconnection from the internet, which bars attendees from participating in collaborative efforts of finding solutions to a project. Meeting interruptions due to any of these reasons may cause a cross-collaboration team to work beyond the scheduled timelines in order to complete the project. That can delay project discussions and subsequently decision making, which might have significant cost implications.

3. Language and Cultural Differences

The use of online collaboration software has made it easier for companies to bring together employees from different countries to collaborate in a given project. While that might be a good strategy to improve performance, differences in language and culture can limit the engagement of employees working in different regions. That means online collaboration cannot offer meaningful solutions in this case.

4. Incidences of Group Think

Bringing stakeholders from different departments and region to work together may undoubtedly inspire fresh perspectives on the project. However, there is always the threat of group think, where stronger personalities may take over the discussions, persuade and supplant the ideas of others. Such online collaborations might lead to the bosses believing the outcome is a group effort yet it's something that was agreed upon by a few. That might end up lowering the performance of a project as important ideas may be left out in the process.

Conclusion

While the benefits of online collaboration are many, there are potential drawbacks that come along too. That does not mean companies should avoid adopting the online collaboration software. Rather, they should seek to understand how applicable the software is to the business. The effective use of online collaborations basically depends on how the business analyses the problems and the strategies it puts in place to eradicate them. By adopting online collaboration software, a business can take advantage of convenient hosting of meetings, swift project management and improved savings on communication. But in order to keep the system working, the business should focus on fixing the issues of quality video streaming, internet/software breakdown and language and cultural barriers. This is all any size of business needs to do.

What is internet for ecommerce function

What are advantages of online shopping? Due to rapid growth of technology, business organizations have switched over from the traditional method of selling goods to electronic method of selling goods. Business organizations use internet as a main vehicle to conduct commercial transact . Its advantages include: Online stores do not have space constraints and a wide variety of products can be displayed on websites. It helps the analytical buyers to purchase a product after a good search. Convenience of online shopping, it means that customers can purchase items from the comfort of their own homes or work place. Shopping is made easier and convenient for the customer through internet. It is also easy to cancel the transactions.

The following table depicts the factors which motivate the online shoppers to buy products online.

Top 6 reasons given by shoppers in buying through internet

● Saves time and efforts.
● Convenience of Shopping at home.
● Wide variety / range of products are available.
● Good discounts / lower prices.
● Get detailed information of the product.
● We can compare various models / brands.

2. No pressure shopping

Generally, in physical stores, the sales representatives try to influence the buyers to buy the product. There can be some kind of pressure, whereas the customers are not pressurized in any way in online stores.

3. Online shopping saves time

Customers do not have to stand in queues in cash counters to pay for the products that have been purchased by them. They can shop from their home or work place and do not have to spend time traveling. The customers can also look for the products that are required by them by entering the key words or using search engines.

4. Comparisons

Companies display the whole range of products offered by them to attract customers with different tastes and needs. This enables the buyers to choose from a variety of models after comparing the finish, features and price of the products on display, Sometimes, price comparisons are also available online.

5. Availability of online shop

The mall is open on 365 x 24 x 7. So, time does not act as a barrier, wherever the vendor and buyers are.

6. Online tracking

Online consumers can track the order status and delivery status tracking of shipping is also available.

7. Online shopping saves money

To attract customers to shop online, e-tailers and marketers offer discounts to the customers. Due to elimination of maintenance, real-estate cost, the retailers are able to sell the products with attractive discounts through online. Sometimes, large online shopping sites offer store comparison.

Disadvantages of online shopping

Ease of use is the prime reason that drives the success of e-commerce. Though internet provides a quick and easy way to purchase a product, some people prefer to use this technology only in a limited way. They regard internet as a means for gathering more information about a product before buying it in a shop. Some people also fear that they might get addicted to online shopping.

The major disadvantages of online shopping are as follows.

1. Delay in delivery

Long duration and lack of proper inventory management result in delays in shipment. Though the duration of selecting, buying and paying for an online product may not take more than 15 minutes; the delivery of the product to customer' s doorstep takes about 1-3 weeks. This frustrates the customer and prevents them from shopping online.

2. Lack of significant discounts in online shops

Physical stores offer discounts to customers and attract them so this makes it difficult for e-tailors to compete with the offline platforms.

3. Lack of touch and feel of merchandise in online shopping

Lack of touch-feel-try creates concerns over the quality of the product on offer. Online shopping is not quite suitable for clothes as the customers cannot try them on.

4. Lack of interactivity in online shopping

Physical stores allow price negotiations between buyers and the seller. The show room sales attendant representatives provide personal attention to customers and help them in purchasing goods. Certain online shopping mart offers service to talk to a sales representative,

5. Lack of shopping experience

The traditional shopping exercise provides lot of fun in the form of showroom atmosphere, smart sales attendants, scent and sounds that cannot be experienced through a website. Indians generally enjoy shopping. Consumers look forward to it as an opportunity to go out and shop.

6. Lack of close examination in online shopping

A customer has to buy a product without seeing actually how it looks like. Customers may click and buy some product that is not really required by them. The electronic images of a product are sometimes misleading. The color, appearance in real may not match with the electronic images. People like to visit physical stores and prefer to have close examination of good, though it consumes time. The electronic images vary from physical appearance when people buy goods based on electronic images.

7. Frauds in online shopping

Sometimes, there is disappearance of shopping site itself. In addition to above, the online payments are not much secured. So, it is essential for e-marketers and retailers to pay attention to this issue to boost the growth of e-commerce. The rate of cyber crimes has been increasing and customers' credit card details and bank details have been misused which raise privacy issues. Customers have to be careful in revealing their personal information. Some of the e-tailors are unreliable.

The disadvantages of online shopping will not hinder its growth, Online shopping helped businesses to recover from the recession. Merchants should pay attention to the stumbling blocks and ensure secure payment system to make online shopping effective, The following advice may be followed by the E-merchants and by the online shoppers.

Advantages and Disadvantages of Ecommerce

E-commerce, or the act of selling goods or services online as opposed to selling at brick and mortar establishments, has reshaped the modern marketplace in recent years, but this new form of trade comes with its own sets of advantages and disadvantages over traditional methods. It's important, then, for businesses to look beyond the hype and develop their own perspectives on the true value of e-commerce—to business and to consumers—because interestingly, there are many advantages for consumers that might actually be a disadvantage for e-commerce businesses. Among the top advantages for starting an e-commerce business are eliminating geographical limitations, gaining new customers with search engine visibility, lower costs for maintenance and rent, and higher capacity for goods and deliveries while the core disadvantages of starting an e-commerce business include losing the personal touch of physical retailers, delaying goods or services deliveries, and limiting availability of merchandise as some goods cannot be sold online. Explore the following article to discover whether or not venturing into e-commerce is right for your business.

Advantages to Physical Retailers

The Internet might be the single most important facet of modern society, governing everything from political discourse and higher education to the way we conduct ourselves and our businesses. It's no wonder, then, that switching your business to an e-commerce model would come with a huge amount of advantages.

On top of eliminating the need for long lines at physical stores, e-commerce sites allow people who are not situated in major urban areas access to stores located remotely. E-commerce, as a result, opens new markets for your business, allowing you to develop a new business model geared toward your expanding consumer base, especially one that relies on good e-commerce Search Engine Optimization to drive more free traffic to the site through consumers' use of search engines.

Since you also eliminate the need for a physical store, your business can save money on rent and upkeep like utilities and maintenance. Additionally, because there is no limit to the number of items that can be sold online, your store's stock can expand exponentially by moving to an e-commerce model, and the store can remain open 24/7 so consumers can browse your wares at their leisure.

The most important advantages to e-commerce, consumers can also purchase digital goods like music albums, videos, or books instantaneously, and stores can now sell unlimited copies of these digital items. This also cuts down on things like employee payroll expenses because you no longer need to have dozens of employees a week on-site to sell albums, books, or movies. E-commerce also allows your business to scale up easier than physical retailers as they are not bound by physical limitations like inventory storage space. Of course, logistics gets tougher as a business grows, but one can scale up its logistics, too, with the choice of the right third-party logistics provider. Since the e-commerce merchant captures contact information in the form of email, sending out automated and customized emails is quite easy. Additionally, these businesses and metrics allow for superior store customization by using cookies and other methods of monitoring a consumer's behavior, because the entire supply chain can be interlinked with business to business e-commerce systems, procurement becomes faster, transparent, and cheaper, and there's no need to handle currency notes or cash, which further cuts down on costs and opportunities for accounting errors.

Finally, e-commerce allows your business to track logistics, which is key to a successful e-commerce company, as well as sell low-volume goods. Although conventional retail focuses on stocking fast-moving goods, the economics of e-commerce permits slow-moving and even obsolete products to be included in the catalog.

While it may appear that e-commerce is the perfect choice to solve your business problems, there are still a number of disadvantages to switching from selling at a physical location to using online retail. Many consumers still prefer visiting brick and mortar shops because of their personal touch and the relationship customers get to develop with a retail location. Additionally, many customers want to experience the product before purchase, especially when it comes to clothing, but e-commerce eliminates that luxury.

Security and credit card fraud are also huge risks when dealing with online shopping—consumers run the risk of identity fraud and other hazards as their personal details are captured by e-commerce businesses while businesses run the risk of phishing attacks and other forms of security fraud; both can suffer from credit card fraud. As a result, consumers also fear their inability to identify scams and scammers, meaning that your website has to be extraordinarily protected and verified for most consumers to trust using it.

If shopping is about instant gratification, then consumers are left empty-handed for some time after making a purchase on an e-commerce website as they often have to either pay more for expedited shipping or wait out several days while the postal service does its job. Additionally, if they are unsatisfied with their order, many e-commerce retailers have to issue a refund, which requires your business to expand its reverse logistics functions, meaning the shipping back of goods and refunding of costs.

Speaking of costs, there's a multiplicity of regulations and taxation that comes with opening an e-commerce shop, and regulators are still not clear about the tax implications of e-commerce transactions, which is especially true when the seller and buyer are located in different territories.

What ecommerce benefits to consumers and weaknesses to ecommerce businessmen? Some concerns don't necessarily fit in just the pro's or con's side of the argument—these unique issues present an advantage to shoppers and consumers while increasing difficulty for businesses, meaning that while more customers might be coming to the shop, the business is suffering in another way. While it's easier for consumers to compare prices because of several shopping search engines and websites, sellers might find it too restrictive to their business revenues as many get filtered out of the consumer's consideration set. Though there is nothing about e-commerce that makes it intrinsically oriented to discounts, the way online business has evolved has led to lowered prices online, which acts as an advantage for the buyer, but a disadvantage for the seller.

The consumer experiences the convenience of having goods home-delivered, but the logistics involved with delivering each individual item adds substantial strain to the e-commerce business operation, making it great for profits and customer retention but terrible for logistics and management.

There are several businesses in the marketplace that trade solely online. In setting up an online business, the owner will need to go through the same procedures as a traditional business, in formulating a business plan, by crafting a mission statement and through handling other administrative matters. However, there are a number of advantages and disadvantages of operating an online business, points worth considering as you prepare to launch your enterprise.

Reduced Costs

The main advantage of having an online business is the cost difference when compared to setting up a traditional office-based company. While there are fees associated with securing a domain and setting up a website, these are minimal in comparison to leasing and maintaining physical premises.

Reduced Staff Requirements

Whereas in a physical retail outlet the owner would need to recruit a number of sales staff, with an online business a lot of the work is carried out automatically. For example, purchasing an item online does not require a cashier to take payment: a purchaser simply enters his or her card details and the item is paid for within minutes.

Wider Range

With an online business is that you can market your company on a global scale, reaching potential customers in other countries and continents. You will need to have systems in place in order to dispatch your goods or services to these far-away locations, however. Nevertheless, whereas a physical business can only advertise to customers in a local area, having an online business means you can expose your company to a large number of potential customers.

Saturated Marketplace

Having an online presence does, however, mean that you are surrounded by other businesses within your industry, all desperate to expose their company to a wide audience. As a result, your business may become lost in a sea of similar companies, in which case you will need to discover a product or element to your firm that gives you an edge over your competitors.

Lack of Interaction

With a physical presence staff members can interact with customers face to face. This can impress the purchaser and prompt them to share their positive experiences with others. Some purchasers may simply prefer face-to-face interaction, as opposed to purchasing their goods online. You may struggle to develop a meaningful relationship with a purchaser when you operate an online business.

Support Systems

If a customer purchases an item from a physical store, only to later discover it is faulty, they can return the product to the store for an exchange or refund by means of a relatively easy process. However, if an online purchaser finds that their goods are faulty, it could be several days until the issue is rectified, especially if you have no customer care system in operation. You will need to implement a structured policy and system for refunding faulty goods to avoid customer frustration.

Internet Connectivity

You could stand to lose a lot of time and money if, for some reason, your website goes down and cannot be fixed for hours, or even days. This could cause potential customers to be dissuaded from buying a product from you if they receive an error message when trying to visit your website, and they may communicate their poor experience with friends and family.

Will e-commerce replace traditional retail business in India? Why? Will Books get out of fashion because there is a Kindle nowadays? Will Netflix (or Amazon Prime) replace Cinema Halls? What do you think? Or will you completely stop going to office because there is something called virtual meeting? All of this is happening, and someday sooner than we believe they will overtake the human interaction required to achieve the same output. Yes, the human emotions would die that day!

There is no easy answer to this question, especially when we are at a juncture where things are changing at a rapid pace in everything which has a digital version attached to it. Considering that human society is designed in a way which requires people to stay together and co-operate in order to get through a day, all the things which we come across in our daily lives requires a human interaction to be considered completed. Earlier we had no option but to meet face to face and get things done, but then we got unique technology tools & devices which could eliminate the need for our physical presence and replace that human identity and authenticity by establishing the trust technologically. Phones have long replaced the effort required for me to visit a LPG dealer and place an order. Or when my washing machine fails, I do not think twice before placing a service request and I am completely convinced that some human being sitting on the other side of the phone will make sure to send someone to repair my washing machine.

Can e-commerce bring benefits to India businessmen? They feel that they don't need to waste their time. Their Phone will reach where I will be located three days from now. Human life is always about customization. And it is customization which needs a human touch and a face to face interaction. Will technology ever be able to fill this gap? Certainly. And if not technology, such gaps will be filled by smart businessmen. Slowly and Steadily, all the commerce will be done over the wire (or wireless), and all that needs is a smart businessman to make it real.

Advantages and disadvantages of online retailing

Online retailing is growing at an astonishing rate, with online sales now accounting for around one quarter of the total retail market. Retailers who ignore e-commerce may see their trade lessening as customers continue to shift to ordering products online. However you need to think carefully and weigh all the advantages and disadvantages - backed by good market research - before deciding on whether or not to trade online.

Advantages of online retail

The benefits of retailing online include:

● Easy access to market - in many ways the access to market for entrepreneurs has never been easier. Online marketplaces such as eBay and Amazon allow anyone to set up a simple online shop and sell products within minutes. See ● selling through online marketplaces.

● Reduced overheads - selling online can remove the need for expensive retail premises and customer-facing staff, allowing you to invest in better marketing and customer experience on your e-commerce site.

● Potential for rapid growth - selling on the internet means traditional constraints to retail growth - eg finding and paying for larger - are not major factors. With a good digital marketing strategy and a plan a scale up order fulfilment systems, you can respond and boost growing sales. See ● planning for e-commerce.

● Widen your market / export - one major advantage over premises-based retailers is the ability expand your market beyond local customers very quickly. You may discover a strong demand for your products in other countries which you can respond to by targeted marketing, offering your website in a different language, or perhaps partnering with an overseas company. See ● basics of exporting.

● Customer intelligence - ability to use online marketing tools to target new customers and website analysis tools to gain insight into your customers' needs. For advice on improving your customer's on-site experience see ● measuring your online marketing.

Disadvantages of online retail

Some negatives of online retail include:

● Website costs - planning, designing, creating, hosting, securing and maintaining a professional e-commerce website isn't cheap, especially if you expect large and growing sales volumes. See ● common e-commerce pitfalls.

● Infrastructure costs - even if you aren't paying the cost of customer-facing premises, you'll need to think about the costs of physical space for order fulfilment, warehousing goods, dealing with returns and staffing for these tasks. See ● fulfilling online orders.

● Security and fraud - the growth of online retail market has attracted the attention of sophisticated criminal elements. The reputation of your business could be fatally damaged if you don't invest in the latest security systems to protect your website and transaction processes. See ● e-commerce pitfalls - security weaknesses.

● Legal issues - getting to grips with e-commerce and the law can be a challenge and you'll need to be aware of, and plan to cope with, the additional customer rights which are attached to online sales. See ● the law and selling online.

● Advertising costs - while online marketing can be a very efficient way of getting the right customers to your products, it demands a generous budget. This is especially true if you are competing in a crowded sector or for popular keywords. See ● pay-per-click and paid search advertising.

● Customer trust - it can be difficult to establish a trusted brand name, especially without a physical business with a track record and face-to-face interaction between customers and sales staff. You need to consider the costs or setting up a good customer service system as part of your online offering. See ● manage your customer service.

E-commerce offers many ways retailers can reach consumers and conduct business without the need for a brick-and-mortar storefront. Today, it's almost economic suicide for any retailer not to be able to sell online. However, before you enter the world of e-commerce, be familiar with the advantages and disadvantages of selling online.

Advantages of E-Commerce

retailers can increase their sales and profits faster than a brick and mortar establishment because selling online offers the advantage of being open twenty-four hours a day, seven days a week. Selling online also allows retailers to sell their merchandise in any part of the world without additional expense. This means e-retailers can expand into global markets or target an extremely focused segment, such as selling burkas to Middle Eastern women. While the small retail store on Main Street would never dream of competing with a national chain retailer, a mom-and-pop shop may find itself on a more level playing field with its big-box competitors.

People can find your brand and interact with it when you establish an online presence, including tapping into a whole new (potential) customer base. Much of online traffic is organic, meaning that if you build your e-store correctly, customers will find you without spending a dime. All you need is a robust Facebook, Twitter, or other social media platform to spread the news. Also, while traditional advertising is very costly, if you do get involved in digital advertising, the cost is nominal.

Disadvantages of Selling Online

One of the biggest disadvantages of selling online is the continued battle with security. Shoppers are becoming more relaxed with providing their personal and credit card information, but security concerns are still keeping many consumers from shopping online. Retailers selling online exclusively may have to work harder to build trust and establish a relationship with their customers. Personal interaction is limited when online selling and there is plenty of competition in cyberspace. Store owners may find it very difficult to find repeat customers. As online retailers expand their customer base to include shoppers in other countries, they also increase the difficulties in delivering their goods. The retailer is responsible for all deliverables and if the customer does not receive their products immediately, it is ultimately the retailer's responsibility to resolve the issue.

Online Banking - Advantages and Disadvantages

The World Wide Web has permeated virtually every aspect of modern life. If you have access to a computer with an Internet connection, an almost limitless amount of goods, services and entertainment choices are at your fingertips. You can do just about anything online, including your banking and financial transactions. But is this wise? Just how comfortable are you conducting your banking business in cyberspace? After all, online banking has both advantages and disadvantages, namely:

Advantages

● It's generally secure. But make sure that the website you're using has a valid security certificate. This let's you know that the site is protected from cyber-thieves looking to steal your personal and financial information.

● You have twenty-four-hour access. When your neighborhood ● bank closes, you can still access your account and make transactions online. It's a very convenient alternative for those that can't get to the bank during normal hours because of their work schedule, health or any other reason.

● You can access your account from virtually anywhere. If you're on a business trip or vacationing away from home, you can still keep a watchful on your money and financial transactions - regardless of your location.

● Conducting business online is generally faster than going to the bank. Long teller lines can be time-consuming, especially on a Pay Day. But online, there are no lines to contend with. You can access your account instantly and at your leisure.

● Many features and services are typically available online. For example, with just a few clicks you can apply for ● loans, check the progress of your ● investments, review ● interest rates and gather other important information that may be spread out over several different brochures in the local bank.

Disadvantages

● Yes, online banking is generally secure, but it certainly isn't always secure. ● Identity theft is running rampant, and banks are by no means immune. And once your information is compromised, it can take months or even years to correct the damage, not to mention possibly costing you thousands of dollars, as well.

● Some online banks are more stable than others. Not all online setups are an extension of a brick-and-mortar bank. Some operate completely in cyberspace, without the benefit of an branch that you can actually visit if need be. With no way to physically check out the operation, you must be sure to thoroughly do your homework about the bank's background before giving them any of your money.

● Before using a banking site that you aren't familiar with, check to make sure that their deposits are-insured. If not, you could possibly lose all of your deposits if the bank goes under, or its major shareholders decide to take an extended vacation in Switzerland.

● Customer service can be below the quality that you're used to. Some people simply take comfort in being able to talk to another human being face-to-face if they experience a problem. Although most major banks employ a dedicated customer service department specifically for online users, going through the dreaded telephone menu can still be quite irritating to many. Again, some are considerably better (or worse) than others.

● Not all online transactions are immediate. Online banking is subject to the same business-day parameters as traditional banking. Therefore, printing out and keeping receipts is still very important, even when banking online.

Online banking does have pros and cons. However, it's not only the wave of the future, it's the wave right now, and the clock isn't likely to go backward. If you take reasonable care to safeguard your personal and financial information, you'll likely find that online banking is a convenient tool that you can easily live with. Eventually, you'll probably even wonder how you ever lived without it.

With increasing the need of eCommerce industry, every businessman is looking to have an online store where they can sell their range of products and services. One can get a lot of benefits by opting for eCommerce as it delivers a comprehensive range of benefits to retailers and merchants

Electronic Commerce is also known as e-commerce that consists of the purchasing and selling of products or services through electronic systems like computer networks and the Internet. In this modern world of technology, e-commerce is becoming a very significant option for many businesses as there are lots of companies that are interested in developing their online stores.

With increasing demand for online purchasing, more and more businesses are moving to e-store from brick and mortar stores. In the US, more than 60% of people are purchasing goods online from the comfort of their home and this figure is increasing constantly. By considering this percentage, we can say that e-commerce is expanding tremendously because of its complete range of benefits that any industry vertical can enjoy. Today, e-Commerce has revolutionized the way companies are doing business. Now, consumers can purchase almost anything online 24*7 a day and get an ultimate shopping experience. Before you opt for an e-Commerce business, have a look on its comprehensive benefits that you can enjoy:

Convenience & Easiness:

For many people in the world, e-Commerce becomes one of the preferred ways of shopping as they enjoy their online because of its easiness and convenience. They are allowed to buy products or services from their home at any time of day or night The best thing about it is buying options that are quick, convenient and user-friendly with the ability to transfer funds online. Because of its convenience, consumers can save their lots of time as well as money by searching their products easily and making purchasing online.

Offer Product Datasheets:

Consumers can also get description and details from an online product catalog. For your customers, it is very much important to get information about the product no matter whether the time of day and day of the week. Through information, your customers and prospects are making decision to purchase your products or not.

Attract New Customers with Search Engine Visibility:

As we all know that physical retail is run by branding and relationships. But, online retail is also driving by traffic that comes from search engines. For customers, it is not very so common to follow a link in the search engine results and land up on an ecommerce website that they never heard of.

Comprise Warranty Information:

No matter whether you are looking to choose including warranty information with product descriptions and datasheets or providing it from within an ecommerce shopping cart, you need to make sure that customers must be aware of important terms and conditions that are associated with their purchase.

Decreasing cost of inventory Management:

With e-commerce business, the suppliers can decrease the cost of managing their inventory of goods that they can automate the inventory management using web-based management system. Indirectly, they can save their operational costs.

Keep Eye on Consumers' Buying Habit:

The best thing is e-commerce retailers can easily keep a constant eye on consumers' buying habits and interests to tailors their offer suit to consumers' requirements. By satisfying their needs constantly, you can improve your ongoing relationship with them and build long-lasting relationships.

Competence:

For effective business transactions, e-commerce is an efficient and competence method. Setting-up cost is extremely low as compare to expanding your business with more brick and mortar locations. Very few licenses and permits are required to start-up an online business than physical store. You can save your lots of money by using fewer employees to perform operations like billing customers, managing inventory and more.

Allow Happy Customers to Sell Your Products:

With lots of customers' reviews and product ratings, you can easily increase your sells as new customers find that your products are good and effective. Make sure that you mention your clients' testimonials, reviews and product ratings as such things can help your new customers to purchase your products.

Selling Products Across the World:

If you are running a physical store, it will be limited by the geographical area that you can service, but with an e-Commerce website, you can sell your products and services across the world. The entire world is your playground, where you can sell your complete range of products without any geographical limits. Moreover, the remaining limitation of geography has dissolved by commerce that is also known as mobile commerce.

Stay open 24*7/365 days:

One of the most important benefits that ecommerce merchants can enjoy is store timings are now 24/7/365 as they can run e-commerce websites all the time. By this way, they can increase their sales by boosting their number of orders. However, it is also beneficial for customers as they can purchase products whenever they want no matter whether it is early morning or midnight.

Economy:

Now, you don't have to invest your money in the physical store, insurance or infrastructure as all you need is a wonderful idea, unique products and well-designed website to reach your precious customers to sell your products and services. We can say that this makes an e-commerce a lot more economical and reasonable.

Boost Brand Awareness:

As like e-commerce business can help B2B organizations to get new customers, so it will be helpful for e-commerce businesses to boost their brand awareness in the market. Developing pages that can be indexed by search engines crawlers is one of the best ways to enhance your website' search engine optimization and enhance the target audience on your site.

Decrease Costs:

One of the most positive things about eCommerce is that you can decrease the costs of your business. Below are some of the costs that you can reduce by opting for ecommerce:

● Advertising & Marketing Cost: If you opt for ecommerce, you don't have to spend your money on advertising and marketing. However, organic search engine traffic, social media traffic and pay-per-click are some of the advertising channels that are cost-effective.

● Personnel: A complete automation of check-out, billing, inventory management, payments and other type of operational costs lower the total number of employees that you require to run your ecommerce business.

● Eliminate Travel Cost: Now, customers do not have to travel long distances to reach their desired stores as ecommerce allows them to visit the e-store anytime without traveling. With few mouse clicks, customers can make their purchase and have wonderful shopping experience.

Offer Huge Information:

One of the best benefits of ecommerce for customers is they can get huge information that is not possible in a physical store. We all know that it is quite difficult to equip employees to respond to customers who are looking for information on different product lines.

But ecommerce websites offer additional information to their customers without any hassle. All the given information is provided by vendors so that their customers find it easy to purchase products with information.

Analytics:

We can say that business 2 business offers an excellent platform to organizations to launch their complete range of analytics campaign. Through ecommerce, organizations can easily calculate and evaluate sales effectiveness, customer effectiveness, marketing campaigns, product mix, customer engagement and more.

Expand Market for Niche Products:

It is difficult for buyers and sellers to find each other in the physical world, but it becomes very easy for them with the inception of e-store. Customers can search their required products on the web and can purchase it from any corner of the world. No matter what kind of product customers are looking, they can find all types of products without any hassle.

Scalability:

With effective ecommerce solution, you and your organization grow and scale easily to meet market demand as well as customer requirements by introducing different sales channels and reaching market segments.

Ability of Multi-site:

With ecommerce platform, it becomes easy for businesses to launch channel specific and particular brand ecommerce website. This ability enables you to provide co-branded websites for your specific customers and allows for websites catering to specific international spectators.

IN conclusion, future internet remote working mode and online business will be more popular and it can be easier accepted to be used by working people and businessmen in our society , due to they can bring time saving and cost saving functions to them.

Computer technology related service consumer negtive emotion factors

Technology negative influence reasons

● 1.1 Online technology negative influence

Nowadays , internet is a popular tool to be provided to human to apply, e.g. online commerce brings businessmen to do online business trading, online searching information brings anyone can find information in short time, online studying can brings online learning chance and none classroom attendance to students. However, if we often do any online behavior, it will influence our mental and physical health to be poor, e.g. often spending time to use internet for social media contact. This interactive technologies will influence every young people's brain, behavior and attitude to be poor because they often spend time to use computer at home. Then, this digital technologies will lead them to lack nervous to study or learn any new knowledge, when who are students if they often apply computer to learn and they do not need to contact classmates and teachers in classrooms. Consequently, their school examination results will be possible influenced to be bad if they often apply computer to learn because they do not spend other time to any recreational activities or contacting people to make friends activities in their daily life.

It brings these two questions:

(1) Will internet often be used use to influence young people's mental and physical health to be poor?

(2) Has it bring direct negative impact relationship when young people

often spend time to use interest to do learning and information research behavior to cause poor mental and physical health?

Nowadays, human often uses internet which is one part of our habit. Our lives have become increasingly abuse in technology. Much of our communication and research is now online, much of our leisure and entertainment is provided by the internet and video games , and many of use internet find our mobile phones have become one essential part of our connectivity and everyday organizes to control our normal behaviors and to influence my normal life style poorly.

With these changes in lifestyle questions are it will arise negative influence about what technology may bring negative influence to us. Some of these questions bring potential detrimental effects, which had being unpredicted crisis in which the human brain is under threat from the modern world. Considerately, it influences the teenagers learning behaviors and attitudes to be poor. It seems that they have possible cause negative impact effect relationship between internet abuse habit behavior and poor mental and physical health as well as poor learning attitude and poor learning behaviors to young students.

The main factor of often doing internet playing behavior will have disadvantages to young people, because they will apply the internet tools to play video games to enjoy greater attention. This reflects a special case of environmental factor influence on whose mind and brain and health to be poor. Otherwise, if young people only spend some time to apply internet tools to do any reasonable need and meaning behavior, e.g. searching jobs from internet or searching any university written articles for study reference for learning intention or working seeking intention. Then, internet is a good tool to help them to develop their further career . Even, internet will train their brain and mind is more clear and clever and health to get advantages during who do any searching behavior for studying or learning intention from internet channel.

In conclusion, internet communication technology will bring either positive or negative influence to any users, it is depended on the user how to spend whose time to do any researching data or studying behavior in their daily time spending arrangement . Such as often playing game behavior or watching movie behavior and listening music entertainment behavior , which will have negative influence to any internet users' mind and physical health to be poor. Otherwise, sometimes searching jobs or seeking teaching articles or newspapers to read for learning intention from internet tool, which will have positive influence to any internet users. Hence, internet technology must not bring negative influence to human, it can also bring positive influence to human. It is depended on how we spend time to apply this high technology communication tools to do the beneficial mind and learning training behavior from this technological communication tool.

● How technology could contribute to bring poor standard of living to influence our societies

The effects of technology will have possible to bring global poor standard of living challenges. On the positive influence, especially science-based technology has offered a better world through the elimination of disease and material improvements to standards of living. But, on the negative influence, it will cause resource extraction, dangerous materials and pollution of air, water and oil have created conditions for unprecedented environmental to cause damage to the biosphere, when human applies any technologic tools to damage our earth natural environment in order to gain any profit for business aims.

Although technology brings businessmen to earn more profit, when who apply high technology to raise productivity and performance and efficiency to workers, e.g. artificial intelligence manufacturing robots, or they apply internet to sell their products (ecommerce), but technology also brings these disadvantages: Despite the ongoing technological revolution, the majority of the world population still lives in poverty with inadequate food, poor housing and less energy supply, illness increase , due to technological manufacturing can influence clean water and fresh air to be polluted to influence human's bodies to be un-health. Specially, the populations in Africa, Asia development countries, illness and death ratio both is risen by water and air pollution in these development countries nowadays.

Thus, it seems that it has relationship to bring negative influence to us between technology and air/water pollution and rising illnesses and deaths. Also, human needs to consider technology will support and enhance productivity and performance and efficiency , but it also influence human quality of standard to be poor challenge as the same time occurrence.

However, I suggest that businessmen ought reduce to invest much productivity by technological manufacturing improvement method, who ought concern environment pollution challenges how to avoid to apply technology to bring negative influence to all human's poor health challenge for long time. If human can apply technology, such as positive tool to solve problems or knowledge of how to create things, such as to brew beer , good taste soft drink or fruit or to make an atomic bomb, and culture (or understanding of the world, our value-systems), e.g. agriculture , irrigation and clean water management and navigation technological skill improvement. It means knowledge, technology becomes understanding of how to make and use tools and instruments becomes encodes as technological knowledge and know-how.

Consequently, human's positive and responsible behavior will change technology tools to develop of modern scientific knowledge, based on observations, hypotheses and generalizations on the natural laws concerning the behavior of materials and the living environment.

How to avoid to technology brings
negative influence on children

● Technology negative influence to children

In this world, it becomes impossible to escape the constant connection with others, aside from completely dis-connective from it, and into the unknown. Thus, parents need to know how their children using technological tools of behavior, which will influence impact on their children positively or negatively.

Nowadays, laptops and smartphones are now in the hands of children or young as ten age, and the eight to eighteen age young people that this group spends on average of ten hours and forty-five minutes or day exposed to media.

Whether their high amount of contact electronic media behavior is a good thing or not. So what is the right answer? Which side has the correct insight? When we may not have the immediate answer, one must look into both sides of the argument and determine what the correct path for today's children is. Thus, it brings thing effect, such as: one decision is about technology use will affect today's children as they develop.

Whether technology in classroom is truly a benefit for students. The benefits include it can enrich basic skills. Students who have access to technology become more quickly in the material and , such as are able to absorb the information more quickly. Electronic material can be more stimulating and interactive for children, it is motivational since it provides ease to students in study conducted of advanced learning technology students have found to have more interested to attempt to do writing behavior.

Nowadays, children can use technology as a supplement with traditional education, but it is as not replacement. In fact, computers have been specifically useful, for they allow us to manipulate items, such as text to meet the needs of individual students. For example, text can be made larger so it can be seen easier and also read aloud for deaf students. Moreover, recently, specific devices have been engineers to cater to students with specific disabilities. Thus, it seems that the introduction of technology into modern culture has drastically shifted social norms to include technology into children's daily lives.

However, when technology had been applied essentially into children's daily live. Technology also had bad points. Today, it is not uncommon to bring children playing on their portable video game systems, when at a restaurant with their family or to see a child operating a computer better than some adults. If children were abuse to use computer to video game wherever they go to any places, such as restaurant, school, toilet, catching transportation tool to sit down to play video games by mobiles habitually. It will bring this social challenge: Can technology influence children choose not to pursue to spend much time to learn, instead of often spending time to play video games for entertainment aim by mobiles habitually.

Technology will part of word of the rest of our foreseeable lives. But if children often accustomed to apply technology tool to play any video games from mobiles and internet tool. Consequently, they will often devote nervous and time to spend to play any video games from mobiles conveniently any time. Just like there have to be rules of conduct in real life, there have not to be smart rule of conduct in digital life to children.

The pursue of this internet and video games entertainment technology will force or encourage children to the playing video games from internet skills to navigate it and keep up with it as they get old. Hence, to judge electronic media is beneficial or harmful to children's learning stage . It is depended on how the child chooses to apply computer and/or internet technology from electronic media tool. If the child often use internet and computer or mobile tool to go to anywhere to concentrate on playing video games. Then, I believe that it will bring harm to the child's future learning development. Otherwise, if the child often use internet and computer or mobile tool to learn or seek any education articles in classroom or library or at home, these electronic tools are as technology advances to learn media. Then , it will be beneficial to the child's future learning development.

Technology negative influence to low knowledge learner to feel difficult to adopt future new technological labor market

Nowadays, information technology development is rapid. It brings this question: Will it bring negative influence to low knowledge learner to feel difficult to adopt future new technological labor market, special in underdevelopment of culture countries' labor markets?

To answer this question, firstly, we need to know what the underdevelopment of culture countries' labor market means before to answer this question. Culture means adaptive behavior, has been an integral feature of the human species through its evolution, it is shared, learned, symbolic, and transmitted cross generationally. In another sense, culture refers to all non-biological aspects of human existence, including economics, politics and technology. Underdevelopment of culture countries' labor market means what labors are needed to the under knowledge or educational level countries' labor markets.

There are very strong beliefs that the adoption and usage of information technology has performed positive effects on the development of any country, but it is not present that it will can bring negative effects on the underdevelopment of the culture countries, e.g. Africa, island places' living people, these places are not reactive or are not reaching technology mature stage. So, it brings these questions:

● What if the rate of adoption exceeds society's or individual's ability to adapt, when the rapid introduction of information technology?

● What if economic benefits are distributed in ways that are socially destabilizing?

● What if income distribution is unfair, with higher skilled personal becoming better compensated, when many people are deskilled and effectively unemployed of jobs comparable to their current jobs and at salaries comparable to what they are earning today?

● Can their low knowledgeable workers feel difficult to learn any high technological skill to prepare their future job demand in these underdevelopment countries?

It seems rapid information technology to underdevelopment culture countries , which have chances to cause social challenges. Such as low skilled workers' unemployment , even office workers' salaries or technology manufacturing factory workers' wages will be reduced if who would not adapt the new technology development to follow the new technology influence to impact their work culture or method.

Thus, it also seems that culture can't exist without some form of society, i.e. culture us social. Therefore, cultural factors are observed in the society as providing to the production of its members who need to apply technological tools to manufacture products or serve their clients in their job responsibilities, e.g. factory workers, restaurant waiters etc. low skilled and learned workers. They need to learn how to apply new technology to work, e.g. computer skill or artificial intelligent skill.

So, it explains why rapid technology development will influence the low culture under development countries' low knowledge and low skillful workers to feel difficult to adapt how to learn to apply new technology production in themselves countries' technological job nature development change . Then , it will cause social challenges, such as unemployment, reducing wages, dismiss them, raising domestic labor market competition.

Moreover, some scientists concerned with the negative labor competition impact effect of information technology on the underdevelopment countries' low knowledgeable level of workers rather than the economic contribution of IT, because when many low knowledgeable level of workers feel difficult to learn technological skill to do their jobs, then they will be dismissed possible to bring social unemployment number to be increased and shortage of labor in these underdevelopment culture countries . In essence, they was asking if IT would erode this unique possession , even if it seems to contribute to their economic development.

Consequently, the intensive use of computer by the low knowledgeable skillful labors before the realization of whose thought –high technological production method itself may prevent the low knowledgeable workers' productive form being able to develop as a creatively thinking personally. This is a negative example of a mental process to them, which has been defined earlier.

In conclusion, the development of a new information society to under development culture countries would then raise a number of fundamental problems, one of which could be how to formulate and create optional cognitive preconditions for successful low knowledgeable labor' upgrade of high technological skill in short term. There are some pf the problems faced by developing nations who are still to development their technological production skill to low knowledgeable workers to let them feel difficult properly, let alone creating optimal preconditions for a successful mental process of low knowledge labor-computer interaction. At present, the adoption of IT in developing counties needed to be concern how to adapt whose countries' information technological labor users' production skill change.

The negative impact of smartphones/ mobiles and
desktop/ laptop on human health and life

● Avoidance to driving and speaking mobile at the same time

Nowadays, the smartphones being a very new invention of humanity, became an inherent part of human's life. The smartphone combines different features. It allows users to keep pictures, memories, personal information correspondence, health and financial data in one place. Smartphones also become an integral part of modern telecommunications facilities. In some regions of the world, they are the most reliable only of available places. The phones allow people to maintain continuous communication without interruption of their movement and distances. However, recent scientific facts and research analysis of the smartphones' usage has disadvantages to influence human health and life.

The main key points indicate the effect of electromagnetic waves on human brains, effect of handheld device usage on human's upper extremities, back and neck. A significant neglect influence between the total time spend using mobile device each day and pain in the right shoulder and between times spent internet browsing and pain at the base of the right thumb. Moreover, mass cellphone calls enhance risk to human safety, e.g. when they are driving and listening and talking to touch mobiles at the same time. The drivers' driving and phoning calls behavior at the same time which will be very dangerous of their speaking and driving to cause traffic accident occurrence in possible. Thus, drivers can not neglect to avoid to do the mobile speaking and driving behavior at the same time when they are driving to reduce their traffic accident occurrence to cause their death or hurt in possible.

● What are the negative effect of electromagnetic waves on human brains from smartphone influence

Scientists proved that the smartphone is a source of the eminence of electromagnetic waves. Numerous studies have been conducted in the past years to identify the effect of electromagnetic waves emitted from the cell phones on human health.

However, it has not proved smartphone can influence our health certainly. As soon as mobile phones more and more part of our lives, the world is continuing research to prove whether cell phones are harmful to human health.

Today, there is no official statement announced by laboratory or medical center to answer this question: The complexity of the analysis of the statistical data makes the task more difficult for researchers. The impact of harmful radiation emitted from cell phones is still being studies.

Nowadays, human are accepted to use mobile phone in any time, any where popularly. Although, mobile is a good small size and convenient carrying of communication tool for human to use when we need to make phone calls to anyone in anywhere and any time conveniently. But, I feel that it will harm human health when we often use this communication tool any time.

However, some doctors indicate cell phones can cause brain cancer risk easily. But they have not any evidences to prove it is truth nowadays. Hence, the statement that cell phones can cause cancer has been not confirmed. The studies failed to prove that cellphones make a major risk develop cancer among frequent users. The main issues when conducting studies are some people may not accurately report the usage as they don't exactly remember how often they use the cell phone excluding speaker phone , and it is still difficult to measure the impact of other factors that may accelerate the cancer development for excessive cell phone users.

Although, it is not proved that cellphone can use brain cancer to human when we often use. But some scientists or medical professionals have proved that the cell phone users often use cell phones , it is possible to cause human physical illnesses, such as upper extremities, back and neck caused unhealthy and pain.

A smartphone or handhelds device combines advanced computing capability, such as internet communication, information retrieval, video, e-commerce and other features, that make device highly popular among people. According to Pew research center investigating, it showed that the number of smartphone owners comprises 56% of American adults in 2013 year and their average daily use of the device is about 195 minutes. The number of cellphone users increase every year. Various studies show the connection between cellphones usage and physical illness of the users' health. Some studies report that users complain about a headache, hand tremor and finger discomfort and pain of physical illnesses numbers increasing.

In fact, most mobile hand-held device users complain of discomfort at least on one area of upper extremities, back or neck. Long –term usage of the device leads to additional tension on tenders , muscles and tissue etc. different kind of physical illnesses. Moreover, in research conducted by a group of Korean scientists from Inji University focused that an effect of cellphone on hand-held device users was a significant association between the total time spend using a mobile device each day and pain in the right shoulder, and between times spend internet browsing and pain at the base of the right thumb.

● The laptop and desktop negative influence

On the laptop and desktop negative influence aspect, although telecommuting and telework communication technology is popular to be applied to our daily life. For example, they are modern alternative to office arrangement, employees work from home office, café, garden, carpark , even car.

According to scientists showed that nowadays, there are 20 to 30 million people who work from their home at least one day each week. Another 15 to 20 million work when they are on the road, 10 to 20 million runs some form of home business and 15 to 20 million work at home part of the time. IN most cases, people use desktop and laptop in their home office.

However, modified cellphones or smartphones are also substitutes to a home office. In fact, in principle of computers, it makes the workplace safer and convenient to compare mobile phones. There are different examples of adaption desktop or laptop computers to health needs of these users when bring their computers to go to anywhere to use in common, e.g. ergonomically designed keyboards design, pad bolster, mouse etc. design to adapt to their carrying to use their laptop or desktop needs. However, laptop or desktop computer products have not proved any serious harmful to influence human health to compare mobile phones at this moment.

Consequently , although technology can create different kind of jobs to let human to do, or assist human to communicate conveniently, e.g. mobile or artificial intelligent robot assist human to do any clerical job duties or learning more easily, .e.g. internet or laptop or desktop or owning mobile and laptop function computer products. There high technological products can bring benefits to satisfy human needs, .e.g. raising productivity efficiencies for workers, providing far distance overseas phone calls telecommunication, searching data or electronic business running from internet channel. But human can not neglect that these high technological products whether will bring negative influence to our mental or physical health when we often use them in possible. Thus, often using high technologies products to influence our health issue will be one important matter to be our future consideration.

Future internet function development trend
● Online television
Online television channels, platforms, devices experiences and choice will be positioning entertainment consumer market for the foreseeabl future. The reason is onlin ebook, music entertainment has been popular. Why does online television won't be popular?
Bloomberg business week website (2013) indicated that the evaluation of control technological development of portability technological tool: from 1975 year , the astraltune product had been populaar. The, 1979 year, Sony walkman had reached the 200 million sold number. Next, 1994 year, the smartphone had reached 1.4 billion users. Following 2001 year, the Apple ipod had reached 350 million sold. Then, 2010 year, the Apple ipod had reached 100 million sold. However, in watching television/movie entertainment consumption consumers could have different choice, e.g. from 1975 year, consumers can choose VCR entertainment tapes to watch movies or television programs. Then, from 1995 year, consumers can choose DVD , following from 2007 year consumers can choose Netflix streaming recording cameras to record any movies or television programs to watch. It had reached 30 million subscription numbers. Following from 2012 year, entertainment consumers can choose Acreo FM internet signal to watch TV.
Anyway, the entertainment watching facilities development had been following this trend: Capacity from 1981 year, the capacity is broadband. then, from 1999 year, capacity is WiFi, it had 61% of households share market. Next, from 2001 year, the capacity is 3G technology, many people like to download any movies or TV programes to mobile phone to watch. Till to nowadays, the mobile phone capacity is improved to 4G technology, the mobile phone internet user number had reached 59 million current

subscribers. So, it implies that many entertainment consumers like to use internet to download any movies or TV programs to mobile phones or laptops to watch.

It implies future internet development trend which can be used to entertainment industry. Hence, the future of television ought have implications for the component of a media company, when it applies internet technology to operate, such as IT service management, disaster recovery, digital content security, cloud etc. technological development.

Interactive advertising bureau (2013) indicated the devices used to view online television among US digital video viewers by type Mar 2013 1% of respondent(s), laptp had 58%, internet-connected TV had 47%, desktop has 39%, smartphone had 28%, tablet had 28% , ipodtouch had 14%.

Hence, it implied many entertainment consumers prefer to use laptop or internet connected to watch online TV television or movie in the future. These two channels will be the most popular online TV/movie entertainment channels in the future. Moreover, future internet technology development ought concentrate on improving it's speed, quality, performance to satisfy any laptop or internet connect TV entertainment consumers. Hence, future internet technology development ought concentrate on improving it's speed, quality, performance to satisfy any laptop or internet connect TV entertainment consumers.

● Internet innovative logistic industry

What is future potential benefits and limitations of using internet to logistic operaters? The users pay attention to two new developments that may have a very large impact on the development of logistic has been pointed out, i.e. To the " internet of everything" and to the so-called fourth industrial revolution. Will internet be popular used by logistic transportation industry?

Nowadays, logistic transportation industry is facing challenges, factors include possibly quickest onset of transportation action, high efficiency as well as flexibility, whose main function is the maximinal adaptation to client needs, e.g. delivering any products or documents to any countries' clients in the most time and no any error to deliver the products or documents to the wrong receivers.

However, internet is increasingly influenced by the skillful management of modern technologies to assist delivering in efficiency. It is based on complex and comprehensive data sources, arising from and influencing the development of modern trends. So, logistic industry needs have internet technology to help modern production, processing and logistics processes to satisfy the expectations of stakeholders.

The internet of things (IOT) is a new modes of communication, information connection between people and things, but in particular connection between objects (things). Hence, IOT management systems have a very wide range of applications and in terms of logistics, in a direct or in direct way many cover, among other, smart cities, intelligent industry, intelligent enterprises, intelligent buildings.

In the future, the group of significant trends in logistics include: big data/ open data, cloud logistics; autonomous logistics, 3D printing, robotics and automation; internet of things; localization and local intelligence; wearable technology;augmented reality; low-cost sensor technology; crypto-currencies and crypto-payment. Hence, future logistics industry will need internet technology assistance to develop any businesses. For example, DHL logistic delivering firm, the first 6 trends belong to a group that will impact on : Firstly, big data/open data, it is a degree of digitization enterprise data can be shared in an unprecedented way. Integrated data streams in the supply chain of many logistic suppliers and open data sources have a very high potential for logistics operations, improvement of operational efficiency, full control over the suppl chain, assets and personal , the possibility of more accurate forecasts, and adjustment in real time.

Secondly, what is cloud logistics? It meets the challenges of complex diistributed , uncertans less predictable logistic conditions, reduction of the total cost of IT services (including the cost of installation, updatin , maintenance fees)., service risk minimization, faster and simply implementation, better reliability and security.

Thirdly, automonus logistic: It is stand-alone devices can be applied throughout. The supply chain from " the warehouse of the future" through auto-driven vehicles. Following the example of autopilots to unmanned supplies.

Fourthly, 3D printing is technology chnging the logistics by adding new manufacturing " mthods and possibl emergence of new market segments, such as the digital magazone.

Firthly, robotics and automation is the new generation of robots and automated solution will significantly better performance offers a serious alternative to manual labor, reducing time consuming actitivied aim. So, these will be internet is how applied to logistics industry trend in the future.

● Six key forces or " Drivers of change" impact on future internet development

In the future, there will have to key drivers of change impact on future internet development, it includes : the internet and the physical world, artificial intelligence, cyber threats, the internet economy, networks, standards and interoperability and role of government. However, thesedrivers will have three areas of impact include: digital divides, personal freedoms and rights and media and society.

However, future internet technology will have these threats to influence its development. They include: civil society is seen as more important to raise needs, internet must remain user centric to raise competition, it is critical for individual safety and for the future internet economy, new thinking , new approaches and new models are needed across the board from internet policy to addressing digital divides from security approaches to economic regulation, multi-stakeholder needs will change increasing frequenty, internet users wil consider data collection and privacy in confidence.

In the future, artifical intelligent development will incresse internet needs in possible. The advent of artificial intelligence (AI) promises new opportunities, ranging from new services and breakthroughs in science to the augmentation of human intelligence in digitial world. For example, when there is significant hype about the possibilities hat (AI) may bring voices of concern to apply internet technology assistance. Hence, human must ensure that humans remain in the " internet and (AI) driver's technology combination ."

Consequently, the hyperconnected internet economy that results will see traditionl industries to lead future new internet market leaders from around the globl driving innovation and entreprensurship. Hence, future internet and (AI) will be technological driven economy, it depends on how scientists improve their innovation.

However, scientists ethical consideration will be one important issue when they decide how to apply internet and (AI) technology. If they choose to apply them to war aspect, it is very horror matter to human's future safety. Hence, developing (AI) and internet technological countries need to consider scientist's behaviors in order to avoid war occurrence to cause human's death in future one day.

Hence, scientists ought follow this direction to develop internet technology. The future internet is needed to promise social development , economic prosperity and technologies that can ampify the best of humanity. But, it also brings about to solve challenges and questions to achieve to aim to raise human's social welfare or beneficial final direction.

What will be the certain factors to shape the future of the internet development? It includes as below: Social economic opportunity factor, it refers this ability how to connect people is essential to the internet's value as a platform for innovation, creativity and economic opportunity. How can the drivers of change encompass internet technological , economic, regulatory, security and network related challenges for the future internet . The drivers of change may include, such as how the internet economy development, what the role of government is, what the internet and physical world will shape, how internet assists artificial intelligent development, how to fight cyber threats, how networks standards and interoperable developments.

Future hospital, transportation, manufacturing etc. industries development factor how these industries develop, it will influence how internet needs. Because the rapid change will disrupt businesses and increse pressure on societies , particularly models and the nature of work will be profoundly changed to influence internet change needs. It is far from clear whether this internet technology driven assistance will favour existing internet platforms or bring greater competition and internet entrepreneurship.

How the internet economy will increase efficiencies, productivity and create new opportunities factor. Internet technology will reshape economies in ways stakeholders, and particularly governments may be ill-equipped to keep up with. And as technology drives automation, traditional jobs and the local economies that rely on them will be at risk. So, the future internet economy will depend on new approaches to skills and education. For example, traditional manufacturing sectors that were once relatively insulated must evolve to succeed in an increasingly connected internet economy. As devices and applicances are built to be network ready, the internet live needs us between manufacturing and manufacturing technological company increasing. Companies will need to adopt a technology mindset as they are from replacing parts to updating software to manufacture efficiently by internet and artificial intelligent technology assistance. Also, business is trying to protect against disruptions to their business models, for example, in the tussle between Google's automated cars and the automobile industry. For one, it's another application of sensor technology for the other , it's a change in mindset.

In the future, most widely used online services and platforms deeped their market position or face competition and possible displacement by new players? Could these internet companies face new competition from traditional industries as online in a world of IOT? Can internet platform be popular to be used for advertisements for businesses? (AI)/new generation of entrepreneurs like to use technology to solve local problems, reach global markets and drive innovation. Hence, online (internet) data search can be the best tool to help them to achieve their intention. I believe that it has not other technology can be replace internet to search lot of data in the short time within 10 years. Hence, internet of things (IOT) ought follo this direction to improve its quality to attract many clients. (entrepreneurs) to use this data serch service.

Moreover, artificial intelligence will be popular to be used. It will be beneficial to internet to be used. For example, a society completely based on data collection on the business. Humans lose some self-determination through automated choices by connected machines. So, our community across all stakeholder groups and regions believes that automation generated through data analytics technology will have greater influence on human behavior and decision making. So (AI) and internet can be cooperate to assist themselves to serve human. For example, (AI) could bring about a fundmental reshaping of decision-making as policy development's increasingly data driven. AS (AI) and automation drive significant structural change across industries, the nature of work will change. Many existing jobs may be displaced as (AI) moves beyond user data to changing how products and services are delivered from internet assistance. The communication between machine to machine increases pressures to cut costs and people are being replaced. This is only going to increase with time. There are economic benefits , but also challenges to employees.

Hence, if the internet platforms of today can become dominant across infrastructure, services and applications, user choice and control over their online experience, as well as availability and deliversity of information and content could be popular factor to influence internet economy. When search companies reach such a level of scalability, it is difficult for others to complete with them. For example, customers may find it is difficult to move from one provider or platform to another. This will cause in the loss of choice and constraints on innovation and lead to internet fragmentation. This is a trend to toward an ecosystem of users and developers, in which you can have the big winners or something similar to walled gardens. But there will always be some disruption tahta fragments this garden and creates a new paradigm. So , the reach and resources of internet platforms mean that startups will be acquired in their infancy, before they can disrupt the bigger players.

Will any internet companies replace Google, yahoo internet companies' services? This question is if smaller entrepreneurs are able to compare in an able to compete in an uncertain environment of investment analysis to the opportunities, these creates are ranging from new big data search service to the applied to intelligence in the digital world. So, artificial intelligence will be creative destruction. Many jobs will be also be eliminated by (AI) technological invention, but it can generate new jobs and jobs from internet , big data serch services assistance.

● Future trend of mobile and internet development

Morgn Stanley reserch indicated that future past mobile vs. desttop internet user development trend within 5 years. Mobile internet users number was from 400 million 2007 year climbed up to 1,900 million 2015 year. Otherwise, desktop internet users number was from 1,000 millon 2007 year climbed up to 1,7500 million 2015 year. Hence, it implied that , although desktop internet user number was more than mobile internet user number in 2007 yer, but till to 2015 year,mobile internet user number was more than desktop internet user number. It reflect many people had accepted to apply mobile tool to do any internet search behaviors. It is possible that it will be popular to apply mobile tool to do internet search behaviors for long time in the future.

It brings this interesting question: Why do global internet users prefer to spend more time to apply mobile tools to do search behaviors from internet? I shall indicate that this technological teaching method example, such as how smart mobile phones and internet technolgy had changed the old phenomena of learning model in educational industry. The traditional phenomena of learning model was that teaching innovation means unit cost of teaching, success teaching evidence means number of teaching units deployed, every student can free access open teaching contents from internet channel of desktop tools, every student learning can be achieved every delivery and display from internet learning, every teacher training needs to achieve the first and last discussion to every student from internet online teaching tool. Hence, many schools will accept to teach students from online teaching channel. Every student can turn on desktop to link to internet tool to learn at home conveniently. So, internet learning students do not need to go to schools, due to internet learning tool is similar to classroom to let teachers can apply internet channel to teach their students as well as students can listen their one teacher teach what in the same time when they open computer to link internet to see their teacher face and listen what who teach them after they log in their school website from internet channel conveniently. Hence, every group of students who can see teacher and listen what their teacher is teaching them in the same time after they turn on desktop to link to internet at home.

Some scientists also predict future mobie internet can be applied in educational and communication industries from 2020 year. Mobile internet can be applied to these aspects: education security, labguages, radio distributed systems, networking.

How can mobile internet be applied to children age education industry? I shall explain what what pocket school means. Pocketschool is not a name of device to be applied to different device for a different context, it is not a name software varies of open software contents, it is an initiative to help underrepresented children and migitate digital, education and economic divides. For a kind of mobile math learning game education method, it is a critical thinking math teaching method to children. Every child student can turn on mobile to learn how to apply simply math equation to calculation from mobile internet. Hence, future mobile internet tool won't only be applied to playing game aspect, it can be applied on education game aspect to let children to feel fun to learn from themselves. So, children can apply mobile internet to learn from device recognition to solve problem through collaborations, e.g. children cn apply moile internet tool to learn writting story ot telling story to increase learning internet or training to be authors. Mobile internet can also be applied to medical aspect, e.g. seeing any x ray images of brains , bones or any part of bodies, when medical photographs are delivered to download to the patient's mobile from the hospital easily.

In conclusion, in the future mobile internet will be popular used by mobile users and internet market must be expand to mobile tool market, instead of computer tool market.

● Digital Pollution prediction tool development

Can internet (digital) technology be fueled by the social, mobile, cloud, big data gathering and growing demand for anytime, anywhere access to information to help scientists to predict when or why or how any natural environment bad climate change occurrence and find any solutions to avoid any pollution is caused which can reach the serious level by human's damage natural environment behaviors?

Nowadays, the evolution of digital tool development, human can apply this tool to gather big data to help any businesses to decide to best activity to reduce loss, or to analyze information to get the more accurate result. In the future, I believe that digital technology can be applied to help scientist to gather nature climate and environment change data to analyze when the climate will be changed to be worse. Even, when water and /or air and/or soil and/or noise different kinds of pollution will be serious to influence the country's people's health, e.g. water is polluted to drink or air is polluted to breathe or soil is polluted to grow food or noise is serious to influence our mental health. Even, digital big data can help scientists to find the reasons why the country's air and/or water and/or soil and/or noise pollution is caused and attempt to find any solutions more accurate to avoid the serious level of any pollution occurrence.

Moreover, in the micro −economic benefits, digital tool will develop to be used to predict the level of water/air/soil/noise pollution to assist policy decision makers to do any effective policies to response to these nature climate change challenges that cities face, include climate change and poverty, will be essential to making cities of the future competition.

Thus, digital technology seems to be future one kind of the most suitable climate change or environment pollution big data gathering predict tool to compare other climate change predict technological tools.

● Future digital technology prediction tool development trend

Nowadays, cloud, big data demand is growing to be satisfy to any different businesses or personal needs. In the future, it seems to be applied to help scientists to attempt to gather any big data to save to cloud (internet saving channel) , to analyze why ,when, how to cause the water/air/soil/noise pollution will reach the serious level and , to find the best solution to solve the causes of any pollutions accurately.

Digital technology will be one good prediction tool to help scientists, even who are not scientists to gather data to do any analyses concern climate change or environment pollution easily. It's advantage is any people who do not need to spend more time to learn and feel difficult to learn how to apply this technological tool to compare other difficult learning of technological climate prediction tools generally. Since, internet (digital) is one kind of popular and cheap technological product to be used, any people can free change to use it when who are using in public library , school library, any transportation tools, such as bus, ferry, tram, train, taxi private cars, or restaurant, shopping centers etc. different public places. Hence, gathering data activities are very convenient and easily to any people and it is one good prediction to predict when ,how, why natural environment change and climate change and pollution causes when people can bring whose laptops to go to anywhere to apply internet (digital) tool to gather any climate and environment data change immediately.

Factors influence Canada computer market development

● Canada and Norway Similar behavioral consumption model

Nowadays, Canada and Norway both countries have similar economic development models. I shall indicate what reasons to support my view point to believe that they have similar consumption model in their societies as below:

They have a strong trade and investment relationship are built on complementary resources, similar levels of development and shared interests and values. Hence, these both macro-economic and micro economic factors will influence Canada and Norway countries overall both social consumption models to be similar to influence themselves people (consumers) daily behavioral consumptions are more similar.

Because both Norway and Canada are advanced economies, basic trade is augmented by research and opportunities to help both countries deal with similar geography and climate. It causes Canada export or import success. Thus, Canada's trade success which will depend on Norway trade cooperation. Also, Norway's export to Canada will influence Canadian social consumption model to be similar to Norway's social consumption model as well as Canada's export to Norway will influence Norway social consumption model to be similar to Canada's social consumption model. For example, Norway's investment in Canada supports Canadian GDP and jobs. In spite of the heavily materials, based outputs of both countries. The relationship makes a unique contribution to the knowledge and innovation economy.

In fact, Canadian and Norway people whose life habits are very similar. Moreover, Norway's impact on the Canadian economy includes on these aspect: Technology, telecommunications, utilities, consumer services, oil and gas and financials. It will influence Canadian general social consumption model after Norway consumption model on these Norway similar industries investment are brought to Canada to influence Canadian's daily life or life habitual changes to cause follow Norway people's consumption model or attitude in daily life. (Canadian Aquaculture Industry Alliance) indicated for example, agriculture is an important sector for the Canadian economy, providing jobs and investment in every province, as well as the Yukon.

The aquaculture sector employs over 8,000 Canadians, overwhelming in British Columbia, New Brunswicky and New foundland and Cabrador. It seems aquaculture sector is one factor to influence Canadian's behavioral consumption model.

Canada and Norway negotiated a path of closer trade relations through the Canada-European Free Trade Association (CEFTA) agreement in 2009. This could be strengthened through updated foreign investment protection and promotion rules, such as through a foreign investment promotion and protection agreement. Due to Canada and Norway have trade and investment relationship have trade and investment relationship. It will influence Canadian's life habits and consumption people's consumption model after Norway's business investment is introduced to Canada.

For example of Norway industries communication development to influence Canadian's consumption desire changes include as: Information and communication technology aspect; Canadian Trade Communication Service (2012) indicated that as a society, Norwegians are some of the top per capita users of information and communications technology (ICT) in the world, and they also have some of the highest spending per capita on ICT. Norway ranks sixth on the international telecommunication Union's ICT Development Index, which ranks countries' performance in terms of ICT infrastructure, use and skills. Norway is an advanced ICT country with related industries that are based on globally competitive.

Nowadays, ICT expertise has developed around the country's more traditional sectors like oil and gas, aquaculture and the shipping industry. However, it also has expertise in niche areas, such as food mobile banking solutions, micro payment and customer relationship management (CRM) technologies. Because of the ICT synergies, Ontario's technology corridor in South Western Ontario provides attractive investment options for Norwegian companies. Encompassing the greater Toronoto Area and Kitchener-Waterloo cities in Canada, this region is known for its high tasks expertise and entrepreneurial spirit. Hence, it seems Norway's communication industry development will influence some Canadians who live in Toronoto or Waterloo etc. large cities' consumption model to follow Northway people's consumption model in mobile cell useful time, habitual usage mobile phone calls, e.g. average 100 hours increase to 200 hours or more per month, due to cheap mobile phone call charge factor; long distance phone call increasing time to use, due to cheap distance phone call charge factor; food consumption channel on internet ecommerce shopping consumption model.

Canadians also often use internet to see movies, listen music or reading or searching information etc. different entertainment aim at homes, due to cheap internet charges to home internet users. Hence, after Norway communication industry is invested to develop in Canada, it will possible to cause many Canadian change their behavioral consumption model in Canada communication industry consumption market.

● Living standard, productivity and
competitiveness to international
comparison factor

Why does living standard, productivity and competitiveness to international comparison factor influence Canadians' behavioral consumption change model? What is productivity mean? Productivity measures the efficiency with which production inputs, such as labor and capital are being used in an economy to produce a given level of output. The key determinants of productivity include" the education, training and experience, the workers and the the amount and types of equipment available to them, as well as technological innovation and changes in both organizational and management practices.

In this view point, these determinants are influenced by broader factors, such as competition openness market. The term " competitiveness" means as a measure of a country's advantages or disadvantages in selling its products or services in international market. Hence, Canadian's consumption behaviors will be influenced by how it's products are produced as well as its competitiveness with internationals, which are interconnected that contribute to strong Canada's economic growth and rising living standards. For example, in the year, if Canada's productivity effort is raised and export or import number is more than last year, its domestic Canadian who are living to cause who have more jobs to do. Then, they have more effort to consume, due to their living standards are risen in this year, who need to consume anything to satisfy whose better living of standard demand.

Another example, I assume that the more efficiently Canadian businesses use resources to produce products and service in this year. That is the more productive, they are the greater their advantage in selling those products and services in international markets, that is the most competition, they will be. Then, Canadian will have more different kinds of products to choose to buy from local manufacturers' products supply. The more product choices influence will bring many Canadian choose to buy local products more than overseas foreign import products. The reasons are possible what local products are cheaper than foreign import products, local products have much different kinds of unique choice, more than foreign similar kinds of products. It will have more local different kinds of product choices will influence.

The trend of buying desires to Canadian's consumption is to be changed foreign manufacturing product import who will trend to choose to buy Canadian's domestic manufacturing products in the year. Hence, Canadian's manufacturing more different kind of unique product choice will influence Canadian who desire to buy foreign manufacturing import products to change to desire to buy Canada domestic manufacturing products, due to they can provide more different kinds of products choice to sell to them in this year. Past, they can not buy many of any these Canadian domestic manufacturing products traditionally. Consequently, in the year, raising productivity and raising living standard and raising competitive effort factor will influence Canadians change their behavioral consumption model in this year.

When these high technological products can be manufactured more number and sell more in Canada after future ten years. then, these high technological products can sell cheaper price, due to Canada's artificial intelligent manufacturing skill has reach the mature stage. Hence, Canada artificial intelligent scientists can innovate high qualify and low cost material to manufacturing kind of artificial intelligent robots in order to sell more number and reasonable cheap price for this kind of (AI) research and development high technological products after future ten years research and development process. Consequently, it will influence future Canada (AI) home consumers acceptance to choose to buy any kinds of (AI) robots to assist housewives to share their home workload for Canadian families in popular after future ten years. Moreover, future Canada (AI) robot products will be also popular to use for different functions for any businessmen, e.g. shopping center (AI) robot cleaning service, houses or offices or any building (AI) robot cleaning service; restaurant (AI) robot cooker's cooking service replaces to human cookers. (AI) non-manual automatic transportation vehicle send products to deliver to different places; (AI) robots deliver product to suitable locations in warehouses. Hence, future after ten years, when Canada innovate to research (AI) robots technology to be success. Then (AI) robots will be popular to be used to Canada domestic some (AI) users and business (AI) users both. Canadian's consumption model will be accepted to high technological (AI) consumption model as well as innovation will influence future Canadian how to choose to apply high technological product, such as (AI) robots will be used to replace human general job duties in office or home or business function to replace themselves tasks for main consumption intention in future their daily high (AI) technological innovation life trend model.

● Innovation policy factor influences Canadian behavioral consumption model

How can Canada policy decision makers innovate Canada social consumption model? Nowadays, Canada policy makers are giving increasing attention to innovation. Innovation strategies are being designed in more countries. International policy learning or innovation related issues becomes an important tool for industrial policy development. To answer above question, I shall ask whether it has relationship between innovation and consumption desire in any countries.

Such as Canada innovation case, the economic structure of Sweden and Canada differ with respect to e.g. industrial structure, where the Canadian industry is more characterized by small businesses when Sweden's industry is dominated by way large and international companies. These structural functions have very strong impacts or national innovation policies and strategies that lead to different solutions, which offer valuable prototypes for learning.

However, both countries are have similarities as well as differences between them. They are facing a growth challenges, Sweden needs to increase both the number of start-ups and growing companies, when Canada's environment strength seems to close to US, its foremost competition and also its biggest export market. The economic structure of Sweden and Canada differ with respect to e.g. industrial structure, where the Canadian industry is more characterized by small business when Sweden's industry is dominated by international companies.

The importance for small businesses of a measure corresponds to the correlation between the function of the measure and the circumstances for the targeted group in Canada. Canada innovation policy achieves to small business target group, e.g. integrated business, technology advice, which implies a network of people with different competences, but easily assess through a low number of entry points. The efficiency in the use of public research and development resources is related to the approach to commercialization of results in science and research in universities and research institutes that are publicity funded or owned.

Hence, in micro economy view point, Canada government innovate technology to assist many small business development, it will encourage many small business target group businesses to attempt to enter themselves local sale market in Canada. Then, there are many small businesses exist in Canada, it can influence Canada consumers have much different similar kinds of product choice to buy in anywhere easily and conveniently. The advantages are some consumers who do not need to drive cars to go to very far distance to their homes to buy cheap or expensive products because there are many small business stores provide different similar kind of products to let them buy more easily and conveniently. Consequently, it will influence many Canada consumers' consumption desires to be risen , due to who do not need to drive cars to anywhere to buy, who can choose to walk to buy any different kinds of similar products in short time.

Hence, innovation policy can encourage way small businesses set up to cause some Canadian who live far from large cities people, whose consumption desires are also influenced to be increased. The improved macro-economic situation has also made possible, e.g. strategies tax reduction, large increase in research and development expenditure, strengthened the venture capital sector and measures to increase highly qualifies labor through support for graduate university studies and improvements to Canada's immigration policies. These changes will also influence Canadian's behavioral consumption change model. For example, Canada innovation strategy related to education strategy and mainly industry and research and development policies. The focus on these four areas: Canada's knowledge performance skills, the innovation environment, and the need to strength the innovation capacity of communities. The strategy mainly focus on investment development on innovation issues on research and development, such as any technological industry development. Hence, after future ten years, Canada will be possible one high technological development country to follow US, UK, German etc. high technological development countries. In the future, when Canada's research and development success, some high technological products use be possible to be manufactured from Canada's manufacturers, e.g. any artificial intelligent products, non-manual driving vehicles, robots,.

● Immigrant economic and social factor influences Canadian consumption model changes

Canada immigrant brings Canada negative with the deterioration in economic outcomes, such as the changing mix of source regions and related issues, such as language and school quality, dealing returns to foreign experience and the deterioration in economic outcomes for all be labor market entrants of which immigrants are a special case. Due to immigrant brings negative influences to Canada's economy development, it will influence Canadian has negative consumption attitude, because economic downturn to cause Canadian domestic low education workers will lose jobs, due to foreign low educations Canada can pay cheaper wages to compare Canada domestic low educational workers. Hence, Canada's employers can choose to employ the low educational workers to replace domestic Canada low education workers. Then, it will cause many Canada low education workers unemployed and they will feel difficulty to find new jobs to do, due to they need to compete with foreign Canada immigrant job seekers.

Thus, long -term many Canadian low educational worker unemployment challenge will cause low consumption desire social challenge, and many Canada small businesses will lose these domestic Canadian low education consumers (target consumer group) to cause their businesses fails in possible. Hence, long-term serious many foreign low educational sudden immigrate to Canada, which will be possible to cause many low educational Canadian lose jobs to cause their consumption desire to be less consumption to buy any not essential products or not essential entertainment.

● High impact firms accelerate Canadian competitiveness influence technological product consumer behavioral changes

Many US technological products are exported to Canada to bring much weaker. Canadian domestic technological firms' technological product attractive effort, it reflects a competitiveness challenge for Canadian firms. These US technological products are sold to Canada, it will also influence

Canadian consumption model changing, such as the Canadian technological product consumers' habitually choices to buy any domestic manufacturing technological product, it is possible that are US technological products are imported to Canada market to increase different kinds of US high technological products for Canadian to choose to buy. They will influence the habitual Canadians who are traditional any Canadian high technological product consumers, who will change consumption model to choose to buy US different kind of technological product, even their prices are possible higher than Canadian high technological manufacturing products. It is possible that Canadian domestic high technological product manufacturers who can not manufacture any better functions or more safe or more beautiful or unique high technological products to compare US high technological product manufacturers.

Hence, although Canada can earn much imports income to raise GDP every year growth from US high technological product imports, but long term bulk of US high technological product imports, which will influence Canada domestic high technological product manufacturers' income to be reduced when they still choose to buy their products in local possible, due to they encounter US high technological product manufacturers' competitiveness every year. It implies Canada domestic high technological product manufacturers need to concern their consumer choices will increase and whether Canada is still their original market to sell their high technological products in the future.

Implementing Canada's rural development policy in a knowledge-driven economic consumption behaviors.

Nowadays, Canada government considers have to implement rural development to encourage consumption to raise economic growth. It aims to improve Canada's economic restructure and increase competitive effort in global, e.g. agriculture, forestry, mining and fishing sectors etc. However, Canada government will encounter these challenges to need to solve in order to implement its rural development strategy more easily. These challenges include resource depletion, substitution of synthetics for natural commodities, substitution of capital for labor in production, relocation of natural resource industries to low-cost jurisdictions in the developing world, and low level prices on global markets, which are no longer mitigated by subsidies, trade protection and business incentives.

What is knowledge-driven regional economic development mean? (like forestry, fishing, agri-business etc. , diversification of the rural economies through service industries and tourism, development of small and micro enterprises, exploitation of the potentials for search and development, selective infrastructure development and social development in especial better access to health care and education).

Why knowledge-driven rural development will encourage rural consumption to Canadian. There reasons include knowledge-driven manufacturing can influence Canada rural consumers to feel base fresh shopping feeling, it is different and better consumption model to compare traditional rural consumption model. For example, Canada rural development strategy is targeted at knowledge production exchange and commerce in rural consumption market. It involves entrepreneurs, researchers and venture capitalists within, for instance, the agri-business and bio -products, energy and agriculture. Thus, Canada rural business development will have possible to influence any rural favorable product consumers to raise whose desires to choose to buy any fresh idea or undiscovered rural products in this Canada rural consumption market.

● How can greening of the Canadian economy to influence businesses' behavioral changes

Will Canada economy development raise Canadian green environment consumption desires? to answer this question: we need to know what green consumption means, it can be explained to develop in a low carbon, resource-efficient social consumption desire. Canada needs to know why Canadian feel who needs environment consumption. The reasons include supporting environmental protection, innovating improved assurance criteria and methods to deepen enterprise responsiveness to the green economy agenda, motivating stakeholder engagement and the use of best practices and standards to give better understanding of the views and the actions of all those affected by the green economy, driving through leadership in the area od challenge and opportunities posed by the green economy through focused research and skills development.

Canada government also needs to know Canadian is facing a series of major environment and social challenges. Such as: the need to produce more food to feed growing populations; how to manage of competing demand global fresh water supplies; the significant and expanding challenges of climate changes. Thus, when Canada government lets Canadian to know why green environment protection rural consumption model will protect global environmental climate changes to avoid worse and our natural resources won't waste to use to cause shortage possibility. Thus, Canadian will change consumption behaviors to reduce waste to use. Canada government can promote climate change effects to let Canadian to know include: increased risks of extreme weather events, effects on infections disease dynamics, rising sea levels leading to rain of land and water sources. Thus, such as how to protect earth environment and nature resource shortage issue, Canada government needs to promote it is human responsibility to reduce to waste to consume any resources. To let Canadian to reduce waste from their consumption behaviors. It is social education which concerns human, such as Canadian how to avoid waste from their traditional consumption behavioral model to change green environment protection consumption model in their daily life. Then, Canada will have much natural resource to supply for Canadian to use and Canada's natural environment will also keep clean, when Canadian feel need to change their waste consumption habitual behaviors for themselves in order to give benefits and welfares and raising green economic growth for themselves country.

● Increase productivity growth influences to increase social consumption in Canada

Canada's recent productivity performance is insufficient to ensure that future generations will enjoy the growth in incomes that current generations are accustomed to. The productivity growth influential factor includes the most important determinant of how increased material living standards; it is also critical to ensuring that adequate fiscal pressures associated with population aging. Thus, when Canada can increase productivity growth, then it will have enough products to supply to Canadian to consume. The question is how to raise productivity growth?

As its root, productivity growth is driven by innovation and investment in capital equipment and Canada is behind most other industrialized nations on both of these. With regard to innovation, sharp proposes expanding federal technology transfer programs that assist firms in exploiting best practice innovations. With regard to capital investment, sharp identifies high taxes at the main proposes abolition of sales tax on machinery and equipment, this tax advantage can give economic benefits to encourage Canada businesses entrepreneurs to invest businesses to do in Canada. Thus, it can encourage business investment migration to bring Canada's productivity growth. However, the effect of productivity growth will be the only means to ensure not only the increasing living standards or increasing social consumption to which Canadians are accustomed, but also the resources needed to meet the fiscal pressures brought on by population aging, due to productivity growth must need more resources to be supplied to manufacture any products ensure.

Thus, if Canada expected consumption can be grown, it needs to solve resources shortage challenge to ensure it has any resources to supply to manufacturers to manufacture any products to cause productivity growth aim for long term macro economy development.How can greening of the Canadian economy to influence businesses' behavioral changes

What is greening economy mean? It can be defined to efforts to improve environmental conditions are motivated by government environmental policy, environmental and economic efficiency and corporate responsibility. Thus, apply this definition to Canada, we find a four step greening process that is common across all sectors of the economy. This process suggests that environmental considerations have become heavily influences into the behavior of Canadian firms.

What are characteristics influence how firms approach greening in Canada? For example, greening economy can influence unconventional oil and the mining businesses, we find that demand elasticity, collaboration and international trade considerations are shape greening efforts. A key finding is that environmental initiatives and economic growth are not alternatives, but rather increasingly can complement one another.

How does Canada greening economy influence Canadian businesses' behavioral to be changed? The notion of the green economy and instead focus on the greening of the economy as a basis for assessing the progress being made by businesses and individuals to achieve economic growth with environmental benefits. There are several trends become apparent about the relationship between the environment and the economy in Canada. Such as: Canadian corporates are increasingly any environmental considerations into any decision making. Canadian cooperates consider how to improve environmental efficiency frequently results in cost advantages, how to raise incentives to reduce environmental impact which can be in strong driver of innovation and Canadian corporates consider corporate responsibility is a driver for improving environmental performance. Hence, Canada greening economy policy influences Canadian firms consider have to apply environmental protection methods to achieve any best advantages or benefits to themselves. However, Canada government has implemented to do more conservation, emissions, sustainability successfully. Otherwise, it ought consider how heightened environmental awareness is having a positive impact on environmental outcomes and highlight how green initiatives are increasingly complementing economic growth.

In fact, on the one hand, Canada has a resource-abundant modern industry economy. In the 1600 year to modern forestry , mining and oil and gas extraction, the development of the commodity sector has always played a key role in Canadian economic development and economic growth. So, these industries need many labor to serve to help them to develop their businesses in Canada, e.g. forestry, mining and oil and gas extraction need environment protection in order to achieve Canada natural environment to own enough natural resources to supply to them to produce any products, e.g. Canada needs have enough trees to provide woods to manufacture furniture, natural resources to be supplied to manufacture oil, gas etc. gas energy.

On the other hand, green jobs are necessary to Canadian greening businesses. Green jobs are jobs within industries and businesses that have a positive green impact or at least a significantly lower negative impact than their rival(s), which are most able to capitalize on the growing governmental , business and consumer desire to minimize and mitigate human's effect on the environment.

Consequently, Canada greening economy influences Canadian greening business considers how to raise greening labor individual skills. A green job is one whose predominant function serves one or bot of the following goals. Such as conserve energy or reduce pollution. This includes clean energy alternatives, products or services designed to conserve energy and other natural resources and efforts prevent reduce, control or measure environment damage. In effective, if Canada expected green economy success. It needs to encourage any Canadian related greening product sale businesses how to raise greening labors; skills and how to reduce pollution to keep natural environment more clean in order to achieve more natural resources have enough supply to let them to use to manufacture any products to sell to satisfy Canadian consumers' needs.

How growth strategy influences
Canadian consumption model changes
Canada government commits to deliver growing economy to a strong

middle class consumer target group, such as social middle level income people, who are owning properties and vehicles etc. fixed assets in general. It aims to encourage this target consumer group to increase consumption desires, where then benefits of growth are shared in a fair and equitable manner in Canada's society today. Thus, it aims to encourage this Canadian middle class income target group's consumption desires in order to raise Canada economic growth.

It brings this question: How can Canada government encourage this middle class income target group to raise their consumption desires. It will encounter this macro and micro economic challenges to attract this middle class income target group's consumption desires. Such as Canadian households' high debt levels still represent a key risk to housing and consumer spending, especially if the economy were to face slower income growth. Moreover, increasing levels of household indebtedness and rapid increases in house prices in Canada's largest housing markets which will influence this middle class income consumers' consumption desires to be decreased.

However, Canada government had attempted to achieve these strategies to raise this middle class income target group's consumption desires. these strategies include as below:

(1) To foster greater innovation, the Government is creating innovation Canada, a new platform that will make it easier for Canadian innovators to access and benefit from Government led innovation programs. Supporting business led innovation which will facilitate collaboration between innovators and potential clients on research, development and demonstration activities that pursue major commercial opportunities, establishing a new strategies innovation fund will encourage and simplify existing business innovation programming and focus on attracting and supporting new high-quality business investments and launching the Pan-Canadian artificial intelligence strategy which aims to promote collaboration between Canada's main centers of expertise and position. Canada is as a world-leading destination for companies seeking to invest in artificial intelligence and innovation.

In addition , the Government is established on invest in Canada Hub, new federal body dedicated to attracting leading global firms to Canada, in order to bring more jobs, fresh capital and new innovative technologies to the Canadian economy. Thus, it seems that Canada promote to artificial intelligent products market to attract middle class, even high class income people to feel that they have needs to buy any kind of (AI) products to use. Also, it encourage (AI) technology firms to set up in Canada in order to raise more (AI) related work chance to let them to work in order to raise high (AI) technological educational workers' income level to encourage them to consume in Canada domestic consumption market.

(2) To help the Canadian workforce acquire the job skills needed to adopt and succeed to raise more employment chance to cause economic growth in order to raise social consumption desires of these three stages to achieve the final effect to raise social consumption desires. Hence, Canada government focuses on educational innovation aspect, it is expanding the labor market transfer agreement to increase the delivery of skills training and employment services aimed at helping Canadian find and maintain employment. It is also expanding the eligibility for Canada student loans and grants to make post-secondary education more afford for adults returning to school after spending several years in the workforce as well as part time students and students with dependent children.

It is the goal of the government to desire the best possible education outcomes for Canadian to raise whose knowledge level to prepare further to find jobs to work easily. Also, the government is making investment to support in increase in the number of high quality, affordable child care for low and modest income families to allow parents to pursue new opportunities to learn and to return to work. Hence, it is one long term education strategy to aim to raise Canadian knowledge or education level to achieve more Canadian can become the middle class income level consumers to encourage them to have effort to consume to raise economic growth to push economic development.

Consequently, Canada government's growth strategy aims to assist many Canadian have effort to become to be middle, even high income level target consumer group in order to encourage them have effort to raise consumption in Canada's society. It concentrates on implementing long term education and job skill upgrade level to young people as well as innovating high technological artificial intelligent products research development both aspects. Hence, growth strategy needs spend much time to raise long term education level and (AI) technological innovation level in order to achieve to encourage the middle level or high level income target consumers' consumption desires to be raised.

Reference

Canadian Trade Commissioner Service (2012), "

Information and communications technology
profile-Oslo-Norway" Government of Canada:
Department of foreign affairs and international
trade (Now Dept. of foreign affairs trade and
development). June
Canadian Agriculture Industry Alliance: Economic
benefits. http://www.acquaculture.ac/files/economic benefits. php

Airport indoor travelling staying shopping market

Emotional labor factor

Airline service industry, front line travelling passengers service workers' emotional challenge concerns cabin crew and airline ground service employee whose service quality or performance how to serve travelling passengers in order to reach service level or satisfy their service performance needs to be accepted. So, how to influence airline service labour individual emotional matter which will be one major factor to let travelling passengers how they feel satisfactory to the airline service.

The question concerns how to let airline service cabin crews and air ground service employees build long term good emotion to serve their airline travelling passengers. Because
bad emotional airline service labors will damage the whole airline employers' loyalty as well as reducing travelling passengers number in possible.

Will a lot stresses at work cause bad emotion to airline ground service employees? The hospitality industry comprises of travel and tourism and the major segments include lodgings and cuisines (hotels, restaurants), transport(airlines, rentals, cruise and railway companies), travel and tour operators. All of these related travelling industries' employees , they are emotional labor, whose service performance or service attitude will influence future potential travelling passengers' airline choices to the airline operating servicer again. Any airline service employees in these service sector industries, have to interact with their travelling clients, be its customers on a regular emotion reflecting basis. So, they must be patient to listen any travelling passengers' enquires in order to help them to solve any problems considerably.

Emotional labor is managing one's feelings to generate a publicly accepted facial and bodily display of emotion. Emotional labor is an expression of emotion for a wage. Jobs involve face to face or voice to voice interactions with clients (travelling passengers), jobs demanding the employee to produce and alter an emotional state in other person, and jobs allowing the employer to implement certain amount of control over the emotional activities of the employees, produce or create emotional labor among the employees.

Thus, long time bad emotional airline front labors number increasing, it will influence the airline whole service member performance to be its airline passengers. However, many airline organizations have their owning set of norms or policies that determine these feeling rules. These are specially seen in customer service industries. IN long term, these strict policies will let airline front service staffs feel stress or pressure, because they won't feel to be punished in possible, e.g. without salary continue increasing, dismissal (lose jobs), changing to another position to do more simple or boring job duties, if they are discovered that their working service performances are not satisfied to their airline employers in any time.

So, strict airline organizational policies will be one strict or pressure emotional regulation to any airline front service staffs. This emotional regulation refers to a person's capability to accept and understand his or her experience of emotions to get involved in healthy strategies in managing emotions which are uncomfortable whenever required, when they need to contact their airline passengers every day. In fact, it has possible that they will accept unreasonable complaint from their airline passengers, even they perform very good or they have help their airline passengers to solve any enquiries when they feel any needs, they stay in airports any time. So, it has close relationship among airline front service staffs' emotions and the airline's policy as well as their service attitude. Thus, good airline policy will build good airline service staffs' emotions and good service attitude or service behaviour to serve their airline passengers every day in possible.

Any airline organizations can not neglect to consider how to build (keep) good airline front labor emotion issue. Because they are any airlines' representatives, if they can build good

images to let the airline the airline passengers to feel. Then, it will influence many airline passengers to choose to buy the airline tickets to replace other airlines because they like its front airline front staffs' services. SO, any airline organizations need to consider front service staffs' health status and definite psychological or mental diseases more than physical diseases, because many airline front service staffs only need to serve their airline passengers and they do not need to move any heavy things in airports in general. They need to spend more time to contract their passengers more than any things. When their passengers give their passports or/and any related travelling documents, e.g. air tickets to them to check in to find whether they can allow to enter airport restrict areas, and if they give their luggage to them, they also need to help them to measure its size and weight heavy to decide whether they need to pay extra fee and their luggage are permitted either to keep to them together to enter the air planes to fly or separate air planes to fly to destination. So, they need to make accurate judgement need to avoid any error occurrence. They do not allow to do any wrong judgement or error in order to be complain by their airline passengers often. Hence, any airline organizations need have good method to help their airline front service staffs to avoid to do any wrong judgements in order to influence any flights delay or customers' complaints , due to their personal wrong judgement to their passengers cause in possible.

Thus, any airline organizations require to enquire themselves these questions: Is there any influence of emotional labor (surface acting and deep acting) on the general mental health or psychological disease of airline employees? Is these any difference in the experience of emotional labor across demographics (age/gender/mental status/work experience of airline employees influence their service performance? Because above any one factors , such as every airline front service staff individual age, airline service experience, marital status of these factors will influence their emotions to be good or bad to serve their airline passengers every day. Hence , any airline organizations need to investigate every airline front service employee individual background in order to arrange the most suitable policy to train their front line or ground airline service staffs' skill in order to let them to feel less stress or pressure
or they can feel happy to enjoy to serve their airline passengers.

On conclusion, reducing airline front or ground service staffs' psychological stress or mental pressure issue which will be the most effective or the best solution to assist them to raise confidence to serve their airline passengers in airports in long time. I believe that it is the most rapid psychological solution method to assist any one airline front or ground service staff to raise service level in short time.

Airports service environment factor

The environment of airports service environment for the airline services, which will also influence travelling passengers' travelling destinations and travelling frequent times choices. The airport price factor includes income growth, aviation technology and local economic / geographical features of the country's domestic or overseas airports both. IN fact, airports, airports are indeed two sides businesses, it has commercial relationship between both airlines and passengers. So, airports' pricing will influence passengers' travelling demands to the airlines in the country. Any countries' airport(s) need(s) to respond how to help themselves country airlines how to increase passengers number and airlines choices in order to achieve attracting traffic on frequent air planes flying aim. Because the country's travelling passengers number increases , it will influence the country's airport(s) ' income increases indirectly, instead of the countries' any airlines themselves incomes.

Hence, any country's airport(s) will be one good platform to let travelling passengers to stay in the country's airport(s). It means that id the country's airport(s) can build good service image and reasonable products sale price and comfortable shopping environment to attract any countries' passengers feel comfortable and worth to stay in themselves countries' airport(s), when they need to transfer air planes to stay in the country's airport, e.g. one hour to five hours short time, even overnight long time staying. However, if they
feel the country's airport(s) are(is) more comfortable and clean to stay, less noise, as well as they have enough chairs to let them to sit or sleep and large area to let them to work in the airport ground floor.

Moreover, the country's airport(s) can have enough restaurants , bookshops, any electronic or other kinds product shop[s, even cinema etc. shopping or entertainment services to satisfy
the passengers whose eating needs, entertainment needs, shopping needs in the airport. Then, I believe that the country's airport(s) can help itself airlines to attract many passengers
to choose to increase travelling times to the country frequently. For example, when the country's airport passengers feel that the airport restaurant food concessionaires will probably provide enjoy positive external gains from having more flights at the airports, additional or better eating facilities are unlikely to provide external benefits to the airlines by stimulating many more passengers with local origins or destinations to use

the airport. I believe these airport restaurants can influence the choices of transit passengers whether which country will be their transfer air plane's short journey staying airport destination to fly to their final destinations. Although, transit passengers usually stay to the transfer air plane airport in short time, but they hope that these any one transit staying airport can have any restaurants to provide good taste food to them to eat when they feel hungry, if the transfer air plane country's airport can provide enough restaurants and they can have different food taste choice and reasonable price. Then, the airport's restaurants may attract many short time transit passengers to choose to eat their food, even many passengers will like to choose the country's airline to buy tickets to stay short time to wait to transfer another air plane to fly to their final destination to replace another country's airport to stay short time.

Hence, it seems that any countries' airports' entertainment, eating and shopping service environment will influence any countries transit passengers whether they ought either choose to stay short time this country's airport in prefer or another country's airport to stay short time in prefer in order to decide to buy the country's airline air ticket for transfer airplane to another destination. Hence, any airports service environment will influence any countries passengers how to make transit airport destination short time staying choice.

However, I also suggest that an airport will place a lower revenue -over cost burden on that side of the travelling market that benefits the other the most. Assuming one passenger
can earn benefit enjoyed by airlines from an extra- passenger using the airport, the airlines will be willing to pay up to this amount to increase passenger enjoyed benefit feeling.

The airport can extract rent from the airlines up to above their allocated costs for providing the airport short time staying platform (transfer air plane short time staying airport) for eating, entertainment, shopping need service of increasing their destination arriving passengers or transfer another air plane passengers number base. This involves transferring the external benefits derived by airlines from additional passengers using the transfer airport to the another destination airport.

On the another view, from a airport location choice perspective, locating or expanding an airport near a city center can reduce or at least contain passenger access costs . But, because land is
like to be more expensive, the airside costs to airlines are serious higher

and if the various other external costs of aviation are included. Hence, countryside or the airport is built far away from city center in the country. This location is one reasonable location choice, because it can reduce noise to influence people who are living when air planes are often flying or landing on the airport and the rent cost to the airport's any business renters will be influenced to reduce. Then, their food , product or entertainment service prices charge to the airport consumers will also be reduced. Thus, any airports ought nor neglect their building location choices in any countries because they will influence airport business renters sale prices.

Lean maintenance repair and manual
error factor

Any airlines must need air plans to catch passengers to fly to travel. So, any air plans will need often to fly. Every flight will need long time to fly, e.g. short trip needs to fly less than five hours, even long trip needs to fly more than five hours, even ten hours. If many passengers choose the country to travel, the air plan needs to fly
frequently to catch every flight passengers to go to the travelling destination frequently. So, any airlines air plans often need to check whether they have any engine machines has broken, need to be repaired in possible in order to let passengers feel the airline air plans are safe. If the airline's any air plans have occurred any accidents when they are flying, even the accidents cause any one passengers hurt, even death. Then, these flying accidents will let passengers feel life risk to choose this airline's any air plans to catch to fly. IN special, long time trip(s) flight(s). So, lean maintenance and engine check is needed to consider for any one airplane to any airline in order to improve efficiencies and minimize costs, maintenance, repair,
and overhaul services in the aviation industry sector, even avoiding any flying accident occurrence or reducing serious flying accidents occurrence chance to bring any one passenger
hurt, even death when they are catching any one of the airline air plans to travel. Thus, any one of airline safety is one important successful factor to any airlines.

Instead of passenger safety aspect, the flying logistics safety factor is also important. The central tenet of the lean to a flying process can mainfest in a variety of ways , as over stalled
and underused inventory and misallocated labour, time transportation and logistics. From a customer's perspective, value-added activities are

necessary and customers are willing to pay for activities(Bamber, 2000, Glass, 2016). For example, improvements caused by lean introduction in aviation industry in order to avoid misallocated labour time, increasing number of old broken tools, and obsolute jigs and fixtures. Aviation MRO services have been reported by the MIT Lean Aerospace Initiative (2005) to result in:

(1) Set up time: 17 to 85 percent improvement.
(2) Lead time: 16 to 50 percent improvement.
(3) Labour hours: 10 to 71 percent improvement.
(4) Cost: 11 to 50 percent improvement.
(5) Productivity: 27 to 100 percent improvement.
(6) Cycle time: 20 to 97 percent improvement.
(7) Airline airplane manufacturing factory floor space: 25 to 81 percent improvement.
(8) Travel distance (people and products): 42 to 95 percent improvement.
(9) Airplanes engine inventory or work in progress: 31 to 98 percent improvement.
(10) Scape, rework , deflects or inspection: 20 to 80 percent improvement.

Hence, any airlines' airplanes need to be achieve any one of above improvement at least percent level in order to keep airplane's accident occurrence chance to the least level.

Moreover, airplanes' pilot employees their flying experiences or flight numbers factor is also important to influence airplane safe flying issue. Because if the pilot has less flying

expereince or he is not proficient pilot, or his flight number is less. This pilot's individual flying factor will also influence the airplan's safety when he is driving the airplane.

So, any airlines need to consider how to train any one of pilot to be one proficient pilot, because id less experienced pilot , he/she is not proficient to drive any one airplane to fly. Then, the flying accident occurrence chance will also raise. It is one critical successful factor to influence passengers' confidence to choose the airline's airplanes to catch, instead of maintenance repair and checking engines factor.

On conclusion, raising travelling passengers' safe confidences factor will be one critical successful factor to influence any airlines' services level, because flying safety issue

must be one important matter to be considered to any passengers when they decide to choose the airline's airplane to catch to fly to any destinations. If one airline can not guarantee any flying accidents won't occur, to cause any passengers hurt or death. Then, any passengers won't have confidence to feel its others services level can satisfy their basic flying enjoyment

needs. Due to passengers' life cost must be no worth calculation more than other service cost. When they choose to catch the airlines' any one airplane to fly to the another destination form the

country's airport. Hence, the influence of human factor in airport maintenance factor will influence any airlines' services feeling level to their passengers because human factor is one of the safety barrier which is used in order to prevent accidents or incidents of aircraft.

Therefore, the question is to which extent the error caused by human factor is included into the share of errors that are made during aircraft maintenance, such as flying

accidents, incidents, injuries, death, damages related to aircraft operation and maintenance. More airlines' detailed analyses have led to the knowledge that it is necessary to study the

interrelation of repair people, machines, airline factory maintenance and manufacturing working environment, and the air planes production processes. Human is the key factor production

process and in the process of operation of technical means since gives new value to the object of any one airplane manufacturing process.

As a factor, the human is not perfect and introduces unintentional error in the system. It is important to develop a system of ever identification and to work constantly on error

prevention. The works and activities on aircraft maintenance can produce hidden and active errors on the aircraft. Hidden errors are a type of errors that are seemingly invisible during aircraft

flying. Active errors are errors that occur immediately and result in immediate aircraft damage or injury , even death to any travelling passengers.

Hence, non human or without human factors will be less number to compare human factors to cause any flying incidents or accidents occurrence easily, e.g. damaging engine, old engine (no renew engine), fire, crash etc. different kinds of causes. However, the main causes of human errors to cause any flying accidents may include: lack of communication between the pilot(s)

and airport airplane landing staffs, complacency (assessment of work

according to previous working experience), lacking of flying knowledge to the pilot, distraction, lack of
team work, fatigue, lack of materials and technological support), pressure on the work performer, lack of assertiveness (lack of self-confidence or technical approach to work),stress (working under pressure), lack of awareness etc. different human factors. Any one of above human factors will influence any flying accidents cause.

Moreover, instead of human factor, the flying working environment which refers to the space and place for work as well as the conditions of work factor will also influence human
error occurrence increasing chance, e.g. time pressure, equipment and tools enough number supplies, night shift, all of any one work environment factor will also influence human error
occurrence increasing chance in any flight flying. However, the factors that lead to cause of maintenance error may be caused from wrong information system supplies of equipment , aircraft
manufacturer, wrong working equipment and tools, wrong design of aircraft equipment and parts, incorrect working task arrangement, lacking technical education to the aircraft maintenance
workers, employee's bad personality, poor aircraft factory manufacturing working environment, poor airline company organization structure, working management and control and poor
communication etc. different manual or non manual factors.

Hence, all of above any one non manual factors will also raise manual error factor to cause any flying accidents occurrence chances. However, if any airlines hope to satisfy their passengers' flying service level. They must consider non manual and manual both factors for aircraft lean maintenance repair service aspect.

Influence of airside and off airport to airport geographical choice factor

What does airport airside means ? It includes a system of three components: runways, taxiways and agron-gate areas, on which aircraft and aircraft support vehicles operate. It brings this questions: Why can airport airside operation influence passengers feeling to the country's airport
and airline services? How does it influence airport ground service staffs' service performance?

In fact, this airside airport physical area choice has direct relationship between aircraft and apron gate areas of the terminal processing of passenger and cargo. They are major factors to influence operations on runway component. It means that airport ground service staffs' service efficiency, used for the passengers and air fright catching any airplanes processing.

Hence, in a geographical sense, landside and airside capacity on how designing and building og geographical area can bring indirect influence to passengers. They need to enter or indirect influence the airport , in special, many flights are staying on the airport runway as well as many passengers need to leave from the airplanes or enter to the

airplanes in the same time on the airport boundary. Hence, if the airport has good airside design , then many passengers will feel convenient to leave or enter the airport from the airside areas.

Airports are perhaps truly intermodel terminals in the transportatoin system. They provide an intersafe among air highway, rail and even water way travel. They are an important part of the medium and long distance intercity transportation system in our future transportation tools. Hence, it has enough reasons to support airside geographical airside and off airport factors can influence an airport and its airline flying service providers on its capacity as well as how it's capacity can influence passengers' satisfactory level when they arrive

the country's airport. Hence, airport's congestion growth problem that is needed to consider to any airports because when one airport 's congestion is growing.

It will influence passengers service satisfactory level to be fallen down in possible, e.g. capacity is increased by the addition of a new access road, such as additions provide a major increase.

Thus, the stair step growth, it will cause congestion growth because if the airport had used many areas for stair step growth and passengers will have less space to let them to walk on the ground and their airport congestion feeling will also increase when passengers are staying to leave the airport or waiting for check in or check out or waiting to transfer another airplane in the country's airport

The major airside factors to influence travelling passengers whose airport service feeling may include as below:

Availability of enough land for expansion for runways, availability of aids to navigation and air traffic control techniques that could result in reduction of separation between aircraft , noise, aircraft mix, load factor, exclusive use and use of gates , enough airside and outside facilities, availability of airspace, whether aircraft large size is enough capacity and where is location of gates, staffing, equipment freight, environmental protection regulation, and community attitudes toward airside operation.

Thus, whether the airport has enough facilities to satisfy passengers staying in its airport service need, it will have indirect influence further passengers increasing or decreasing

number problem. For example, if the airport terminal functions are spread over a large geographic area, access and facilities have to be expanded to accommodate the spread-out configuration of the terminal or if terminal facilities are grouped together, the access facilities can be congregated into a smaller geographical area.

The capacity of the landside is a function of the terminal design , which has a major influence on the relative to between airside and landside capacity. Also, these off airport factors can also

influence landside capacity, they may include: off airport parking, off airport terminals, urban development pattern, multiple jurisdiction, financial resources etc. issues. The sub factors of the off-airport access functions , they can influence passengers' services feeling to the airport. They may include: user and vehicle characteristics, e.g. occupants per vehicle, separate and preferential guide way subsystems, roadway traffic management, access link to major transportation , transportation connections. All of these airside and off-airport facilities will

influence passengers' servicing feeling when they arrive any countries' airports. Hence, any countries' airports ought not neglect any one of these minor airside facilities of inside airports to outside airports both.

The another geographical choice airport building issue, it is also one critical factor for how the development of airport cities. It will influence passengers' service feeling to any country airport. The questions may include: Why may any country need to develop an airport city? Can it bring economic benefit and attract many passengers to choose to travel the country? Can the airport city reform to raise airport service performance or service level? Airports have become new dynamic centers of economic activity, incorporating several commercial and

entertainment services inside passenger terminals, when developing a hotels and accommodations , office complexes, conference and exhibition centers or leisure facilities choices for

leisure passengers and business passengers both.

Airport-centered development may occur at different spatial scales (from the micro scale of the passenger terminal to the regional or metropolitan scale), thus assuming different

shapes and mainfestations. Different concepts to address these developments can be found in the " airport city", airport corridor, and aerotopolis (Guller, M. & Guller, M, 2003).

I shall explain how airport city concept can help to raise passenger service performance feeling in airports and airlines as below:

In general, airport passengers hope airports ought provide these different kinds service and achievement the lowest satisfactory service quality or performance level to let

them to feel, such as air transport needs have complex airport -neighborhood interactions (in what concerns an eventual development towards the concept of airport city) requires the

identification of thes takeholders involved and an awareness of the relationships between them. Any airport's main task needs to provide traveling, air transport, shipping, entertainment services to

the dual market of airlines and travelers. As such, its primary interaction consists of the supply and demand relationship with the users stakeholder group (passengers and airlines), which results in broad terms in the airports aeronautical revenues. Furthermore, non-aeronautical (commercial) revenues also result from the interactions between airport and users, namely from agents such as cargo and passengers oriented organizations who pay rents or concession feeling to the airport authority, depending on the commercial arrangements binding these agents.

Thus, one successful airport city, it ought provide good neighborhood transport service to travelling passengers, e.g. bus, taxi, ferry etc. public transportation service. It aims to avail any airport passengers can catch any one of these public transportation tools to arrive airport or leave the airport easily. It also needs to provide hotel, conference service for business visitors as well as retail shops, cinemas for shopping visitors or entertainment visitors when they are staying in the country's airport(s). Also, it ought provide facilities to any cargo -oriented

organizations to deliver any cargo in short time rapidly. So, one airport's any neighborhood facilities have relationship to influence any passengers and airport organizations' service performance feeling between different user agents including: service provision (e.g. between passengers and businesses), business transactions, supply and demand (e.g. between public transport providers and passengers and passengers or visitors) and employer-employee relationships (businesses and workforce , such as airport airline ground service workers). Because if they feel that they can work in one comfortable airport working environment, they will feel happy and enjoyable to serve their passengers more everyday. It means that any airports' facilities will have indirect relationship to influence airport ground service workers' psychology to feel either enjoyable or hate to work in the airport environment often.

On conclusion, airports ought need to consider themselves airside and off airport facilities whether they have enough supplies and innovate their facilities to be better , even perfect in order to satisfy any airport visitors, travelers, user organizations and airport ground service employees to enjoy to work and use their services if they hope their service level or performance is satisfied
to their service needs for long term.

Influencing air connectivity to service quality factor

Can air connectivity growth decreases travel costs for attracting travelling passengers, consumers and businesses and facilities global productive growth? This seems to be particularly an issue when airport capacity is scare or when new airports are added to an existing airport system. What is air connectivity ?
Why does air connectivity raise passengers services? How to measure air connective service?

When direct and indirect connectivity relate to the airport connectivity available to local travelling passengers, any airports ought need to raise extra
airline services to raise service quality , e.g. cheaper air ticket price, in-flight service extra service provision, e.g. comfortable and clean and quiet air port waiting environment
service provision and feeling. However, passengers will generally prefer direct, non-stop connections over indirect air connectivity service.

Air connectivity service can assist airlines to raise competitive effort an offer and they provide access to the many destinations with too little demand for a direct flight, such as minimum connecting time differs in quality , due to in-flight time differences, the inconvenience and risk of missing a connection and transfer time for direct or indirect flights. Hence, any airlines can reduce passengers indirect or direct flight in-flight time to wait airplanes arrive to catch when they arrive any airports. This air inflight waiting time shorten service will attract many passengers to choose the airline to catch airplanes if its inflight waiting time to airport passengers is lesser than other airlines' in-flight waiting time in any airports. It can raise airline service quality, due to the airline has many passengers feel in-flight waiting time is shorten than other airlines often.

In fact, airport connectivity is one good concept method to raise passengers' satisfactory service level. One of the important factors for the connectivity of airports may include: The size

and economic strength of the local catchment area how drives outbound demand, size and economic activities as well as tourism attractiveness are an important cariable factor in explaining

inbound demand (including the propensity to flying demand), landside accessibility drives the size of the catchment area that airlines can serve from a particular airport within a certain landside travel time, apart from the socio-economic variables factor, also cultural , political and the historical ties play a role in explaining demand the origin-destination level factor. All of the research on the factors that explain air level, demand at the origin-destination or airport level is widespread, including gravity modelling (e.g. a bed at al., 2001) and regressions on aggregate

airport demand (Dobruszkes, 2011). All of any one factors may be airport connectivity service to influence passengers' service feeling level in airports and airlines both service quality.

ON airport visit costs aspect, airlines also need to consider airport visit costs in their route development strategy. Visit costs may also influence passenger choice behavior when

airlines pass on higher/lower charges to the passenger through air fares. Although, airport visit costs generally represent a limited share of an airline's total operational costs, this share can be more significant for short haul flights as well as fair airlines. All of any one these airport charges and passenger fees variable may influence passengers airlines choice. They may include:

Fees variable, landing charge, parking charge for their vehicles or aircraft, passenger luggage charge, security charge, boarding bridge charge, noise charge, emission charge, airport development service increasing charge, check -in charge, terminal charge, cargo charge. So, if any one of these charges influence the airline ticket price rises, it will influence passengers' air ticket purchase choice to the airline in possible.

On airport service levels aspect, for keeping and attracting passengers, airlines and airports need to compete with services that improve the passengers experience. Such service
factors concern for immigration and luggage, but also relate to the terminals, waiting transfer another air plane time, shopping facilities, toilets, atmosphere and space cleaniness, friendliness of staff and availability of delicated lounges. Together they determine the image of an airport and its perceived value by passengers and airlines.

On airline routes development aspect, it can also influence passengers choices to the airline, e.g. Australia airline had developed long route to England destination. Any Australia
passengers can fly to England route directly. They do not need to transfer another air plane to go to England. Although, flying time is above 12 hours long time, but it can bring available to
passengers. They do not need to spend time to wait another air plane to transfer to go England in Australia any airports. THus, airline route development strategy airline planners require detailed, accurate information to make new route decisions, but airlines usually do not have the resources to fully evaluate every new route market. So, they need a sound well articulated business case, can convince airlines to introduce new air services, as well as airport / destinations can influence the airline planning process.

For example, Interviewer indicates that new routes are a huge investment and risk to an airline in airline economic view point, if the airline had not gathered any data to evaluate
whether the new route is worth to develop and predict passengers' new route choice behavior. It assumed 75% lead factor will influence any new route development in success. It indicates these different aircraft type and seats per flight, annual passenger requirements data for these aircrafts: Boeing 747 aircraft needs to satisfy 400 at least seats per flight and annual passenger requirement need 219, 000, aircraft airbus A340 aircraft needs 280 at least seats per flight and annual passenger requirements need 153,300 , Boesing 767 to 300 aircraft needs 220 at least seats per flight and annual passenger requirements need 120, 450 . Boeing 737 to 700 aircraft needs 76,650 and regional Jet aircraft needs 100 at least seats per flight and annual passenger requirements need 54,750.

Hence, any airlines need have route priorities strategy before they decide which new flight route(s) will be developed , in order to achieve airlines add service in order of expected profitability, different airlines have pursued different strategies, destinations can move up the priority board with: solid research and analysis (always) and incentives (sometimes).However, any airline questions for new routes may include as below:

What is the current, actual market for a potential route?

How much can my airline stimulate the flight flying market?

How will the competition react?

How much market share will achieve?

How will be the connectivity contribution?

Will the new route be a financial success?

Hence, any airlines need to reduce uncertainty and risk, before they decide to develop any new route market.

The air service development process may include as below:

Step one: market assessment, required a quantify the time size of the existing air travel market

step two: strategy, deficiency analysis and detailed route analysis

step three: business case analysis, packaging and presenting the information to airlines

step fourth: evaluate and negotiate airline incentives

It is the final steps an appropriate incentive, in certain circumstances, helps airlines commit to new air service to satisfy any new route passengers' more satisfactory flying needs.

Similarly, the strategy steps follow: benchmark air services, identify deficiencies, identify new route opportunities, identify potential air service providers, assess viability of potential air services and prioritize route opportunities and target carriers.

Any airlines may find any information concerns new route business cases to decide their countries flying new routes choice , such as: catchment area profile: demographics, economy, tourist etc. information, airport profile : traffic and facilities information market profile; market sizes , top city pairs, traffic leakage etc. information, suggested service : frequency , schedule, airport routing information, route analysis: market share, load factor, stimulation potential, self-diversion etc. information, any airlines' past flying routes strategic considerations etc. information in order to predict and evaluate whether how many further passenger number is flying that they accept to choose the new flying routes travelling needs.

Hence, how to design to impact either the supply or demand for any new flight routes that is only important because of the country has less number of passengers accept to choose the new flying route to fly. Then, the new flying route does not needed to be design to supply to the country's travelling passengers because their acceptance to this new flying route ends are very less. However, the demand level is low new flying route needs to satisfy these three qualifying services criteria, such as: Are new routes only? Increase on existing routes? Does it work service rent incentives? Will the new flying route be satisfied to air service to the airline passengers and airport waiting passengers, e.g. strategically important? Marginally (unprofitable) self-sustaining in the short term? New flying routes only? Increase an existing routes? Service rent incentives?

How can airports afford aggressive airline incentive / fee discounts and still fund route development marketing in a difficult economy? I recommend that the solution method may include new flying route design and developing and maximizing non-aeronautical revenue streams both, such as retail and duty free, food and beverage, parking , loyalty and premium programs and land development to airport building. Marketing funding strategy may be an ineffective incentive for travelling destinations. However, it may not differentiate a market, as route marketing incentives are used by over 80% of communities in the U.S. marketing incentives can be: Unilateral airport pays 100% or cooperative airlines matches some portion, funding amounts are often tied on the capacity of inbound seats to be available on the new flight (flying) route. By calculating the economic impact of new visitors (spend at the destination), a destination can calculate the return on investment in cooperative new flight (flying) route market.

On conclusion, air connectivity is one important factor to influence any country's travelling passengers to the airline's service quality or service level in order to achieve new flying (flight) route design , reducing inflight transfer another airplane waiting time in airport, or marketing development in success. So, any airlines can not neglect this air connectivity will influence their passengers' service quality.
Hence, air connectivity factor is also very important to influence any travelling passengers' service satisfactory level.

How to measure and rise airline

service quality

How are airline performing ? Nowadays, the rise of the low cost airlines' competition is serious, due to airlines hope to rise themselves attractions to influence passengers to choose to use their travelling services. So, different airlines have spend long time to build their unique person-to-person passenger services, which passengers use of different airlines, e.g. digital electronic air tickets purchase method. Any airlines hope to make each journey personalized to the individual will gain market share and improve its service quality to be more unique in order to reach the efforts of airlines to build high levels of customer service appears to have been generally noticed by passengers, when they choose to buy the airline's digital electronic ticket or paper air ticket to use its flying service.

Hence, improvement their digital e-ticket purchase experience and communications factor, for example, if any passengers can enter the airline's air ticket purchase website to buy electronic ticket to pre-book seats in the short time rapidly as well as there are enough seats number to supply to them to pre-book. So, they do not need to worry about without any seats to supply to them to catch the airline's flight to fly to anywhere in any time available conveniently. So, it seems that there is plenty of space for airlines to grow and improve their digital experience and communication method to let any passengers to feel, if the airline hopes to let its passengers to feel that it has unique service to compare others airlines.

The aviation industry plays a major role in the aspect of work and leisure to passengers around the global. So, nowadays passengers' demands to any airlines' service quality had been raised. Hence, any airline service industry messengers are under pressure to prove their services are customers oriented service improvement of performance that guarantees competitive advantages to the global travelling marketplace. So, it also implies that any airlines' services performance will be influenced to cause many passengers feel more poor and let passengers dissatisfy the airline's service performance. The, the airline will possible lose many passengers, due to passengers have many airlines choices, they can find any airlines to replace which any one airline to buy air ticket from internet at home immediately.

However, airlines' comfortable seats arrangement service provision feeling factor is still important in preferable to compare other factors, because passengers must need to sit any seats in any air planes. So, whether the air plane can provide new comfortable seats to let passengers to feel this factor is still the most important factor to influence any passengers to choose to the airline's air plane to catch. For example, service comfortability is how passengers observed the quality of service offered them by the airline's cleanliness, quiet zone, shops, restaurants and business pavilion in functioning like staffs, information desk, and in flight announcement are included as tangible features by the passengers (Geraldine et a.,2013). All of these factors are needed often to measure whether their service performances are satisfactory to themselves passengers service needs.

Moreover, the other factors may include service affordability , it can be regarded as given passenger the opportunity to select from inclusive air ticket prices made available to the different group of passengers by the airlines, as a gesture of goodwill , to establish and reinforce customer loyalty and repeat purchases essential for the airline continuity as well as service reliability. it is the probability that airline will carry out its expected function satisfactory as stated in the flight schedule. Hence, there is a strong link between different airlines' service quality variables, airline image and repeat patronage from the passengers.

Service quality is a measure of how well the service level delivered matches passengers expectations to measure service quality based on input from focus groups. It consists of five factors (tangibles, reliability, responsiveness, assurance and empathy). All of these factors will be identifies that how the airline service quality can be satisfactory to its passengers ' psychological and emotion enjoyable service needs.

Any one of these any five service factors will be important to influence the airline's passengers service feeling level to the airline. It means that the passenger will have more chance to choose the airline's service again (repeating purchase its air ticket). Hence, any airlines can not neglect any one of service feeling to its passengers. It needs often to enquire questionnaires to evaluate whether its these five aspects of service quality , if it discovered any of these five aspects of service level is poor, e.g. 5 scale is the best service performance level, then it can attempt to find its error whether which aspects, it needs to very need to reach the 5 scale , the best service performance level when many passengers feel, e.g. enquiring 100 passengers who give 5 scale to reliability service aspect, before reliability service aspect has less than 50% passengers from 100 passengers who feel the airlines concerns this reliable service level aspect questions to be the best. It is one kind of measurement service quality method to any airlines.

Other service performance evaluation factor is satisfaction in the job to every airline front service or ground service staffs to the airline. Job satisfaction describes how content an employee is with his or her job. It is how the employee responses to a job. It can be considered as a part of life satisfaction to one organization, when the employee is working in the organization. Hence, if one airline front service as ground service staff who can feel more job satisfaction to compare his/her prior airline employer. Then, he/she won't be easy to change his/her present airline employer.

However, some factors can influence job satisfaction are pay and benefit, fair performance appraisal, career and promotional opportunities, proper reward and recognition, work-family life balance, the job itself, proper working conditions, leadership chance, autonomy in work.

Job satisfaction can also involve complex number of variables, circumstances, opinions and behavioral tendencies and a variety of work related outcomes, such as commitment, involvement, motivation, satisfaction, attendance. Hence, any airlines also need to concern how let their employees feel job satisfaction issue in order to avoid their leaving turnover number increases, due to job satisfaction and dissatisfaction depend on the expectations what the job supplies for an employee not the nature of the job.

Finally, instead of concerning employees job satisfaction issue, any airlines also need to concern passengers satisfaction issue because it will have any passengers will choose the airline, if it can bring more service satisfaction to let them to feel , then they will become repeat passengers to the airline.

What kinds of factors passengers were looking for and what were the reasons of choosing a specific airline? When one airline often is complained from its passengers. It will have more mistakes to let them to feel or dissatisfy its service. Hence the airlines needs to find which are its mistakes and improve in order to satisfy its passengers' expectations, e.g. finding what are the mistakes to the airlines' serious concern regarding passenger complaints and complaint satisfaction in order to make the airline more likely to meet its passengers' expectation in case of a problem. Hence, any airlines need to concern how to improve its employees' satisfactory service as well as its passengers' satisfactory service both issues as well as how to measure their service quality whether is enough to achieve general service acceptable performance to its passengers.

Reference

A bed, S. Y. A.O. Ba-Fail and S.M. Jasimuddin (2001), " An economatic analysis of international air travel demand in Saudi Arabia". Journal of air transport managmement, vol. 7, pp.143-148.

Bamber, L., & Dale, B.G. Lean production : a study of application in a traditoinal manufacturing environment. Production planning & control, 11 (3), 291-298, 2000.

Dobruszkes, F.M. Lennert and G. Van Hamme (2011). " An analysis of the determinants of air traffic volume for European metropolitan area". Journal of transport geographyy, vol. 19/4/pp.755-762.

Gealdine, O., & David , U.C. (2013). effects of airline service quality on airline image and passengers' loyalty: Findings from Arill Air Nigeria passengers, Journal of hospitality and management tourism, 4(2), 19-28. doi: http://dx.doi: 10.5897/HMT 2013, 0089.

Glass, R., Seifermann, S., & Metternich, J. The spread of lean production in the assembly, Process and maching industry. Procedia CIRP, 55, 278-283, 2016.

Guller, M. & Guller, M. (2003) From Airport to airport city. Editional Gustavo , Gili, Barcel on a.Intervistas Consulting Inc.

Massachusetts Institute Of Technology (MIT), Lean Aerospace Initiative, Available: www.lean.mit.edu, 2005.

CHAPTER SIX